The Scottish Enlightenment

Human Nature, Social Theory and Moral Philosophy

Essays in Honour of Christopher J. Berry

Edited by R. J. W. Mills and
Craig Smith

EDINBURGH
University Press

Edinburgh University Press is one of the leading university presses in the UK. We publish academic books and journals in our selected subject areas across the humanities and social sciences, combining cutting-edge scholarship with high editorial and production values to produce academic works of lasting importance. For more information visit our website: edinburghuniversitypress.com

Edinburgh University Press Ltd
The Tun – Holyrood Road
12(2f) Jackson's Entry
Edinburgh EH8 8PJ

First published in hardback by Edinburgh University Press 2021

Typeset in 11/13 Goudy Old Style by
IDSUK (DataConnection) Ltd

A CIP record for this book is available from the British Library

ISBN 978 1 4744 6731 5 (hardback)
ISBN 978 1 4744 6732 2 (paperback)
ISBN 978 1 4744 6734 6 (webready PDF)
ISBN 978 1 4744 6733 9 (epub)

Contents

Acknowledgements

The editors wish to thank the contributors, the staff at Edinburgh University Press, particularly Carol Macdonald and Kirsty Woods, and the anonymous reviewers for their comments on the initial proposal. This volume was inspired by the work of Christopher J. Berry who, through his teaching and writing, has helped to shape the study of the Scottish Enlightenment and the thinking of the authors whose papers are collected here. The volume is dedicated to him in appreciation.

Notes on Contributors

Roger L. Emerson is Professor Emeritus of History at the University of Western Ontario. He is the author of *Professors, Patronage and Politics: The Aberdeen Universities in the Eighteenth Century* (Aberdeen University Press, 1992) and *An Enlightened Duke: The Life of Archibald Campbell (1692–1761), Earl of Ilay, Third Duke of Argyll* (Humming Earth, 2013).

Fonna Forman is Associate Professor of Political Science and Director, UCSD Center on Global Justice, University of California San Diego.

Ana Marta González is Professor of Moral Philosophy in the Department of Philosophy and Researcher at the Institute for Culture and Society at the University of Navarra, she is also the Academic Leader of the Culture & Lifestyles branch of the Social Trends Institute (New York, Barcelona). Author of *Sociedad civil y normatividad. La teoría social de David Hume* (Dyckinson, 2013), among her recent publications are: 'Value and Obligation Once More: A Critical Assessment of Robert Stern's "Hybrid" Kant' (*Metaphilosophy* 51:1 (2020)) and 'Practical Identity, Obligation and Sociality' (*The Journal of Social Philosophy* 49:4 (Winter 2018).

Ryan Patrick Hanley is Professor of Political Science at Boston College. Prior to joining the faculty at Boston College, he was the Mellon Distinguished Professor of Political Science at Marquette University, and held visiting appointments or fellowships at Yale, Harvard and the University of Chicago. He is a specialist on the political philosophy of the Enlightenment period, and his most recent books include *Our Great Purpose: Adam Smith on Living a Better Life* (Princeton, 2019) and *The Political Philosophy of Fénelon* (Oxford, 2020).

R. J. W. Mills is a Leverhulme Trust Early Career Fellow in History at Queen Mary, University of London.

Naohito Mori is an Associate Professor of History of Political and Economic Thought at Kochi University. His research interests centre on the economic, political and historical writings of David Hume. His publications include the monograph *Hume and His Ambivalent Idea of Civilized Society* (Sobunsha, 2010; in Japanese).

Maria Pia Paganelli is a professor of Economics at Trinity University. She works on Adam Smith, David Hume, and eighteenth-century monetary theories. She wrote *The Routledge Guidebook to Adam Smith's Wealth of Nations* (Routledge, 2020) and co-edited the *Oxford Handbook on Adam Smith* (Oxford University Press, 2013) and *Adam Smith and Rousseau* (Edinburgh University Press, 2018). She served as the president of the History of Economics Society and as the book review editor for the *Journal of the History of Economic Thought*. She is currently the president of the International Adam Smith Society.

Eric Schliesser is Professor of Political Theory at the University of Amsterdam. His research encompasses a variety of themes, ranging from economic statistics in classical Babylon, the history of the natural sciences and forgotten eighteenth-century feminists (both male and female) to political theory and the history of political theory and the assumptions used in mathematical economics. His recent publications include *Adam Smith: Systematic Philosopher and Public Thinker* (Oxford University Press, 2017) and a translation with commentary of Sophie de Grouchy's *Letters on Sympathy* (together with Sandrine Bergès). He keeps a daily blog, *Digressionsnimpressions*.

Craig Smith is the Adam Smith Senior Lecturer in the Scottish Enlightenment at the University of Glasgow. He is the author of *Adam Smith's Political Philosophy: The Invisible Hand and Spontaneous Order* (Routledge, 2006) and *Adam Ferguson and the Idea of Civil Society: Moral Science in the Scottish Enlightenment* (Edinburgh University Press, 2019).

Spyridon Tegos is Assistant Professor of Early Modern Philosophy at the University of Crete, Greece. He is currently preparing a manuscript (in French) on the classical French sources – early modern theatre, belles lettres – of the early liberalism of David Hume and Adam Smith. The project focuses on the social and political relevance of the 'middling rank' and their manners, and traces the issue in the French liberalism of Madame de Staël and Alexis de Tocqueville.

Zhengping Zhang is an Associate Professor in the Department of History in the College of Humanities at Zhejiang University. Her research focuses on the Scottish Enlightenment. She is the author of the book *Passions and Wealth: The Science of Human Nature and the Political Economy of David Hume* (Zhejiang University Press, 2018), and the translator of Christopher Berry's book *The Idea of the Commercial Society in the Scottish Enlightenment* (Chinese version, Zhejiang University Press, 2018) and works by David Hume, Adam Smith and Jack Goody.

Preface: A Political Theory of the Scottish Enlightenment

Fonna Forman

Prefacing a festive volume on Chris Berry's work comes with a tremendous sense of responsibility: setting a tone to celebrate an intellectual hero for generations of scholars who have devoted their lives to the study of the Scottish Enlightenment and the voices who animated it, without lapsing into embarrassing hyperbole.

Chris describes his earliest encounter with Enlightenment attempts to understand modernity less as a bold discovery mission than the fallout of accidental encounter (with Jonathan Harrison, J. S. McClelland and Donald McRae mainly) and an inauspicious search for a PhD topic that might pique the interest of a supervisor. 'I just wondered whether there was a Scottish version of the topic,' he recollects. Coming upon the bibliography of W. C. Lehman's edition of John Millar's *The Origin of the Distinction of Ranks* in the college library, he concluded, 'there might indeed be'.

From the perspective of decades and the explosion of scholarship that followed, it is fair to say that Chris's youthful curiosity was impressive, and that his ultimate approach to exploring Scottish thought as a 'social inquiry' became catalytic, in the grandest sense. There had been some earlier research on the subject – Chris himself credits Gladys Bryson's 1945 monograph, *Man and Society: The Scottish Enquiry of the Eighteenth Century*, a 1965 study of Adam Ferguson by David Kettler, Duncan Forbes's 1966 introduction to the Edinburgh University Press edition of Ferguson's *Essay on the History of Civil Society*, other works by Forbes and Andrew Skinner, engagements with Marxist tropes by Roy Pascal, Ronald L. Meek, E. G. West and Donald Young, and the introduction to Adam Smith's *Moral Sentiments* by David Daiches Raphael and Alec Lawrence Macfie. Chris was among a wave of younger scholars in the 1970s and 80s who began to metabolise this research, and more or less deliberately lay the groundwork for a defined field of inquiry – notably Nicholas Phillipson, Roger Emerson, Hans Medick, Tom Campbell, Donald Winch, J. G. A. Pocock, Albert O.

Hirschman, Knud Haakonssen, John Robertson, John Dwyer and George Elder Davie, among others.

By the 1990s, scholarship on the Scottish Enlightenment had 'lifted off', with path-breaking monographs, articles and scores of PhD dissertations published each year. It was during this period that Chris published *The Idea of Luxury* (1994) and *The Social Theory of the Scottish Enlightenment* (1997). Chris's contributions to this emergent field of intellectual activity can be extrapolated from his own Preface in the 1997 monograph, where he enumerates what he takes to be the concerns of a properly 'social' inquiry of the Scottish Enlightenment: historical theorising, political and economic thought, moral philosophy, and a pervasive concern with cultural issues. While these themes pervade eighteenth-century Scottish thinking, Chris's synthetic approach to them is his greatest contribution. Ideas are not isolated or hermetic, but hang together with other ideas and institutions to produce a distinctive way of thinking about people and society. As genuine members of the Enlightenment this meant a commitment to human progress and civilisation, triumph against superstition and domination, an understanding of order both physical and social, all uniquely refracted in Scottish social theory by their preoccupation with habit and custom, and a deep appreciation for the slow evolution of human institutions and their resistance to rational solutions.

It was during this period in the mid-1990s that I became drawn to Scottish thought. I first encountered Chris's work during dissertation research at the University of Chicago on Adam Smith's *Moral Sentiments*, in conversation with Lauren Brubaker, Ryan Hanley and Eric Schliesser. It was an exciting time to study Smith, as scholarship on the Scottish Enlightenment, and on Hume and Smith in particular, was exploding. Winch, Hirschman, Haakonssen were canonical texts by this point; and yet a new book called *The Social Theory of the Scottish Enlightenment* captivated me. It demonstrated a way of doing history, of asking questions of ideas, that was unconventional among the intellectual historians who were most prominent at the time.

As a young political theorist drawn to the rigour of intellectual history, but struggling with a convention that I suppress from my work the social and political impulses driving my fascination with the Scots, discovering Chris's work was something of an emancipation. Countering a perception that the Scottish Enlightenment belonged to historians (or the occasional wayward philosopher), Chris described himself a 'political theorist', and refused to situate his work squarely in a single discipline or be constrained by its method. The great virtues of political theory are its indeterminacy, its critical agility and its resolve to weave across the domains of history, politics, economy, science, art, medicine, morality, religion, philosophy and culture and to disregard purported margins between them – very much indeed like the Scots themselves. It might be said that Chris's scholarship itself manifests the very best of Scottish social inquiry, so that his subject of inquiry also becomes, in important ways, his method of inquiry – a unique 'Berry method'.

As we celebrate Chris's journey here, we also reflect on where we are headed. In our academic culture of institutionalised silos, where research trajectories are inevitably defined by professional norms, often constrained by a shortage of supervisors capable of overseeing non-traditional and 'cross-disciplinary' projects, or referees capable of evaluating them for their merit, I propose we remain mindful of the transversal impulses of Scottish social science, and resist the inevitable narrowing and over-specialisation of academic research. Foremost, perhaps, is the need to interpret our unique twenty-first-century challenges, as the Scots did theirs, in an inherently integral and cultural way. The dynamics of global poverty, climate change, dramatic migratory shifts, racism and rising 'national hatred' (as Smith described the myopic nationalisms of his own day) are not simply a function of economics, of politics, of ideology, of brain function, or of moral and spiritual decay. Specialists in these 'fields' cannot possibly comprehend our challenges today in isolation, without appreciating the cultural connections and institutions that bind these phenomena together in distinctive ways. The Scots implore us to remain transversal and cultural as we make sense of this phase in the stadial history of modernity.

Introduction: The Work of Christopher J. Berry – An Appreciation

R. J. W. Mills and Craig Smith

The contributions brought together in this collection serve as an appreciation of the work on the Scottish Enlightenment of Professor Christopher J. Berry. This research has been characterised by deep reading and philosophical understanding, an ambitious approach to comprehensiveness, an underlying sensitivity to historical context without descent in antiquarianism, and an ability to demonstrate the pioneering intellectual achievement of a small group of eighteenth-century Scottish thinkers. From detailed studies of the leading lights, of David Hume (1711–76) and Adam Smith (1723–90), through major contributions on specific themes such as language and luxury, to overall syntheses of the enlightened social theory, Berry has made a vitally important contribution to understanding both the era itself and its legacy. This Introduction summarises some of the highlights of Berry's publications, though by no means does it cover all aspects of his contribution. Similarly, our focus here is, for the most part, on Berry's contribution to Scottish Enlightenment studies, and so we mention other aspects of his oeuvre only in passing. The aim is to set the chapters that follow in the context of a developed, career-long scholarly exploration of the ideas of the Scottish Enlightenment.

Berry's entrance into Scottish Enlightenment studies happened at precisely the time the subject was taking on coherent scholarly form. This was somewhat coincidental: studying first at the London School of Economics and then taking on an academic post at Glasgow, Berry was one-step removed from the prominent discourse on the Scots and natural law theory that emerged out of Cambridge and was most famously associated with Duncan Forbes. This distance perhaps contributed to Berry's production of original research outside of the paradigm of the work undertaken in Cambridge. Berry's doctoral research was on the Aberdonian social theorist James Dunbar (1742–98). This led to articles on Dunbar's distinctive contribution to the enlightened Scottish account of sociability, and participation in the Scots' discussion of the sociological influence of climate and theory of language predicated on the development of human nature's analogical faculty. Dunbar emerges as a literatus engaging in sophisticated fashion with the Scottish Enlightenment's characteristic interests, but also as a tinkerer offering distinctive but not original contributions to the Scottish science of society. Stemming from his research on Dunbar's theory of language, Berry's early research included work on enlightened Scottish theories of language more generally – not least in a well-regarded piece examining Adam Smith's 'Considerations concerning the First Formation of Languages' appended to the third edition of Smith's *Theory of Moral Sentiments* (1767).

Hume, Hegel and Human Nature (1982)

Berry's first research monograph, *Hume, Hegel and Human Nature* (The Hague: Martinus Nijhoff, 1982; henceforth *HHHN*), signified the beginning of his interest in the importance of concepts of human nature for political and social theory. *HHHN* explored the emergence of the interpretation of human nature as intelligible only in terms of local social context. While Hume superficially reads like a contextualist theorist of human nature, the emergence of such an interpretation was a distinctly post-Humean development associated not with the Scottish but the late German Enlightenment and reaching its apogee with Georg Wilhelm Friedrich Hegel (1770–1831). The Scottish 'science of man', epitomised by Hume, did not reduce the explanation of human difference down to the specific characteristics of specific cultures. Hume looked beneath social diversity in search of the universal principles of human motivation and behaviour underpinning all human history. Berry's analysis was a contribution to a larger debate over whether late Enlightenment sociologists could be described, following Isaiah Berlin's description of the *Aufklärer* as cultural relativists. The Scots, exemplified by Hume, were not. They did claim that the universal aspects of human nature manifest themselves differently in different local contexts. This did not prevent judgement. Hume ranked societies, for example, according to whether they constrained natural human impulses or whether they were the result of superstition or barbarism.

Hume believed the 'science of man' – Berry clarified what he understood this science to involve in texts discussed below – will inform its practitioners of the proper functioning of human nature. They will learn how to judge the anthropological testimony of social and political diversity against the constant and universal aspects of man. Human nature is not radically malleable. Man is a social creature, but it is not this sociality that constitutes what it is to be human. Enlightenment Europe's growing knowledge of past and present societies did not result in a relativising impulse but a sense that this knowledge could be plotted in coherent and normative trajectories of social change.

Two themes stand out in Berry's account of Hume. Firstly, Hume offered a strikingly naturalistic and organic account of the formation and cohesiveness of society. Societies were not the product of such ahistorical notions as social contracts or rationally deduced systems of justice. They were the result of human nature's inherent propensities working over long periods of time. Society emerged as the unintended consequence of man's propensities to contract habits, secure bonds with sexual partners and children, to seek out social interaction, and to feel sympathy towards others. This is a depoliticised understanding of society, in which it results from a 'network of habitual associations and behaviour patterns' and related 'familial socialisation, education' and adherence to existing 'social ordering' (HHHN, 91). Secondly, Hume explained social diversity in terms of how the universal human passions and propensities are stimulated in different contexts. Here Hume differed from his friend Adam Smith by explaining change less in terms of socio-economic and institutional improvement and more in terms of the transition from barbarism and ignorance towards knowledge, moderation and humanity. Social development was judged, for Hume, in terms of differing degrees of civilisation rather than modes of subsistence.

Whereas Hume stressed the constancy and universality of human nature, Hegel rejected the notion we could speak meaningfully of 'human nature' outside of social contexts. Humans are distinct from Nature because of their spiritual quality: they are the only creatures capable of thought and self-consciousness. But human nature is determined by context or, more specifically, by Volk and State. There is no separation of the individual from these two: their inner thoughts, habits and manners – those things that distinguish them as human – are fundamentally framed by their context. But Hegel rejected both the relativism of such contextualist accounts of human nature (such as Herder's, read in certain lights) and the notion of unintended consequences underpinning Hume's account. To Hegel, world history has a purpose: the actualisation of Geist (loosely, 'spirit') through man's jointly happening growth in individuality, in terms of greater freedom, and universal spirit, in terms of total societal adherence to common goals and values. States can be judged according to this purpose. The Oriental era restricted individual freedom and participation in common goals to the tyrant, the Greek and Roman eras to the few, whereas the Germanic

Protestant era extended them to all. The State reaches its end point when all members can pursue their individual subjectivity freely and reach their status as 'spiritual universal' or someone self-consciously obeying the rationally understood law. And for Hegel, Berry avers, his philosophy of world history is a form of theodicy in which the 'Cunning of Reason', Hume's unintended consequences, actually serve divine purposes.

Human Nature (1986) and The Idea of a Democratic Community (1989)

Berry's two other major publications during the 1980s were contributions to political theory. *Human Nature* (London: Macmillan, 1986) is an analysis of how concepts of human nature inform political thinking. This resulted from a wide-ranging survey of notions of human nature in Western political thought. All ideologies have underlying conceptions of human nature. When these are invoked, it is usually in terms of what is it possible, appropriate or desirable for humans to do (or, likewise, what is impossible, inappropriate or undesirable). Aristotle's (384–322 BC) claim that 'man is a political animal' is both a description of human nature but also a prescription: the political life is the best life for man. Conceptions of human nature hold for characteristics that are true of all humans. This includes even relativist theories of human nature, given that inherent in the notion of relativism (relation) is something universal. Any concept of human nature places some constraints on human beings and limits what is feasible and infeasible in the world of politics. To pick one of Berry's examples, E. O. Wilson holds that his understanding of the socio-biology of human nature shows that anarchism is an impossibility.

The concept of the human, then, is indispensable to political thinking because it established the conceptual space that frames the bounds of the political possible and impossible. To ignore human nature will result in useless political doctrines, but, conversely, all theories of human nature are contentious. A right-wing critic of left-wing rationalist attempts to implement new institutions will make the Burkean charge that they overestimate the fixed and limited powers of human reason; the left-wing retort will be that the right-wing critic obstructs progress by eliding the status quo with the permanent realities of human nature. Overall, we should not expect too much from the concept of human nature. Recourse to our preferred version will not end dispute, but nor is discussion avoidable. Yet, though debate over human nature will never end, this does not mean the debate is not worthwhile. Concepts of human nature can be tested against the criterion of internal consistency and against the weight of agreed and disagreed upon 'facts'. Hobbes's political theory will fail to persuade anyone who disagrees with the claim that the ultimate human motivation is the avoidance of violent death. Thinking about a theory's concept of human nature is a useful analytical way to proceed in critiquing that theory.

The Idea of a Democratic Community (Hemel Hempstead: Harvester Wheatsheaf, 1989) explores the intellectual cartography of the idea of a democratic community that is assumed or implied by critics of liberal capitalist democracies. Berry's project is to outline how this notion is a powerful presence in debates in political theory, one which trades on the assumed conceptual priority of the idea of community and the belief in the existence of a set of communal goods that can be attained in a non-competitive fashion, and yet which lacks a clear conceptual delineation by those who make use of it. The key characteristic is a Hegelian notion of preservative transcendence: the democratic community will replace the selfish individualism of liberal capitalist democracy while at the same time retaining the valuable aspects of liberal society's defence of the status of the individual. The book is a work of analysis rather than a work of advocacy and develops a concept first developed in a 1979 article in *Political Studies* entitled 'Idiotic Politics'.[1] Idiotic politics is a term of art developed by Berry to contrast with the idea of democratic politics. Drawing on the meaning of the Greek root *idiōtēs* ('individual' or 'private citizen'), idiotic politics is individualised politics characterised by a focus on the private sphere and personal interests. It is intentionally pejorative because it is intended to embody the critique of liberalism via the idea of a democratic community. To lead an idiotic life is to live a private life deprived of community. Berry then traces this critique through several of the main currents of contemporary political thinking: through the feminist critique of the public/private divide; the concerns about political apathy and a lack of participation in republican thought; and the idea that excessive individualism undermines the sense of community necessary to sustain the institutions of liberal democracy. While recognising the power of these arguments, Berry is ultimately sceptical about the ability of this critical tradition to develop a coherent response to the reality of competition between individuals seeking to realise their own desires.

The Idea of Luxury (1994)

Berry's next major publication was *The Idea of Luxury: A Conceptual and Historical Study* (Cambridge: Cambridge University Press, 1994), a complicated work with wide-ranging aims and arguments, which traversed several academic disciplines. Berry avoided offering 'some grand synthesising theory of luxury' but provided a 'conceptual framework to serve heuristically as a means of giving some shape to an amorphous subject' (231). The distinction between 'necessity' and 'luxury' is present throughout history, but the precise meaning of those categories is conventional and relational. We can learn a lot about a society through understanding specific relations and conventions, not least because different valuations of needs and desires result in different understandings of political order. A theocracy will have different notions of luxury compared to a socialist state compared to a liberal democracy. At the centre of the Western debate over luxury is a paradigm shift from the ancient and Christian understanding of the 'needful' as the 'normative benchmark' (232) of the good life, with luxury being a threat to virtue, salvation and the public good, towards the modern neutral paradigm which sees in luxury the potential for bringing about economic opulence and political freedom. In the 'ancient paradigm', concepts of luxury were bound up with notions of transgression from living within the fixed, singular and natural framing of the good life. In the latter, desire for luxury was understood as just one further characteristic of human nature to be factored in to understanding man and society. Hume and Smith play key roles. Their accounts of luxury within commercial society provided an alternative way to think about the relationship between consumption, individual ethics and civic life that entirely overturned the traditional paradigm's claims about the deleterious effects of luxury.

Western political thinking inherited overlapping understandings of the negative consequences of luxury consumption from ancient philosophy and Christian theology. Plato (427/423–347 BC) and Aristotle claimed human needs were fixed. Anything that went beyond their satisfaction, as luxury was by definition deemed to do, was actively detrimental. Indeed, Plato's *Republic* can be read as a lengthy diagnosis and proposed cure of the problem of the pursuit of unlimited wealth and luxury through fixing society according to the dictates of reason. To Aristotle, the ultimate end of man is fixed in the life of either the contemplative philosopher or the politically active citizen. All other human action is either subordinate to securing that end, or detrimental to its achievement and can be said to be perverted and corrupt. One of the aspects of the 'modern' paradigm was the jettisoning of this notion of the fixed good life and its depreciation of economic activity. In the subsequent Western millennium, however, it was Roman opprobrium towards luxury that achieved paradigmatic importance. Frugality, simplicity of life, rational self-command over insatiable bodily desires and living within one's means are praised. To the Stoics, the pursuit and consumption of luxury inflames human desires unnaturally.

Luxury disturbs our pursuit of self-command and internal tranquillity by encouraging the pursuit of insatiable desires. To ancient republican political theorists, luxury threatens the civic order by enervating and effeminising citizens – ancient criticism of luxury was heavily gendered, with women associated with the desires and goods that destroyed manliness. Luxury directed citizens away from serving the public good and towards satisfying their own insatiable selfish desires and needed to be controlled – not least by sumptuary laws. Luxury was both a symptom and a cause of the Roman Republic's fall: symptomatic of a turning away from the common good and causing the enervating and emasculation of those who pursued it.

The Christian theology that followed supplemented these accounts by viewing luxury as bound up with postlapsarian human nature. Luxury, framed as indistinguishable from lust, emblematised man's sinful search for worldly pleasures at the expense of the good health of their immortal souls. Compared to pagan Roman republicanism, however, the Christian account of the indefatigability of depraved man's sinful nature saw no opportunity for countervailing manly action. Berry's central text here is Augustine's *City of God* (c. AD 413–16) and its discussion of unruly, wilful sexual desire as evidence of how the bondage of original sin has made humans insatiably carnal. Lust become another aspect of the Roman indictment of luxury because, like the pursuit of wealth or greed or comfort, sexual desire involved a 'rule-trespassing wilfulness' (94).

The normative picture of the luxury-free good life and good society offered by Graeco-Roman and Christian thinkers came under intense challenge by seventeenth-century theorists of human nature. Epitomised by Thomas Hobbes's thought, many early modern writers redescribed humans as creatures of infinite and infinitely changing yet never fully satisfied desires. This process Berry described as the 'de-moralisation' of luxury. The tranquillity proposed by the Stoics was unachievable. Controlling human desire was now framed itself as unnatural: the desire for luxury was just one aspect of normal human nature at work. This development was followed by late seventeenth-century theorists of trade, epitomised by the understudied Nicholas Barbon (c. 1640–99), who stressed the economic benefits accruing from pursuing trade in luxuries. The era's financial and commercial revolutions encouraged criticism of notions of virtue framed as self-denying, civic-minded action. Trade theorists like Barbon argued against traditional accusations that luxury undermined public order by showing its potential material and military benefits for states.

The second stage of the shift from the ancient to the modern paradigm involved 'de-politicisation' of luxury during Enlightenment Europe's extended debate over luxury's costs and benefits. Berry's account focused on the contributions of Bernard Mandeville (1670–1733), Hume and, especially, Smith. Berry actually downplayed Mandeville's importance: the *Fable of the Bees* (1723–9) was primarily a *succès de scandale*. Mandeville did not develop new ideas. He made provocatively explicit claims that were merely beneath the surface in seventeenth-century discourse on luxury. Upholders of traditional republican and Christian virtues were hypocrites because they railed against luxury but celebrated prosperity. But, as Mandeville pointed out, the public goods of industry, wealth and state power were the result of humanity's vices and not their virtues. While mockingly adopting the rigorist moralising language of those he satirised, Mandeville broke the accepted causal link between virtue and public good by arguing that public benefits (praiseworthy) had origins in private vices (blameable) rather than private virtues. The good society – a society of power and plenty – needed to have vicious citizens. In a deliberate echo of Hume's indissoluble chain, Berry noted that for Mandeville the pursuit of self-denying virtue leads to the undesirable linkage of stupidity, sloth and economic stagnation. Indulging in luxury, by contrast, encourages the joint development of industry, excellence of thought, and wealth.

Mandeville greatly energised a pre-existing Europe-wide debate over the economic and political consequences of luxury. But his provocations put luxury's more sober defenders into the difficult position of needing to explain the de-moralisation of luxury without appearing to praise vice. The most sophisticated contributions here were those of Hume and Smith. To Hume, commercial societies are the happiest and the most virtuous. They enjoy three ingredients key to good living, and each to a greater extent than other forms of society. These are indolence and response, action and industry, and the pursuit of pleasure. These benefits are the result of the complicated developmental relationship between refinement, prosperity and civilisation. Luxury is one of the factors driving this relationship forward. In turn, within refined, prosperous and civilised societies, many of the dangers associated with luxury have been lost. In commercial societies with high levels of luxury consumption, the moralising accusation of personal excess is misplaced. The growth in refinement results in the reduction of overindulgence: people learn to enjoy their luxuries in moderate fashion. By comparison, in more primitive societies, such as those celebrated by the traditional paradigm and Mandeville's hypocrites, indulgence tends to be unrefined and excessive. Similarly, the traditional paradigm's attack on urban centres as locales of luxury-fuelled debauchery, voluptuousness and unfiltered self-interest are entirely misplaced. Towns and cities are places of learning, politeness and sociability – again, driven forward, in part, by luxury consumption. And with cities, moreover, come systems of law, public order, police and moral discipline enforced by social norms. In Hume, the traditional paradigm's celebration of the civic-minded action of virtuous political decision-makers is replaced by awareness of the social benefits of individual's private endeavour in pursuing their long-term self-interest.

Hume's celebration of the positive role of luxury was bound up in a comparative sociology demonstrating that contemporary commercial societies were economically and militarily superior to ancient republican models. The trading nation is not emasculated but the most military potent society in human history. Luxury does not undermine martial spirit, as is demonstrated by the contemporary military dominance of the commercial societies of imperial France and Britain. Hume reinterpreted Rome's descent into corruption not as the result of luxury, but of unthinking imperial expansion and poorly framed government. The non-trading nation is militarily weak, and unable to sustain, rouse or educate its people. Its society is underpopulated, indolent and ignorant. The commercial nation will be an effective military power because of the benefits derived from its commerce. Firearms and artillery used by a well-trained standing army will defeat the men of a citizen militia – regardless of the extent of the latter's selfless civic-mindedness. Hume's sociological account shifted the cause of commercial society's power and prosperity away from the traditional political explanation of constitutional arrangements and civic virtue. The benefits derive from private endeavour, especially commercial endeavour, functioning freely within a context of individual political liberty.

Berry's analysis next moved on to Smith. *The Idea of Luxury* sets out many of Berry's important claims which would be expanded and refined in subsequent work. Smith emerges as a modern liberal theorist of liberty and commerce. He explains and celebrates commercial society's ability to bring about unprecedented levels of personal liberty and prosperity for all. The modern world is a world of commerce in which every individual is, at least partly, a merchant. This is, *pace* the traditional accounts of the good life, entirely natural as it allows our 'propensity to truck, barter and exchange one thing for another' to flourish. Our individual freedom to pursue our own self-interest and pursue our natural propensities for trading places us into a network of interdependence. The traditional republican paradigm emphasised economic independence as necessary for the good life and society – to be independent was to be incorruptible. Smith, by contrast, praised economic dependence both because it brought about opulence throughout society and encouraged the organic development of social ethics. The latter could be participated in by all members of a society, and not just the political decision-makers.

Smith developed many of Hume's claims. Commercial societies are militarily more powerful than self-denying ones. The pursuit of luxury can function virtuously if undertaken in moderation. The rationally framed political schemes of the civic humanists were less effective in securing peace, power and prosperity than allowing the pursuit of private self-interest within a legal framework. Smith's account, Berry stressed, additionally emphasised two major social goods resulting from commercial society's free pursuit of luxury. The first was the distribution of the fruits of opulence. Modern free commercial states are not only opulent societies but are ones in which prosperity is enjoyed by most of the population. The second was that commercial society is bound up with a superior form of political freedom. Opulence results from the interdependence of individuals pursuing their economic self-interest. This pursuit depends on the rule of law and the negative virtue of justice (that is, the adherence to the law), and not on political systems that enjoin and rely upon public virtue. For societies to endure, it is sufficient for individuals to follow the rules. Politics takes a backseat.

Hume's and Smith's major contribution to the discussion of luxury was the 'de-politicisation' of public good. The furthering of society's best interests results from actions within the sphere of communal political decision-making. The public good is now the aggregation of individual material well-being. Since material well-being is the consequence of commercial activity, the only course of action for politics to follow is that which encourages the free pursuit of commerce; the production of opulence depends on private liberty and not civic action. Politics has entered its 'liberal mode' (*Idea of Luxury*, 166): the provision of general rules setting up a neutral legal framework enabling individual, principally economic, activity. The focus of morality has shifted as well: the focus is now on everyone's social relationships, and not just the motivations and actions of the citizen elite. In commercial societies we primarily interact with strangers. Our actions are guided by our sympathy and sustained experience of social interaction. While Berry acknowledged that Smith had residual sympathies for both the Stoic and Republican traditions, it is clear that Smith believes modern luxury-pursuing commercial societies are most in tune with human nature, contribute most towards social progress, and are best equipped to bring about opulence and freedom.

Enlightenment notions of socio-economic progress developed the idea that what is a luxury object now will become a needed object in the future. For Hume and Smith, ultimate human needs remain the same, the needed objects change. They provided what Berry termed a 'history of the mode of satisfaction of needs' (*Idea of Luxury*, 182), not of the emergence of new needs. A linen shirt starts off as a luxury item but then becomes a needed item as fashions change, but the need it comes to serve is the avoidance of the shame of not having the clothing a society expects. The underlying need of avoiding shame remains the same, but what satisfied that need changes. In Hegel and Karl Marx (1818–83), we get arguments holding that new needs do develop over time. For Hegel, the needs man shares with animals are fixed, but what marks humans as humans is transcending their animality. As discussed in *HHHN*, humans are radically determined by their contexts. Animal needs are replaced by abstract, social and mental needs. Food becomes not only something to satiate hunger but also a social fact – as exemplified by religious restrictions on eating. Needs are culturally determined requirements. Hegel is critical of Smith's argument that the constant needs of human nature are best satisfied by the opulence and freedom of commercial society. Human needs change: human history is the history of the growing freedom of *Geist*. The story of growing human freedom involves the abandonment of instinctive drives and the growing participation in the universal, rational human will. Philosophy is needed in the final epoch of human history, but it was not in the first. In earlier stages of human development, human needs were the animal ones of the securing the 'physical preconditions of existence'. In the final stage we need autonomy.

Marx's historical materialism maintains that the satisfaction of humanity's first needs immediately leads to the creation of new needs. Human history is the account of new forms of materialistic connection between humans, as determined by needs and the mode of production. Through a patchwork of quotations from various texts, Marx can be read as arguing the Smithian line: luxuries turn into necessities within the context of economic development, and these necessities reflect changing social standards. But Berry argues Marx can be read in a different fashion. Humans are productive and creative creatures who are framed for communal activity. History is partly the 'history of the development of the forces of individuals themselves', but capitalism estranges the individual from her nature as a human by framing her existence in terms of 'animalistic, selfish, egoistic and crude' needs (*Idea of Luxury*, 191). Capitalist economies reduce the proletariat to meeting only their animal needs, whereas the capitalist is able to develop luxurious and refined behaviours. Only the overthrow of private property will enable the transcendence of the joint existence of luxury and privation, and the shift from the satisfaction of animal needs to genuinely human ones for all within a society. Capitalism has created the productive power to enable human flourishing but keeps most people on the level of instrumentalist selfishness. Communism will satisfy people's basic needs, but also enable their satisfaction of the higher needs of their fully realised humanity. In both Hegel and Marx, human nature is historicised as part of the path to culmination in an end stage, be it the Rational State or communism. Because this is a normative process – moving towards a desired end point – the moral language critical of luxury can return.

On top of its influential analysis, *The Idea of Luxury* was indicative of Berry's soundness as a sensitive and historically attuned analyst of past political philosophy. Berry remained sceptical of contemporary meta-interpretations that presented a fault-line in European thinking in which the traditional accounts of luxury were bound up with Christian feudalism and the new accounts of luxury were proffered by bourgeoise proponents of capitalism. It is impossible to identify protagonists within the luxury debate with their supposed class position. Moreover, the luxury debate was precisely that: a *debate*, characterised by different and competing viewpoints, and not one in which class groups coalesced against each other. Accounts that see the new luxury paradigm as being set out by a bourgeoisie defending and extending their commercial interests have already imposed a pre-established explanatory schema. While detailed intellectual history was not his goal, Berry stressed that we needed to avoid turning into pastiches past views if we want to fully understand the social changes we claim to be interested in comprehending.

Social Theory of the Scottish Enlightenment (1997)

Berry's next book, *Social Theory of the Scottish Enlightenment* (Edinburgh: Edinburgh University Press, 1997; henceforth *STSE*) emerged out of an Honours class taught for many years at the University of Glasgow, with the book's examples and illustrations having clarity as a result of sustained polishing in seminar discussion. *Social Theory* updated Gladys Bryson's *Man and Society: The Scottish Inquiry of the Eighteenth Century* (1945) and covered, in accessible prose, the key framing concepts and arguments of Scottish Enlightenment social theory. Berry's enlightened Scots were two to three generations of thinkers writing between the publication of Hume's *Treatise of Human Nature* (1739–1740) and the sixth and final edition of Smith's *Theory of Moral Sentiments* (1790). Berry's Scottish Enlightenment still had Hume and Smith front and centre, but they were joined by extensive discussion of John Millar (1735–1801), Adam Ferguson (1723–1816), Henry Home, Lord Kames (1696–1782), William Robertson (1721–93), James Dunbar, James Beattie (1735–1803), and Robert Wallace (1697–1771); frequent mention of George Turnbull (1698–1748), Hugh Blair (1718–1800) and David Dalrymple, Lord Hailes (1726–92); and occasional notice of

Gilbert Stuart (1742–86) and James Steuart (1707–80). What unified these thinkers was a shared methodological approach to a common set of social and political questions. The Scots were a family of philosophers – far more than Peter Gay's Parisian *philosophes* ever were – and their output was characterised more by their shared interests, aims and arguments than their disputes over particular themes.

The 'science of man' was a theme present in Berry's earlier writings, but here it took centre stage. The enlightened Scots were theorists undertaking social scientific research inspired by the methods and achievements of the natural philosophy of Francis Bacon (1561–1626) and Isaac Newton (1642–1727). Human action and society could be subjected to causal analysis as the subjects of natural philosophy. From Bacon came the natural historical method of data accumulation, the induction of general principles from this data, and his strongly utilitarian focus on using knowledge for improving the human lot. From Newton came the impulse to search for causes hidden beneath social effects and for making links between social causes. Newton inspired the Scots to develop general rules and principles that explained how social institutions emerged, functioned and endured. The enlightened Scots led the way in adapting the systematic investigation of nature and development of causal explanations in the realm of human nature and society. The central method for this study was the form of historical theorising that has been variously termed conjectural, natural or theoretical history. These histories set aside local and parochial themes and aimed to present large-scale trajectories of societal development. These were built on the accumulation of masses of evidence from historical writing and travel literature, and where the historical record did not inform on connections between causes and effects, the Scots appealed to informed conjectures stemming from their already established empirical understanding of man and society.

The principal development discussed was the transition from rude to civilised society. This was underpinned by the notion that the shape of human history is that of progress. The pattern of social change was best rendered intelligible by dividing the history of social institutions into a stadial schema charting development from infancy to maturity. Concomitant with the development of institutions was the development of increasingly complicated thinking. This was the 'natural history of man' – natural not in the sense of humanity being on fixed course of development, but because such development emerged out of 'natural' causes.

Berry stressed the role of property in the Scots' social theories but did so in a way that avoided the earlier scholarship's accusations of determinism levelled at the Scots. Concern with securing subsistence is the immediate object of early human societies. As those societies develop, so new and complicated objects of concern develop. Here concerns about securing, maintaining and extending property are emphasised. Property plays a central role because its organisation frames how both political power and law function both formally (government) and informally (manners, morality). Yet Berry emphasised that, far from privileging one causal factor as determining all others, the Scots understood society to be an interlocking whole. The development of more complicated forms of property required the development of the cognitive abilities of humans and a shift from focusing on the immediately sensible to the abstract. Property was one factor among many.

Building on his earlier arguments in *HHHN*, Berry demonstrated that the Scots as a group believed in constant and universal human nature. Their social theory comprehending the diversity of human practices across societies was predicated upon a belief in an underlying human nature and the methodological position that 'explanatory principles . . . apply across cultures' (*STSE*, 78). The Scots differed on the role of physical causes, especially those of race and climate, on societal differences. But they agreed that decisive explanation for diversity was to be found more in moral than physical causes. Here the Scots' adopted what Berry termed 'soft determinism' (*STSE*, 84): the view that our social contexts, habits and customs frame our beliefs and behaviours in strong ways that frame our putatively 'free' actions.

Berry's Scots are sophisticated theorists of society able to go beyond the myths of much previous political thinking. The reason-based decision-making of social contract theory was dismissed as having little relationship to the historical record: there is no evidence of such contracts ever existing and hence the normative value of social contract theory is negligible. The natural history of man teaches, instead, that humans naturally live in societies and not as atomised individuals in a fictional state of nature. Any convincing normative theory of political authority and obligation must be built on the findings of empirical studies. The theory offered by the Scots is one that sees the emergence of government as the result of long processes of humans interacting with each other in societies, not of rational decision-making. Changes in the quality and function of political authority occurred in an interlocking relationship with other institutions and behaviours. Moreover, political authority is a customary belief resulting from habitual experience developed only gradually.

Because of this emphasis on the slow progress of political development, the Scots' social theory verges on the conservative. Individualistic explanations of the creation of political authority and constitutions or the adulation of a Rousseauian legislator are simplistic and misleading. The Scots aver, by contrast, the 'social institutions' such as modes of government 'are to be explained by social causes' (STSE, 39). Humans are purposive creatures, but the Scots argued that social institutions, including political ones, develop over time in ways unintended by the actors involved. Humans are engaged with their immediate concerns. Such activity produces unintended and unexpected outcomes, often in complex ways far beyond the comprehension of those immediately involved. This is not the same thing as claiming that individuals are determined by their contexts: 'it is one of the hallmarks of the Scottish Enlightenment that ... it recognises both structure and agency' (STSE, 42). The Scots differed, however, over whether the unintended consequences of human action were evidence of a benevolent providence at work.

The Idea of Commercial Society in the Scottish Enlightenment (2013)

Berry's next major work was *The Idea of Commercial Society in the Scottish Enlightenment* (Edinburgh: Edinburgh University Press, 2013; henceforth ICS). This volume developed many of the themes initially set out in *Social Theory*. For reasons of space Berry's extensions and refinements will be only briefly touched on here. Stemming from enlightened Scotland's 'pervasive interest in "improvement"' (ICS, 17), the study of commercial society was one of the principal questions of eighteenth-century Scottish intellectual life. The Scots produced a body of theory of immense sophistication and explanatory power, and which went beyond merely viewing commercial society as a final stage in the natural history of society. Certainly, they inherited from Montesquieu (1689–1755) a sociologist's focus on society as an interlocking mesh of behaviours and institutions. Yet when it came to understanding commercial states, the Scots went far beyond what Montesquieu was able to offer. Commercial society was one not characterised by the primacy of trade only, but also by abstract thinking, social, economic, political and behavioural complexity, and civility, politeness and refinement.

The Scots explored how modern commercial societies differed from the other competing model of the good society: ancient republics. The latter relied more on agriculture than trade; their militaries took the form of civil militias rather than standing armies, and they relied upon slavery rather than political liberty. Commerce in the ancient world referred to the practice of trade, whereas in the modern world it refers to interdependency both in the sociological and technological senses. Modern commercial societies were understood to be a new and superior form of society. For one, they were wealthier than previous societies – they enjoy, in Smith's phrase, a 'universal opulence which extends itself to the lowest ranks of the people'. The crucial source for such opulence is the division of labour. It was the conjunction of sociological (different groups have different roles) and technological (within a production process, different workers do different things) divisions of labour that characterise commercial societies. The division of labour ensured that most of our daily transactions will be between strangers and in situations where the exchange 'will be most reliably effected by mutual appeal to our interests' (ICS, 71). The division of labour increases the productive power of individual labour, and the result is greater material well-being for all. In the process, the Scots scorned the notion that poverty was either ennobling or redemptive.

As well as being wealthier, commercial societies were also freer. They are characterised by individuals acting with reasonable expectations about potential future outcomes. Transactions take place between individuals bound together less by the ties of marriage, kinship or friendship and more by mutual exchange and self-interest. New financial mechanisms emerged in the form of credit, contracts and money to aid impersonal transactional relations developed the means of such actions: contracts, money and credit. Commercial societies require social stability and political consistency in the form of the rule of law. The Scots understood the latter in historical terms, and they charted the changing attitudes towards political authority and law as one of the central themes of the natural history of society. It is in the second stage of societal development that government is introduced, primarily to protect the property of the wealthy. As such it retains an arbitrary, capricious character into the third stage. With the gradual overturning of feudalism and the emergence of commercial society, power ceases to be localised and is transferred to general application in the interests of the majority against the barons and the monarch. Commercial societies offer what Hume termed a 'new plan of liberty': 'liberty under the rule of law, the procedural operation of general laws known previously to all [and] strict administration of justice' (ICS, 126). Modern liberty is something enjoyed by all in the sense that everyone is, as Smith put it, 'left perfectly free to pursue his own interest his own way' (Wealth of Nations IV.ix.51).

For Berry, the Scots' account of commercial society involved developing a new ethical theory suited to that society. The Scots were not celebrants of the untrammelled pursuit of self-interest; they all rejected what Hume termed the 'selfish system' of Hobbes and Mandeville. They supported, instead, what Berry termed a 'moralised economy' (ICS, 131). The key virtue was the negative one of justice: simply by obeying the rules, we ensure the good functioning of both our individual lives and our society. Yet the unique sociological character of commercial society – in which we are dependent on many but friends with only a few individuals – brings its own ways of enforcing social ethics. As Smith most influentially described it in *Theory of Moral Sentiments*, we want others to judge our motivations and actions with sympathy and approval and we, in turn, are constantly assessing with approbation or disapprobation the motivations and actions of others. Our internal conscience is not an inherent facet of human nature, replete with moral coding, but a natural propensity that is learned through social interaction. In a society where we live among and exchange predominantly with strangers, our conscience takes on the form of the 'impartial spectator'.

Key to the Scots' discussion of the morality of commercial society is that they were able to take the sting out of Mandeville's claim that the pursuit of self-interest meant good societies required selfish citizens. Moreover the Scots re-configurated the virtues needed for commercial society so that, for example, Mandeville's selfish citizens became Smith's prudently self-interested, yet sympathetic and benevolent citizens. Individuals in commercial societies are better able to exhibit the Stoic virtue of self-command because they are acting in the presence of strangers. Their approval is hard to win, especially when compared with the indulgence of our friends or family. The interdependency underlying commercial society brings about new manifestations of earlier virtues – justice, say, or self-command. Again, as with the extension of prosperity and liberty, Berry repeatedly stresses in *The Idea of Commercial Society* that one striking aspect of the Scots' account of the morals of commercial society is that the virtuous life is one open to all who participate.

On the whole, the Scots valorised commercial society. Yet Berry dedicated the most substantial chapter of *Idea of Commercial Society* to the debate within Scotland over commerce's dangers and flaws. Ferguson debated with Hume and Smith over whether the political passivity of modern commercial societies, resulting from the overriding concern of pursuing private rather than public goods, endangered or ensured the liberty and opulence that was enjoyed. The Scots debated the pros and cons of luxury, though most avoided appeal to the Republican paradigm – with Lord Kames being the exception. The related issue of military strength was debated. Ferguson and Kames, fearing decline in martial strength and virtues, proposed solutions relating to maintaining a citizen militia; Hume and Smith argued for the superiority of standing armies in terms of training, equipment and cost. Similarly, the Scots discussed the negative consequences of the division of labour. Here Berry cautioned us not to exaggerate the extent of Ferguson's and Smith's concern over the psychological or social consequences of the division of labour – Smith, for example, was definitely not 'saddled with the possession of some profound disquiet about the soul of modern man' (ICS, 175). Finally, the Scots were uniform in being concerned about the deleterious potential of growing public debt. The extent of this fear, however, varied: ranging from Hume's apocalyptic visions of the future to Smith's thinking about pragmatic steps to deal with the problem.

The Scots knew that 'commercial society is not the best of all possible worlds' (ICS, 186), only that it was the best society on record so far. These societies are opulent because of the systemic use of the division of labour. This opulence is diffused, though not equally, throughout society. In this, commercial societies differ from earlier trading-states. Ancient commercial republics relied upon slavery. Early modern states relied on policing of wealth in favour of the wealthy. Modern prosperity, however, developed alongside the rule of law and administration of justice. This involved the institutionalisation of equity contrary to earlier forms of legally enforced social hierarchy. Only through political and legal stability could there be the necessary confidence behind future-oriented market action. The nature of trading interactions in commercial societies in which everyone is a merchant means that much social interaction is impersonal and functional interaction with strangers. This involves a form of liberty in which the individual can go their own way. Commercial societies will be inherently pluralistic. Related to this is the fact that politics, and military affairs, become areas of specialisation. The wealth resulting from the pursuit of self-interest can be utilised to general social good. And with the decline of martial values comes the growth of politeness and refinement and, alongside these, the better treatment of women.

The achievement of the Scots is that this picture is not one to be found elsewhere in Enlightenment Europe. As Berry argues, you will find *philosophes* writing about the spirit of commerce or the origin and development of commerce. You will not find, however, an account of commercial society as a distinct stage of human development built upon a series of interlocking behaviours and institutions. The *philosophes* either discussed trading republics – see Montesquieu's *Spirit of the Laws* (1748) – or discussed commerce as one aspect of a society still dominated by agriculture – see the Physiocrats' economic thought. Commerce plays no starring role in Voltaire's histories of modernity. The Italian political economists, and especially Antonio Genovesi (1713–69), write about commerce as a fourth stage of socio-economic development, but they do not analyse commercial life in any depth. Commercial societies are ones, in the Scots' eyes, that are largely in tune with the propensities of human nature. The pursuit of self-interest, the propensity to truck and barter, the desire for social approbation are all instances of behaviour that function well in commercial societies. Indeed, in such societies there is little force involved in getting people to act. The characteristic interdependency of commercial societies produces major private and social goods without coercion: the driving forces are, largely, the principles of human nature themselves.

David Hume (2013)

Also in 2013, Berry contributed a short introduction on Hume for Blooms-bury's 'Major Conservative and Libertarian Thinkers' series, though he was sceptical about applying the title 'conservative' to Hume. Certainly, there are sisgnificant resemblances between Hume's political theory and subsequent conservative thought. Like much subsequent conservative thought, Hume did argue that idea that institutions and customs constituting the orderliness of society have developed over time, were the unintended result of human action, and were central to the success and replication of society. Similarly, Hume was sceptical of pure reason's problem-solving power, especially when it came to the likelihood of individuals creating better institutions and behaviours from imposed schemes. Habit and custom are more reliably relied upon. With justification, Michael Oakeshott (1901–90) could associate Hume with the 'sceptical style' of politics which emphasises the tried and tested, the existing and the familiar, and a desire for order and tranquillity.

Yet there are very good reasons why Hume should not be classified as a 'conservative' thinker. Purely on historical grounds, Berry noted, Hume could not be viewed as a conservative because this was the anachronistic use of a post-French Revolution label. Hume's thought differed markedly from post-Enlightenment, post-French Revolution conservatism. Berry stressed that Hume's 'science of man' was radical in its goal to transform knowledge. Hume wished to overturn ignorance, prejudice and superstition – he did not respect tradition *qua* tradition. Hume believed the 'science of human nature' could teach us significant new things about how human nature and society works, and this knowledge should inform behaviour. Hume offered a searing critique of religion that sets him apart from any religious-based conservatism. Similarly, Hume had nothing positive to say about that branch of conservatism which stresses the transcendental significance of faith and nation. The 'profundity of [these] differences . . . mean that in the round [Hume's] own thought is misconstrued as conservative'.

Adam Smith: A Very Short Introduction (2018)

Along similar lines Berry contributed the volume on Smith (henceforth
ASVSI) for Oxford University Press's popular 'Very Short Introduction'
series. Because the purpose of the series is to introduce key theorists and
topics to a popular audience, Berry avoided emphasising a particular 'take'
on Smith. He did use the platform, however, to make two large points. The
first was to encourage economists to re-engage with Smith's writings. Berry
lamented the ignorance of economics about its history – epitomised by
the incorrect depiction of Smith as the 'apostle of laissez-faire' economics.
Contemporary economic theory ignores the *Wealth of Nations*, due to the
former's technicality, reliance upon sophisticated mathematical modelling,
and use of the abstract notion of man as *homo economicus*. Smith's overarch-
ing political economic principles still have value, while his moral philosophy could inspire further recent moves in economic thinking away from
model of human action purely being about maximising economic utility.

Berry's second major point was that Smith should be viewed, and
read most productively now, as a key figure in the history of liberalism.
His thought needs to be understood in total. Economic activity takes
place within society; bartering individuals are already socialised humans,
and socialisation involves moralisation. Smith rejected earlier moralised
accounts of economic action, such as the republican critique of luxury,
which viewed such action as morally inferior. He did not, as E. P. Thompson
suggested, morally disinfect economic action. Our pursuit of self-interest
takes place within a framework of moral values, and our desire for praise
means we aim to act virtuously within this framework. Market societies
do have moral codes, and these are superior to previous forms of society.
Moreover, Smith's liberalism involves a commitment to equality in various forms. Commercial societies require equality of economic opportunity
within equality under the law. The result of individual liberty, happily, is the
furthering of the public good. This public good is the wealth of nations: the
pursuit of individual self-interest leads to the improved material well-being
of all. The fruits of prosperity are not distributed equally, but, unlike earlier
accounts of economic activity, all do benefit to some degree. As Berry concludes, 'it is in this conjunction of opulence and liberty that Smith's legacy
lies' (ASVSI, 112).

Essays on Hume, Smith and the Scottish Enlightenment (2018)

Berry's most recent collection of essays (Edinburgh: Edinburgh University
Press, 2018; henceforth EHSSE) brought together articles and chapters

published since the 1970s. When read together, these essays frame the Scots as a group with shared intellectual interests and aims, who could be described as 'social scientists' desiring both 'material betterment' and 'attitudinal progress' through knowledge of humans as moral subjects acting in society (EHSSE, 24). The Scots are resolutely modernist: they use, but do not require the structural assistance of, classical, neoclassical and theological thought. What motivates their thinking most of all is their philosophical interest in commercial society. The Scots' two major contributions to the history of the social sciences are, firstly, viewing society as an interrelated set of institutions and behaviours varying over time and, secondly, their recognition that commercial society was a new form of society.

Despite his work bringing together the Scots' social theory, Berry has been reticent in much of his writing to claim a unique interpretation of the Scottish Enlightenment. Alongside his unwillingness to make exaggerated claims about what his research meant for understanding the Scottish Enlightenment, Berry was lightly critical of ideological and cultural explanations. Marxian interpretations offer only very simplistic readings of the Scots as ideological defenders of a new bourgeois order. Similarly, the cultural reading of the Scottish Enlightenment often has boiled down to competing (but, as Berry notes, hardly cancelling) claims about the importance of the Union or the continuation of pre-1700 institutions and behaviour. The Scots' self-conscious modernity, however, should be taken into consideration. Berry understood himself to be part of the 'intellectual camp' of interpreters of the Scottish Enlightenment, but strongly averred that he did not adopt an 'oppositional posture' (EHSSE, 194) against ideological, cultural or socio-economic readings of the period. He was also critical of the anachronistically applied significance of the Scots, as founders of the modern world or the fathers of, say, economics or sociology. What his research has done, we can confidently claim, is bring together the work of various Scottish social theorists and bring out what unifies their contribution to the history of social thought. In doing so, Berry has done much to show the coherence and familial quality of the Scots' thinking, but also the immensity and sophistication of their intellectual achievements.

The Current Volume

Our contributors are friends, interlocuters, former students and scholars whose own thinking has been shaped by engagement with Berry's writings, and the collection's contents reflect the intellectual stimulation we have enjoyed as a result of reading his work. The volume begins with a chapter from one of Berry's long-standing interlocutors. In another instance of his persuasive argument that Scottish Enlightenment studies needs to focus on the social history of ideas as much as the productions of the literati themselves, Roger Emerson offers some discussion of the historical settings of the 'science of human nature'. Building on the findings of Emerson's many decades of study of eighteenth-century Scottish social and intellectual history, this wide-ranging chapter provides an overview of the 'science of man'. It does so by providing an account of the institutions and social setting of the 'enlightened' men and women involved in the pursuit of the science. This discussion is intertwined with analysis of some of its major themes, including its often-understated inclusion of women within the 'science of man'. While accepting that the science involved the study of men in societies over time as they realise their various potentialities (an interpretation associated with Berry), the chapter also emphasises that its origins were multifarious, and any full account must include the activities of antiquaries and physicians. The chapter concludes with a summary of the factors that occasioned the science's decline at the turn of the nineteenth century as the resurgence of religious sentiment, the growth of Romanticism, and the process of industrialisation converged to undermine its central tenets and purposes.

Berry has done much to demonstrate the thematic and analytical coherence of enlightened Scottish social theory. Our second and third chapters explore two figures not usually given much prominence in accounts of the Scottish 'science of man'. R. J. W. Mills offers a reassessment of the methodological standpoint of James Burnett, Lord Monboddo, and his possible inclusion into the Scottish Enlightenment's 'science of human nature'. Monboddo's philosophical writings and his proto-anthropological approach to the accumulation of evidence suggest that he is of more relevance to our understanding of enlightened Scottish social theory than most literature suggests. Indeed, while the metaphysical underpinnings of Monboddo's 'History of Man' are firmly rooted in ancient Greek philosophy, his approach to the study of human nature and society show him to be an often pioneering theorist. Craig Smith's chapter brings the historical writing of Tobias Smollett into the fold of enlightened Scottish social theory and shows how Smollett was concerned not only with the characteristically enlightened Scottish tropes of social progress from the simple to the complex, the savage to the civilised, but also with the theme of how different stages of development could brush up against each other within a specific society – namely Highland and Lowland Scotland. And, specifically, such overlapping could be found in Smollett's birthplace of Dunbartonshire. Smith surveys Smollett's thought on characteristically enlightened Scottish themes and assesses the extent to which he can be seen as a proponent of the 'Berry' line – he can, to an extent, but Smollett retains a classical moralised conception of luxury that sets him apart from the main literati.

One particularly useful concept that has emerged out of Berry's writings on the Scottish Enlightenment has been the notion of the 'stickiness of institutions' – part of the explanation of how behaviours and institutions endured despite having outlived their usefulness. Spyridon Tegos develops Berry's account by examining the economic and moral outlook of the middling sort as found in the thought of Hume, Smith and Millar. At the centre of Hume's discussion of the values of the middling sort is a unresolved tension between his defence of the middling order's worldview and his positive description of aristocratic French politeness. Tegos notes a darkly ironic tone to Smith's account of the progress of the middling ranks: as they rise through individual industry and talent, the middle and inferior ranks seek to imitate the aristocrats above them and, in the process, become contemptible to all. The meritocratic ethos of the middling sort is symptomatic of their independent spirit, but their resentment and desire to imitate the aristocracy indicates subservience to a different cultural code. Millar, writing in a Smithian vein but also immediately after the French Revolution, saw the middling ranks' manners combining both a servile and irrational imitation of their aristocratic 'betters' but also, concurrently and with opposite effect, enabling the erosion of the hereditary basis of aristocratic power through demands for increased standing. As Berry has shown, and here Tegos develops, the Scottish genealogy of manners could offer a highly complicated account of explicit and concealed social motivations and antagonisms.

Three chapters follow that explore aspects of Adam Smith in the Berry mould as a liberal political theorist and analyst of commercial society. We begin with a chapter that draws a close line between Christopher Berry's academic biography and that of Adam Smith. Berry, like Smith, spent his career as a professor at the University of Glasgow, and Ryan Patrick Hanley examines Smith's thoughts about his time as a professor at Glasgow. Surveying Smith's belief that it was the most honourable, useful and happy period of his life, Hanley makes the case for Smith as a thoughtful and engaged pedagogue who sought to improve his students and to encourage the virtues that they would in turn find useful in the pursuit of honourable and happy lives. Eric Schliesser offers a detailed examination of Adam Smith's views on political leadership. Fitting in with Berry's account of Smith as a leading early liberal political thinker, Schliesser views Smith's account of political leadership as one with distinctly liberal characteristics. A leader's role is to further the happiness of all citizens. As such, Smith's

political leaders do have important moral commitments: Smith advocates
a concept of good governance in which the citizenry's moral improvement
is of central concern. This is not in a Rousseauian sense of making citizens
virtuous, but in the distinctly Smithian sense of encouraging a good society.
And, as Schliesser shows, Smith is concerned as much with the qualities of
bad political leadership and the evils of bureaucracy. Maria Pia Paganelli's
contribution engages with Berry's account of the Scots' reconfiguration of
the virtues, and explores how punctuality became a virtue within Adam
Smith's view of commercial society. Central here is the notion of opportunity cost, which Paganelli explores through illustrative examples. In pre-
commercial societies, where there are few constraints on time aside from
the slow changing of the seasons and exchange was very limited, there was
nothing lost by being late. This changed in commercial societies, where
the benefit for a merchant of being consistently on time in an economic
arrangement characterised by large numbers of transactions vastly out-
weighed any benefits derived from being late. A reputation for punctuality
became a necessary for virtue to succeeded in commercial society.

David Hume's moral and historical thought is the subject of the next
two chapters. Naohito Mori's chapter explores the binding together of
'civility and slavery' in Hume's thought on the civilising process. Mori
shows that Hume emphasised the necessary subjugation of barbarous
peoples through the enforced establishment of the rule of law which
in turn thereby allowed for the development of civilisation. Barbarous
peoples – Mori emphasises Hume's discussion of Ireland in *The History
of England* – can only be civilised through conquest and a colonial relationship. Hume's argument here, Mori suggests, raises some interesting questions about Hume's status as an 'enlightened' thinker and can
be read productively against the emphasis on 'progressive histories of
liberty' that ignore the role of violent interventions.

Continuing with Hume, and arguing against the usual depiction of
Book II of Hume's *Treatise* as containing an analysis of the psychological mechanism behind moral appraisals and evaluations subsequently
discussed in Book III 'Of Morals', Ana Marta González situates Hume's
application of his 'science of man' to the study of the passions as a
significant forerunner to the sociology of emotions. She explores why
Hume develops his typology of the passions in the *Treatise* by starting
with the indirect passions of pride and humility. Key here is the need to
understand humans in their social settings. Hume's book on the passions,
therefore, is central to his empirical approach to the study of human and
social matters, and the *Treatise*'s continuing relevance for the contemporary sociology of emotions.

Berry's research has been translated into several languages, and he has been very active in developing links with researchers in other parts of the world. The final chapter examines the ongoing relevance of Scottish Enlightenment studies. Reflective of this, Zhang Zheng-ping's chapter surveys the various stages in the Chinese study of David Hume's philosophy and historical writing since the 1930s. Clearly, Hume studies in China is bound up with changing political events, though pure academic interest has also played a role. A pre-Marxist phase saw Hume treated as primarily as a philosopher associated with Immanuel Kant. From the 1950s, Marxist scholars attacked Hume's scepticism, though from the 1980s this was supplemented by a sense of Hume as a key figure in the history of European philosophy. Work since 2000 has been interested in Hume's political and economic thought, but this is reflective not of any politically instructed interest but because of the increase in translations and the growth of Hume and Scottish Enlightenment studies more generally. The accounts of slow, non-revolutionary, transformation from agricultural to commercial society found in the literati has proved informative reading for a China that is undergoing a comparable transformation. Since the 1930s, Chinese translators and thinkers have approached Hume as a philosopher with something to say about contemporary Chinese problems.

Taken together these chapters indicate the scope and depth of Christopher Berry's influence on the course of Scottish Enlightenment studies. They demonstrate the achievements of a career dedicated to the enlightened idea of the improvement and dissemination of knowledge. They also show that the themes and concepts that he has developed in his writings continue to prompt fruitful lines of inquiry: something that is indeed worthy of scholarly celebration.

Note

1. Christopher J. Berry, 'Idiotic Politics', *Political Studies* 27 (1979), pp. 550–63.

1

Scottish Enlightenment Settings for the Discussion of the 'Science of Man'

Roger L. Emerson

Introduction

Let me begin with some personal remarks. I met Chris Berry late in 1971 or early in 1972 when he was still a graduate student and I was still trying to figure out what the Scottish Enlightenment was all about. We went for a pint and talked about James Dunbar who was largely unknown to anyone but Chris at that point. Thanks to Chris, that would change. I was glad to receive articles from him on Dunbar and made a point of looking up the Berrys whenever I was in Glasgow. They were hospitable, and eventually I often stayed with them when I was there. They even nursed me for several days when I could not walk on a sprained ankle. We swapped articles and books and met now and then at conferences. We shared a concern with Scottish thought but we went our own ways – although I think we shared a broad conception of 'the science of man'.[1] It was more than Hume's epistemic basis for a discussion of the foundation of all knowledge. As others conceived it, the science of man drew on many fields to create a systematic way of understanding humanity and its products.

The 'Science of Man', the 'Science of Women' and Enlightened Scots

By the 'science of man' is often meant the empirical study of the human condition as manifested in our bodies and minds, in our beliefs and activities as those are affected by the climatic and social institutions in which we live.[2] While they are not always noticed, it should also include women. For Hume, who did not coin the term 'science of man',[3] men and women were not so different, a point to which we will return. Human nature may be unchanging, but the manifestations of it in societies are not – as he pointed out in several contexts.[4] The science of man establishes the characteristics of our physical human nature, but also the bounds and limits of our minds – our thoughts, knowledge, tastes and actions. It is partly medical but also embraces the rational psychology of *The Treatise of Human Nature* (1739, 1740) and its rewritten form, *Essays and Treatises on Several Subjects* (1757).[5] In another sense, it is the study of men in societies over time as they realise their various potentialities.[6] It deals with the preconditions for the development of peoples, their progresses or the likelihood of regressions, and the diagnosis of social ills. And it offers guides for remedying those ills.

The science of man is tied not only to the rational minds of human beings but also to their passions, which, like ideas, may vary with sex and change in their complexity and in their expression over time.[7] The science of man is comparative and needs data from past periods and different present contexts in order to make comparisons and to plot changes. It was secular for most Scots because it is fact-based and rooted neither in speculations nor faith – though George Turnbull, Thomas Reid and others might have objected to that claim. Although it makes some metaphysical assumptions, it gives rise to theories resting on observed facts. The theories should be testable. It addresses both the prospects of societies and of the individuals who live in them. For those reasons, we should pursue it – out of curiosity and in order to understand our circumstances and to control our destinies. That we can create such a science was suggested to Scots by the successes of other sciences in the period after circa 1600. It drew upon many fields of thought but was pursued mostly by men.

The science of man, while it concerns women, was probably not abstractly addressed by any Scotswoman writing discursive philosophical prose in the eighteenth century. There were, I believe, only two eighteenth-century Scottish women philosophers who addressed epistemological problems – Catharine Trotter Cockburn (1674–1749) and Lady Mary Primrose Shepherd (1777–1847). Neither dealt with physiology and, only at a stretch, with the science of man. The first was a successful woman of letters and a follower of Locke and Samuel Clarke. She wrote plays and was a moralist of sorts, but she is unlikely to have thought the world had a 'science of man', though men and women were the stuff of tragedy and comedy and had a destiny beyond this vale of tears. Lady Mary published in the nineteenth century and was friendly with the Reverend William Whewell and his Cambridge friends. Like them, she was a believer in inductive science as an agent for doing good, and would, no doubt, have joined the British Association for the Advancement of Science had it allowed women. Her outlook was that, as knowledge accumulated, life ought to improve, but, I believe, she did not write on the science of man, although she was concerned with Hume's views on causation and with theories of perception.

Few women had enough education to think about the topics addressed in the science of man. None had the medical knowledge or skills to think about physiology. The first Scottish-educated female Doctor of Medicine qualified only in 1896 (about 150 years after the first woman received an MD at the University of Halle, in 1754) and died in the 1950s. One might argue that the only resident woman scientist in eighteenth-century Edinburgh was almost certainly an Irishwoman, Elizabeth Fulham (or Fulhame), who worked on chemistry for a few years.[8] More than half the people did not and could not think scientifically about the problems covered in this chapter. However, some notable women addressed some of our issues in other ways. To them we shall return, but first we should survey the work of others thinking about the plight of Scots in the 1680s.

By the 1680s, a number of Scottish antiquaries, led by the great lawyer Sir George Mackenzie (1636–91) and Sir Robert Sibbald, MD, had begun to collect materials for a better national history and an adequate geography of the kingdom. They wanted to defend Scottish political and religious independence and Scottish honour. From those efforts came maps, place-name studies, chorographies (regional and local studies), a book on Scottish warriors, and lists of authors and poets – all aimed at the writing of a better national history which would trace Scots from barbarous ages to the present time of relative refinement in Lowland Scotland.[9] Those antiquarians were sure this history would also show that Scots were never subjugated by the Romans or English. Scots also had, from the earliest times, a church which went back to the time of the Apostles (in their case, to St Andrew) and was coeval with, but independent of, the Church of Rome. Scotland had a respectable culture (or cultures) running back into the distant past. The antiquaries, surveyors, collectors and other workers showed that progress had occurred in every aspect of life. Scots had changed as religious, economic, political and social changes were made or came about. This sort of patriotic work was a source for the 'science of man' unrelated to contemporary or earlier natural jurisprudence or to the work we associate with Montesquieu's *Spirit of the Laws* or Hume's new approaches to politics set out in his *Essays* (1741, 1742, 1752). All those efforts also reflected the categories for understanding peoples derived from classical writers and handed down and popularised in works such as Charles Rollin's *Ancient History* (written before 1713 but published 1730–8). There, the animating 'spirit of peoples' is expressed in various sectors of their cultures but the dynamic interplay given to those sectors by Hume and Montesquieu is missing. Rollin's *Ancient History* was widely read in eighteenth-century Scotland.[10]

Antiquaries by 1700 were also collecting songs and poems to preserve a knowledge of, and to show the stages of, Scottish culture and the feelings people had had towards one another in the past. In Scotland, this meant paying attention to when the bloody war songs of the Gaels give way to the refined verses of more polite courtiers – some of whom were equally ruthless. In some places, change did not come until well after 1700.[11] Songs and poems glorying less in blood, but reflecting warfare in Scotland among the clans and nobles, were published early in the eighteenth century by James Watson, Robert Freebairn, Allan Ramsay senior and Thomas Ruddiman.[12] They continued to come out throughout the eighteenth century. Ramsay's *The Ever Green* (Volume II, 1724) actually contained a short, fake epic written by a woman, Lady Elizabeth Wardlaw, who claimed 'Hardyknute' was a very old Scottish poem describing the repelling of thirteenth-century Norse invaders. It fitted into the publisher's agenda of showing the heroism, manners and sentiments – in short, the different culture – of an earlier period. Ramsay and other publishers were clear about their objectives. Later, women also understood them very well. Collecting and publishing poems and songs attracted many female contributors who, like men, continued to make comparisons between the present and the past.[13] The chief collectors of the musical legacy of the past from circa 1740–1800 were probably women.[14] To fill in the lacunae of the past was to supply data and to pen footnotes to the science of man written by others.

The collectors' work also helped, by the late eighteenth century, to cast the history of Scottish into a progressive form. Music offers an example. William Tytler, and others active in the Musical Society of Edinburgh, showed great respect for the earliest balladeers and musicians.[15] We should not mourn the past or praise too much people whom we have surpassed. Histories and antiquarian works show us a past we can understand but to which we should not want to return. Sir Walter Scott understood and sympathised with the people of the past. Like other Romantics, he regarded it with more warmth than did most of the enlightened but, like them, he had few illusions about its shortcomings. Scott was, after all, a man who lit his house with gas made in an outbuilding in the grounds of Abbotsford.

Other literary figures addressed the science of man more indirectly in novels and poems in which women are shown to be progressing, along with men, owing to more education, growing refinement and economic changes. What was generally of interest to the female authors were the blockages to progress – un-comprehending parents, unjust inheritance laws, lack of education, and lack of freedom and opportunities for self-realisation.[16] However, most Scottish women writers put limits on all those. Tories, like Mrs Anne Grant of Laggan (1755–1838), thought women might do more but ought never to have political power or much authority in other spheres. They were to be more or less passive beneficiaries of male efforts to create progress. Mrs Grant derided Mary Wollstone-craft and railed against the revolutionaries of Paris and London. Things would get better, but this would not, should not, change fundamentally the prerogatives of men.

More progressive moralists touched on the science of man in novels which tended to come late in the century. Elizabeth Hamilton (1756–1816), a friend and follower of Dugald Stewart (1753–1828), is the person who comes first to mind. She, too, disliked revolutions and found Woll-stonecraft a derivative thinker, but she believed there was room for much improvement – which, again, would stop short of equality between men and women for the reasons commonly given. Women lacked the strength, endurance, perhaps even the mental capacity, to be the equals of men. Still, as mothers, they needed to know more and have well-founded and correct political and religious views. And they deserved better treatment. Mrs Hamilton argued for all that in her books and essays. She was also interested in improving the habits and character of poor people and was active in newly founded Edinburgh charities for women. In her historical novel *Vipsania Agrippina* (1804; the title referring to Agrippina the Elder (c. 14 BC – AD 33)), she was also interested in showing how Christianity had greatly improved the manners and morals of the Romans, indeed, of all who converted. What Montesquieu had found true in the world of the Franks in the time of Gregory of Tours, she found earlier in Roman history. Christianity civilised people. The history of a woman could shed light on the science of man, but no Scottish woman probably went as far in the direction of equality as did David Hume, who thought there ought to be more equality between the sexes – even in their sexual behaviour.[17]

Elsewhere, I have shown that there was a steady stream of discussion about the status, abilities and potentialities of women in eighteenth-century Scotland.[18] Most of that tended to reflect social and legal changes which had improved the lot of women – greater rights for single women, marginally more control over their property, better educations and kinder treatment. The most sophisticated and general versions of such views were presented by John Millar, who saw all statuses changing with economic conditions which formed new beliefs or changed old ones.[19] However, most who thought about it stopped short of saying women were or could be the mental equals of men. Perhaps Hume came closest to saying that. The reasoning minds of men and women may be the same but their passions differ because female constitutions are more delicate. Moreover, societies concerned for the security of inherited property did not and perhaps could not allow women to be equals – but Hume made the people of his social world more equal than did others.[20] His enemy, the Aberdeen philosopher James Beattie, argued that in every family throughout time the moral standards were the same – those God gave us by the prophets and then in the Bible. There needed to be a final authority. In family life, that role belonged to the person who was strongest and best able to protect others, to those who controlled property, and to those with the most education. Women were and ought to be inferior to men.[21] Of course, many Christians and others informed by a Classical heritage, which relegated women to inferior positions, agreed.

For neither Hume nor Beattie was there a sense that the science of man could condone or lead to an equality of the sexes or to the sort of society imagined by William Godwin in which sex differences would recede as people became un-sexual as they overcame their irrational instincts. One could hope for continued improvement in manners, such as had been seen in the West as it progressed from barbarism to civility and refinement. One could hope that the non-Western world would travel that road and that women would no longer be treated brutally, stoned for adultery, divorced by husbands at will, sold or enslaved. The science of man showed that was likely, and it told people what changes had made that journey possible. Progress in civility was more likely than equality between the sexes – except perhaps in the value of their souls.

Medical Men and the Science of Men and Women

Beattie's 'strength' and Hume's 'constitution' point to physical or bodily differences. Those took up the time of medical men in ways that impinged on the science of man by lending medical support for its often progressive stance but also by trying to understand the differences between men and women. Scottish medicine had long been solicitous of women. The attention paid to midwifery and the diseases of women went up over the course of the eighteenth century. However, Scottish doctors had long been active in describing the anatomy of pregnant women and foetuses – which contributed to the celebrity of the Edinburgh professors Alexander Monro primus and secundus and the Glasgow-trained surgeons William Smellie and William Hunter.[22] Smellie popularised the works of Hugh Chamberlen the elder (c. 1632–after 1720), a royal physician and inventor and user of obstetrical forceps, and of François Mauriceau (1637–1709), a Parisian whose textbook was long used in Scotland. All those men were important medical educators who trained or contributed to the training of many later Scottish medical men.

Both Edinburgh and Glasgow had courses for midwives taught by men associated with the medical schools, the Royal Colleges in Edinburgh, and the Faculty of Physicians and Surgeons in Glasgow. The Edinburgh courses began in 1726, when Joseph Gibson was appointed to teach midwives and medical students.[23] No one in Edinburgh was to practise midwifery after that date without a licence.[24] However, Edinburgh is known to have examined and licensed only one midwife; its policing was ineffective.[25] Midwives were licensed in Glasgow by 1740, but, again, most midwives probably held no licences. Some have seen those moves as an undue assertion of male prerogatives and the ousting of women from a traditional role. I invite any who hold that view to look at the records of, say, the Glasgow Faculty and at records of the burghs. If they do, they will find cases which were mishandled by midwives, in which babies were not turned in the womb to facilitate deliveries, in which ignorant people made decisions which even a little learning would have led them to avoid. And, of course, we should remember that the courses given were initially for midwives and not solely for MDs or surgeons.[26] Medical students did not rush to take the courses. Indeed, they tended to avoid them.

To aid in teaching, the MDs and surgeons created and used wickerwork women which gave birth to leather-covered dolls.[27] When students had learned how to turn babies, use forceps, and do other procedures on dummies, they were introduced to the wards and to real women. The midwifery courses were not long, probably not highly intensive, but they lengthened over the century. What killed women were not the deficiencies of women or men trained in the schools but the fact that puerperal fever and other infections were spread by both, though more often by doctors and surgeons than by midwives. A majority of the sick people seen by MDs and surgeons had infections which medics themselves had unwittingly spread. By the end of the century, this too was being addressed. Smellie, in his influential textbooks, urged more cleanliness, fresh air and less bizarre feeding of the very young. By 1800, most large Scottish hospitals prided themselves for having lying-in wards in which more babies were being born.

Dr Alexander Gordon of Aberdeen (1752–99), in 1795, had also come to the conclusion that fresh air and cleanliness would be helpful at childbirths, although midwives and other doctors recommended not much in the way of extra cleanliness and urged confinement to very warm rooms and little movement for the mother for a week after giving birth. Gordon had studied an Aberdeen epidemic and drew proper conclusions, despite the miasma theory of disease which held that miasmas caused puerperal fevers.[28] His mortality rate in such cases fell to 30 per cent – about as good as it would get until Ignaz Semmelweis, unwittingly, introduced a germicide for hand washing in 1847.

If the argument for female midwives rested on custom, there were, by 1740 at the latest, a lot of experienced male midwives who knew as much as or more than the women midwives about bringing babies into the world. Their numbers grew and their success was often considerable. It is remarkable that, of the 145 mostly middle- and upper-class women whom I have described elsewhere, about 110 seem to have been mothers but only one or two seem to have died as the result of difficult or botched births.[29] Others lost babies, but the women and children did not die as a result of birthing. Given their general affluence, many would have been cared for by surgeons and MDs, not midwives. Now the reporting may be deficient, but most of those women lived well past their childbearing years, dying of the diseases of old age; those who did not live so long generally died of consumption, fevers or infections. There had been progress in important aspects of medicine which derived from empirical analyses and the application of better science. Still, opinions persisted that women were more affected by the passions, more sensitive and usually less rational.

Scottish midwifery gave attention to a range of medical conditions afflicting children and women. In other fields of medicine more attention was given to diseases of women and new cures for them.[30] Among the latter were studies of fevers[31] and 'obstructed menses', for which some were prescribing electrical shocks as a novel cure.[32] Books like William Buchan's *Domestic Medicine* (1st edition, 1769)[33] shifted attention away from hysteric complaints to nervous diseases which afflicted both sexes – hysteria was now redefined for men as melancholia. The cure prescribed was often the same for both sexes – more activity, a stricter diet and diversions. In the first edition of the *Encyclopaedia Britannica* (1770s), most diseases among women described relate to the sexual organs and to menstruation. By the third edition (1788–97), that had changed somewhat. Infections and fevers now took up more time – there were now more of them known and known to affect both sexes.

The progress of surgery and medicine also fed into the progressive story of human achievements and so buttressed the belief that there could be a science of man, part of which dealt with a history of his and her characteristic illnesses. Some diseases were cultural and related to national diets, such as depression and melancholy, 'the English disease'. Diets could be changed. Others were sexually based: infected mammary glands did not affect men, and women did not have prostate problems. Some diseases were occupational, like 'mill reek' (usually lead poisoning), and could be prevented or made less common.[34] Still more diseases were unreal and rested on historical errors now passé. Among those were religious manias and/or demonic possession. The progress of reason would eliminate those. Medical progress had allowed human diseases to be assigned to periods and had related them to social stages, classed them more effectively, and sometimes treated them better with new drugs or medicines, such as zinc ointments, digitalis and quinine. Medicine was progressive and shed increasing light on human nature and its prospects, both bodily and moral.

As medicine progressed, it also led to new operations. It is astonishing to read accounts of operations performed against great odds to save women or the wounded. An effort to remove an abdominal growth, which was killing the female patient, was made in the west of Scotland in 1701 by Robert Houston, later a Fellow of the Royal Society – and resulted in the first ovariotomy. This heroic operation, undertaken with the consent of the woman, cured her. She did not even develop a serious infection in the wound, which had been sterilised with brandy.[35] Not many years later, Alexander Monro primus removed a cancerous breast from one of his patients; he believed this gave her three years more of life, though in the end she died of the cancer. He also published on 'bloody lymph in cancerous Breasts', part of a series of studies on the lymphatic system.[36] Those things went on elsewhere as any reader of Fanny Burney's *Diaries* will know. Attention was given to caesarean sections and to puerperal fevers.[37] Surgical interventions were rare but were performed because the lives they were meant to save were seen as precious and the pain caused by the disease was unendurable both to the women and their men. They were also facilitated because of advances in anatomy and in the control of bleeding, and perhaps the improvement in scalpels and other instruments.

Medical progress had improved the treatment of some diseases and had relativised them to a degree, but the science of man had still to consider the climates in which peoples lived and which might shape their characters. As noticed above (note 11), Hume had addressed that topic, as had many others. Indeed, climate and its importance was a subject much canvassed in the period – as it had been since Classical times. The men in the Philosophical Society of Edinburgh (PSE) published papers in which the presumptive effects of climate were noticed.[38] Both the *Edinburgh Medical Essays* and the *Essays and Observations, Physical and Literary* gave advice about weather journals which some members kept over many years.[39] Other club men in Aberdeen and Glasgow discussed the topic.[40]

It was thought that climate affected the nature, characters and cultures of men and the diseases which afflicted them. It might explain the differences of pigmentation in the races. Had Negroes become dark through exposure to intense tropical sunshine or were they created dark? An answer could also shed light on whether there was a single science of man or one for each race. Scots were interested contributors to theories of race for more than intellectual reasons. Many upper-class Scots owned slaves in the West Indies and were naturally curious about the nature of the people they had bought – and what they owed them. Henry Home, Lord Kames, wrote at length on race which he thought was a basic fact of human natures and probably derived from the separate creations of men fitted by God for the climates they were to inhabit. Some, like Montesquieu, held that the character for peoples was partially dependent on the climates in which they lived. Cold shrivelled nerves and tissues while excessive warmth made for tropical indolence. If that was so, then this needed to be considered in developing any science of man. Scots, I think, tended to disbelieve the grander claims about climate but not in its medical importance. Yaws was an African disease; the fevers of the Roman Campagna were caused by the exhalations of the marshes; other diseases were also related to climates or varied seasonally with the weather – which annually brought malaria and flu seasons to Scots.[41]

Climate and weather were also important in other contexts. Disastrous weather had often been seen as a sign of God's judgement on sinful humans. Might it be explained as a consequence of moving air masses which were predictable? Record-keeping was essential to trace over vast distances the movement of air masses and the weather they brought. The PSE guided those who wanted to keep records. Meteorological work sponsored by the Royal Society or by groups like the Palatine Meteorological Society in Mannheim worked that street. The weather was of interest to all and had important consequences for agriculture, trade and shipping.

Minds, Societies and Prospects

While female bodies were different, both sexes suffered mostly from the same diseases and experienced climates in much the same fashion. However, when it came to minds, those of men and women seemed more alike in 1800 than in 1700. One of the things they both needed was more and better educations. Most of the interesting Scottish women writers argued for improved educations; so did many men. The future of man should include better-educated women. That had begun in some schools but also with experiments in the colleges. The Evangelical Glasgow Professor of Natural Philosophy, John Anderson, thought ladies should not be barred from science courses and proposed to give, in the second half of the school year 1795/96, a course for women. He did not live to teach that, but it was later taught at the Andersonian Institution created by his bequests. There, women were allowed to enrol in two courses, one on 'Natural and Experimental Philosophy', in which abstract mathematical reasoning was minimised, and the other on chemistry, which was illustrated by experiments. In both, decorum was to be strictly preserved. The courses were serious affairs since the cost of the courses was two guineas each.[42] While the courses were initially taken by over 400 women, there was probably something faddish about them. Enrolments dropped, and in 1807/08 only fifty women were taking natural philosophy – along with 120 men. By 1811, the ladies could take a mathematics course. Later in the century, more subjects were opened to them.[43]

But what men and women had most in common were the social worlds in which they lived. That point was made by many by the 1770s, notably by William Robertson in his *History of America* (1777) and, in other contexts, by the Edinburgh medical man William Alexander, in his *History of Women* (1779). Robertson traced the treatment of the savage women by men in the American tribes. From drudging chattels and slaves in some tribes, they became more independent as savages became more civilised. In his conjectural history, the treatment of women improved, because of economic development, increased knowledge, and peace and civility. Eventually, East Indians would get rid of suttee. As education and a sameness of condition in commercial societies conditioned the lives of all, men and women became more alike in what they did. The laws which regulated their actions would treat them more alike. Laws reflected economic changes. Alexander worked this street, too. He ambitiously took in more of the world but showed the same things. What Robertson had noted were general and universal patterns which defined part of the science of mankind which had to be reoriented to include both sexes and the characters they came to have.[44] With time, women in India and among the American Indians would be more respected. For men like Robertson, this was providential.

What was not clear to others was the certainty and course of this progress. For Hume in the mid-century, religion among the vulgar had a pattern of cyclical change, with monotheism giving way to polytheism and that, in turn, giving way to a restriction of the gods at last to one.[45] The process might then reverse. If it did so, there might be alternations of periods of freedom with others of repression, times of good trade and bad. The course of history had been generally upward, but it was contingent and one could not be sure progress was inevitable.[46] For Hume, vicious luxury and its attendant inequalities, political and economic stupidity, superstitious and enthusiastic religions, and, perhaps, warfare, arising out of jealousies of trade and empire, made the course of history problematic. For others, luxury, division of labours, inequalities and lack of civic commitments might end the prosperity of a people. There was no certainty that it would become the lot of happier others. For Adam Ferguson, societies with class differences were healthy but turbulent, wars often beneficial. Not for him Smith's bland assurance that peace and commercial prosperity were a sine qua non for a good social existence. Empire and constant efforts to dominate might well be, for Britain, the key to success in the foreseeable future. But, in the long run, things might turn out badly.[47] Whatever the end, it would impinge on characters, prospects and attitudes. The science of men and women might not be progressive or even stable.

Most of those topics were addressed in papers read to one intellectual group or another along with a miscellany of other subjects.[48] The antiquarian papers deserve special attention because they point to wide interest in their subjects and because they contributed to a more detailed appreciation of many aspects of the past. Even the most heavily scientific and technical of the Scottish clubs, the PSE, spent time on antiquities and historical subjects beginning with the Romans. They assumed, supported and elaborated a conjectural history of man.

Some PSE papers dealt with the presence of Romans in Scotland (23 February 1737, 6 December 1739). Others discussed their forts and furniture (?/?/1738), coins (3 July and 6 November 1740, 7 April 1741), and Roman and ancient British temples (?1748). Some dealt with the languages of the ancient Britons (4 November 1742), others with the burial customs of the Romans, pagans and Christians.[49] Other antiquarian concerns surface in the questions given to those going in 1742/43 to map the Orkney Islands for the Earl of Morton. When, in 1743, Alexander Bryce drew and published the map resulting from that expedition, he noted Viking relics in the islands – as well as establishing that the northern coast of Scotland was twelve miles from where most maps showed it. Such work and enquiries went on throughout the century.

Alexander Fraser Tytler's *An Account of Some Extraordinary Structures on the Tops of Hills in the Highlands; with Remarks on the Progress of the Arts among the Ancient Inhabitants of Scotland* (1790) made change in the Highlands clear – with the message that there should be more of it.[50] About the same time, the Society of Antiquaries of Scotland (1783-), heard similar papers. In 1793, it published the great book of General William Roy, *Military Antiquities of the Romans in North Britain*, the landmark work in this field since it carefully noted and commented on many known ancient sites and what had happened to some of them. Most students of the

Highlands thought the north was still full of barbarians left over from an earlier age and needing civilisation and improvements in every way. One could study the past in the Highlands but the point of doing so was to change it – to make it and the Highlanders more peaceful, productive and civil. Roy had spent much of his life in that work, mapping the Highlands to insure their quiescence. Civilising the Highlanders had been seen as imperative as early as the 1500s but by the later eighteenth century the topic was fraught with controversy.[51]

Other society papers shaded off into history proper, such as Robert Wallace's 'Dissertation on the Numbers of Mankind', read to the PSE in 1744 or 1745.[52] Wallace thought there had been a decline in numbers which reflected the worsened condition of modern peoples – a claim Hume rebutted several years later in his more famous essay, 'Of the Populousness of Ancient Nations'.[53] Other likely papers dealt with weights and measures over time (1763, 1769), a topic often related to commerce.

Some PSE papers and Scottish newspaper accounts pointed to interests in mechanical novelties such as windmills, improved ploughs, new steam pumps, tile drain pipes, ventilating machines for mines, Franklin stoves, electrical generators, seismographs, meteorological devices, and medical inventions from trocars to stomach pumps. Those extended the range of human activity, produced more leisure or better therapies or reflected other changes in societies and for their members.

Akin to those were papers on ways to improve navigation and communications. On 2 February 1738 and again on 7 May 1741, the PSE discussed the shape of the Earth, knowing it would improve maps and make navigation safer. Some astronomy papers fall into the same class. So too did papers on the North-west and North-east Passage such as one by Dr (later Sir) John Pringle discussed in May or June 1741. Hurricanes, earthquakes and storms in the Caribbean were all noticed and barometric readings given. A seismograph invented by David Wark was discussed,[54] as were water levels noticed in the aftermath of the Lisbon Earthquake.[55] Scots had long discussed a cross Scotland canal and did so again on 5 July 1747. The PSE also heard papers on improving river navigation, a concern of the 3rd Duke of Argyll.[56] Those were all things which changed the prospects of mankind and, so, bore upon the science of man because man is shaped by the world in which he lives and acts.

The picture is the same if one looks to Glasgow or Aberdeen. About 15 per cent of the discourses given in the Glasgow Literary Society (GLS) for the years for which we have records between 1752 and 1801 dealt with antiquarian, historical or conjectural historical topics. A few more, relating to politics and economics, may have done so.[57] At the Aberdeen

Philosophical Society ('the Wise Club'), the historical and conjectural historical topics included papers on the origins of language (10 October 1768) and writing (11 May 1762), Rousseau on inequality (12 April 1758; 3 March 1770) and the history of mankind (25 March, 1765; 25 November 1766). Other papers dealt with Linnaeus and would have touched on the divisions between men and animals and the races of mankind and how they came to be.[58]

The most important mid-century club for non-scientific and medical men was the Select Society of Edinburgh. There, too many members touched on topics impinging on the science of man – one needs only to remember that Hume, Robertson, Kames, Adam Ferguson and most of the university's most respected professors were members. They found counterparts elsewhere in the GLS and the Wise Club, such as John Millar or, a bit later, Robert Hamilton, Professor of Mathematics at Marischal College.

An End to the Science of Man?

The science of man suffered shocks from a number of developments at the end of the eighteenth century in Scotland. Some related to conjectural histories but Romanticism was also important. Romanticism gave a twist to the sort of rational psychology which had tried to establish a universal human nature capable of making logical decisions about social issues. If Sir Isaiah Berlin was correct, Romanticisms destroyed the notions that there were single answers to all questions, that they could be found using uniquely right methods, and that the answers formed a coherent set of true propositions which could be known to be true. For Romantics, there were more ways to truth – which was no longer always one. Knowledge is not virtue, and one standard of behaviour will not fit all cultures. Suddenly not all languages could express the same things, and the people of differing nations were unique and quite unlike one another.[59] Such nations needed the protection of states which would allow different cultures and peoples to flourish autonomously.[60]

The upsurge in religious feelings in the wake of the French Revolution also made things difficult for the science of man. It did so by questioning the ability of men to perceive things as they really are. We are too sinful, or otherwise unable to construct an orderly social world from the sensations which constitute experience.

The doctrine of unintended consequences resurfaced as something providential – with the ordering of things beyond our understanding or control. Insecurities about order were supplemented by the sort of pessimism which came from Malthus and the new economics of men who saw the functioning of economies not as within, and bound by, some moral and political constraints, but as autonomous and working by 'iron laws' without the possibility of much amelioration. There was no certainty that misery could be avoided by most working men or that class war could be avoided. The aristocratic order that Adam Ferguson had imagined might now lead to wars of empire and to social turmoil, consequences which even Adam Ferguson could not have approved.

It is also difficult to see how the new order of things organised by industries relying on sciences such as chemistry could lead to a world in which the old science of man could be important. It had grown up in an unindustrialised world and was pursued and articulated by men who, while often tied to industry and commerce, did not have their thinking dominated by those. In the end, the GLS was not a viable club and was replaced by the Commercial and Literary Society of Glasgow and by groups such as the Glasgow Philosophical Club. The first dealt with matters of trade, the sciences which supported it, and with public policies which furthered it. This was a club looking for more production and greater markets; it was not much interested in the science of man and its related topics.[61] The second was largely a club dealing in science, chemistry in particular. Glasgow, the most modern city in Scotland, was a harbinger of things to come. So too was the appearance of the first working men's institute in the form of the Andersonian Institution. It served the practical needs of a skilled workforce but did not teach the moral philosophy which had embraced the science of man. In the more specialised world of the nineteenth century, that would be replaced by theories of progress or by more empirical sciences turning into sociology, anthropology and ethnography – all three tinged with racism and eventually social Darwinism. In so far as there was a possible science of man, it was a unified social science – something not yet realised and for many an ideal not worth pursuing.

While Hume had thought the passions dictated ends and reason the means to realise them, now neither were as autonomous as he had found them. His sense of how men shaped their worlds was replaced by something cruder, the hedonic calculus of Bentham, which now poised a powerful counterweight to the philosophy of common sense which had generally replaced the logic and moral philosophy of men like Hume and Smith. It was more compatible with religious views while keeping most of the supports for science. But, intimations of another world beyond our ken inform the poems of many by the early 1800s. A more religious world was also a more authoritarian one.

Most of those developments took place in London which, in a more integrated Britain, took precedence over Scottish cities as the place where intellectuals congregated to define or redefine British culture. Scots were becoming intellectually less important and showed a willingness to follow London, to which much of Scotland's talent drained away. The science of man did not flourish in this new environment, though it has in the scholarship on the Scottish Enlightenment, thanks to Chris and others who share his interests.

Notes

1. See, esp., Christopher Berry, 'The Rise of the Human Sciences', in Aaron Garrett and James Harris (eds), *Scottish Philosophy in the Eighteenth Century*, vol. I (Oxford: Oxford University Press, 2015), pp. 283–322.
2. In the eighteenth century, 'climate' still included everything peculiar to a region of the Earth – geographic characteristics, weather and what we now think of as climates. For a recent contribution to the literature on 'the science of man', see Tamás Demeter, *David Hume and the Culture of Scottish Newtonianism*, Brill Studies in Intellectual History, vol. 259 (Leiden: Brill, Brill and Boston, 2016).
3. See Berry, 'The Rise of the Human Sciences', p. 283.
4. For example, 'Of National Characters' (1748), 'A Dialogue' (1751) and 'Populousness of Ancient Nations' (1752). Hume's *History of England* is notable for paying little attention to many shapers of national character other than those who created or changed social institutions and the beliefs they encouraged. Even legislators, like Alfred or Edward I, only shaped people as they built schools, gave laws, and encouraged trade and the arts. To be effective, they created institutions.
5. The philosophical materials have recently been republished from the 1778 edition, along with the *Natural History of Religion*, in a volume edited by Lorne Falkenstein and Neil McArthur, entitled *Essays and Treatises on Philosophical Subjects* (Peterborough, ON: Broadview Editions, 2013).
6. This side of it has been nicely described by Chris Berry, 'Rise of the Human Sciences'.
7. The recent Edinburgh Project to study this subject is described at www.scienceofman.ed.ac.uk/summary.html. This project resulted in a volume edited by Thomas Ahnert and Susan Manning, *Character, Self, and Sociability in the Scottish Enlightenment* (London: Palgrave Macmillan, 2011). The project blurb says that 'the roots of the Science of Man lie in the natural jurisprudence of late seventeenth-century Europe' but that the Scots were its most distinguished developers. That origin seems to me only one among many.
8. All that is known about her is contained in or may be inferred from her book, *Essays on Combustion with a view to the new art of dying* [sic] *and painting, Wherein the Phlogistic and Antiphlogistic Hypotheses are proved erroneous* (London, 1794). This was reviewed in England, France and Germany and is now thought of as a pioneering work in the analysis of catalysis.

9. See Roger L. Emerson, 'Sir Robert Sibbald, Kt., The Royal Society of Scotland and the Origins of the Scottish Enlightenment', *Annals of Science* 45 (1988), pp. 41–72, 53–5, 59–60. Scots were not alone in doing what they did. Seventeenth-century England saw earlier, but similar, efforts at surveying, mapping, studying regions and promoting science in order to make improvements. The Danish Enlightenment started in much the same way with Ludvig Holberg introducing modern science, writing a national history, supporting survey work, and writing polite essays and better plays. In Bordeaux, the Academy grew out of efforts in the 1680s to survey the region and write a history of Guyenne which would establish its historical rights. Later, the city also supported concerts and a new library. There was often a prehistory for these efforts, one nicely described, for Scotland, by William Ferguson in 'Humanism and New Looks at Old History' and 'George Buchanan, Humanist and Historian', Chapters 4 and 5, respectively, in *The Identity of the Scottish Nation: An Historic Quest* (Edinburgh: Edinburgh University Press, 1998), pp. 56–97. This activity continued. It may be said to have culminated in its first phase in General William Roy's *Military Survey of Scotland* (1747–55) and his further work into the 1780s. Then, British maps had to be corrected when they were connected to the triangulation maps produced by the French. That surveying culminated in *The Statistical Account of Scotland* (1791–99), produced by Sir John Sinclair, and finally in the Ordnance Survey project (1791–; 1843–82).

10. Hume cited this work in his first book, *A Treatise of Human Nature* (1739, 1740); most of his friends read it as well. See Roger L. Emerson, 'Hume's Intellectual Development: Part II', in Emerson (ed.), *Essays on David Hume, Medical Men and the Scottish Enlightenment* (Farnham: Ashgate, 2009), pp. 102–5, 109.

11. The Irish and Highlanders were often compared to American Indians in the eighteenth century; see Roger L. Emerson, 'American Indians, Frenchmen and Scots Philosophers', in Roseanne Runte (ed.), *Studies in Eighteenth-Century Culture*, vol. 9 (Madison: University of Wisconsin Press, 1979), pp. 211–36. As late as 1745, an exultant Gaelic poet could taunt his clan's enemies in the following way:

> Have you forgotten that battle at Lochy,
> When we with our blades mowed you down like oats standing?
> And likewise Auldearn, where mighty MacColla [Alasdair MacCollair [?–1647)]
> Left your hero from Lawers [Col. Sir Mungo Campbell, c. 1600–45] lying lifeless and silent,
> That rebel from hell with his regiment accurst! You scattered and fled like sheep from a martin, On the day of Kilsyth your panic was fearful . . .
> We left not alive a single survivor

> Of the breed of MacCailein [Campbells] we met in that battle; May
>> they gain such a triumph every time that they meet us,
> In skirmish or battle, in the heat of pursuing
> Ours the sword's victory, theirs but the pen's.
>
> Alexander MacDonald, 1745

Ossian, too, was a head-splitter for whom 'the remembrance of battles was pleasant to the soul'. Lowland Scots lived with the knowledge, or illusion, that the barbarians were still with them just north of the Highland Line.

12. See 'Ramsay the Antiquary', ch. V in vol. IV of *The Works of Allan Ramsay*, 6 vols, ed. Burns Martin and John W. Oliver and Alexander Kinghorn and Alexander Law (Scottish Text Society, 1944–74), pp. 128–52. Ramsay was intent on preserving verse forms, old language, history and the beauty of past work. See also Alasdair A. Macdonald, 'The Revival of Scotland's Older Literature', in *The Edinburgh History of the Book in Scotland* [EHBS], 3 vols, General Editor, Bill Bell: Vol II, *Enlightenment and Expansion*, ed. Stephen W. Brown and Warren McDougall (Edinburgh: Edinburgh University Press, 2012), pp. 551–69. There are other sections in EHBS which deal with music publications to which women also contributed. Still useful is Douglas Duncan, *Thomas Ruddiman: A Study in Scottish Scholarship in the Early Eighteenth Century* (Edinburgh: Oliver & Boyd, 1965) and Stuart Piggot, 'The Ancestors of Jonathan Oldbuck', in *Ruins in a Landscape: Essays in Antiquarianism* (Edinburgh: Edinburgh University Press, 1976), pp. 133–59.

13. Notable among later female collectors were Elizabeth St Clair Dalrymple, Mrs Anna Gordon Brown of Falkland, Anne Grant of Laggan, and Caroline Oliphant, the Baroness Nairne [Mrs Bogan of Bogan]. More of them are listed in Roger L. Emerson and Jennifer Macleod, 'The Musick Club and the Edinburgh Musical Society c.1690–1800', *Book of the Old Edinburgh Club*, n.s. 10 (2014), p. 60, n. 76.

14. This has been argued briefly in *Neglected Scots* and in the monograph on the Edinburgh Musical Society which I wrote with Jennifer Macleod: see our 'The Musick Club', pp. 45–105.

15. Tytler edited *The Poetical Remains of James I, King of Scotland* (1394–1447) and was the discoverer of 'The King s Quhair'. 'In 1783, he published his work on James and a "Dissertation on the Scottish Music", which gave Scots a way to understand songs from James's time. After saying "The genius of the Scots has in nothing shone more conspicuously than in poetry and musick", he went on to begin his account of the simplicity and sublimity of Scottish music and poetry by noticing Ossian. Following that period [allegedly the third century], the rudeness of the early ages was refined by men like James I who introduced rules and wrote airs for the poems he wrote. Scots in lamenting their troubles in love and war, or celebrating their joyous moments – or just being clever in the manipulations of verse forms, melodies and harmonies – created national cultures which, in Tytler's mind, even influenced the Italians before the time

of Tasso. Chivalry, the Church, the multiplicity of little noble courts (each with its bard and each emulous of all the others), produced a musical culture which it was important to recover and to keep alive. Others had long shared his liking for old songs.' Mostly quoted from Emerson and Macleod, 'The Musick Club', p. 55.

16. For an impressive example of this, see Margaret Cullen's *Home: A Novel* (1802); see also Jane Rendall, 'Family, Politics and Reform in Margaret Cullen's *Home: A Novel* (1802)', in Katie Barclay and Debbi Simenton (eds), *Women in Eighteenth-Century Scotland* (Farnham: Ashgate, 2013), pp. 75–93, and the same author's 'The Reputation of William Cullen (1710–1790): Family, Politics, and Biography of an "ornate physician"', in *The Scottish Historical Review* 93 (2014), pp. 262–85.

17. When Hume talks about reason, minds are sexless. Passions relate more to nerves and bodies and bodies differ. See 'On the Rise and Progress of the Arts and Sciences', in David Hume, *Essays Moral and Political and Literary*, ed. Eugene Miller, rev. edn (Indianapolis: Liberty Classics, 1987), p. 133. See also the forthcoming essay by Lorne Falkenstein on this topic, 'Without Gallantry and Without Jealousy: The Development of Hume's Account of Sexual Virtues and Vices', *Hume Studies*, 41, 2 (2015), 137–70. This contains a careful tracing of Hume's changing view on the relation between the sexes from the *Treatise* to its last rewritten form in the *Essays and Treatises on Several Subjects* (1753–6; Hume's last edition was published in 1777). The only woman who justified what would have been thought a libertine position was Jean Home Heron whose views were summarised by James Boswell for Jean-Jacques Rousseau. See Frederick A. Pottle, *James Boswell: The Earlier Years, 1740–1769* (New York: McGraw-Hill, 1966), pp. 77–9.

18. See 'The Other Half: Women in Eighteenth-Century Scotland', ch. 4 of Emerson, *Neglected Scots*, pp. 177–233.

19. The Scots were never simple economic determinists.

20. Falkenstein concludes in his 'Without Gallantry and Without Jealousy': '[Hume's] emphasis is on the condemnation of male gallantry and jealousy rather than the praise of female chastity and modesty. In an open society the temptations to infidelity can be too great to be resisted and all are better served when lapses are covered by secrecy and pretense rather than exposed for punishment or infamy. But while neither men nor women can be expected to be chaste, both can be expected to be modest and discrete, and men have a special obligation to refrain from hunting for sexual partners and special obligations to suppress sexual jealousy and anxieties about paternity.'

21. James Beattie, *Elements of Moral Science*, 2 vols (Baltimore: William Warner, 1813), vol. II, part III, para. 586; p. 301.

22. All of these men published on female anatomy: Monro primus, *Osteology, A treatise on the Anatomy of the Human Bones* (Edinburgh, 1726; six editions by 1758, several translations); 'An Essay on the Nutrition of Foetuses …', in *Edinburgh Medical Essays and Observations*, Vol. II (Ruddiman, Edinburgh,

1737) [hereafter *EME*]; Monro secundus, 'Additional Observations on Gravid Uterii by Alexander Monro . . .', in *Essays and Observations Physical and Literary* [hereafter *EOPL*], vol. I (Hamilton and Balfour, Edinburgh, 1754), pp. 426–35 ['additional' to others made and published by his brother Donald Monro, a London physician]; William Smellie (1697–1763), *A treatise on the theory and practice of midwifery* (1752; vol. II, 1754, vol. III, 1764; French translations); A collection of [over 300] cases and observations in midwifery (1754); and *A Sett of Anatomical Tables* (London 1754, several translations); William Hunter (1718–83), *Anatomy of the Gravid Uterus* (London, 1753, many editions and translations). Collectively, there was nothing by English doctors to equal their achievement. No one before Smellie so thoroughly discussed midwifery and the problems encountered in deliveries. No better accounts of the anatomy of pregnant women and foetuses existed than his and Hunter's. What is also new is the attention to saving the mother in difficult deliveries. Forceps and craniotomy scissors were meant to be a means to that end. Smellie improved both instruments with the aim of helping more women survive difficult births. By the 1770s, such books were regularly reviewed by the widely read *Edinburgh Medical Commentaries*, edited by Andrew Duncan (1744–1828). That periodical ran, under various names, well into the nineteenth century.

23.   Gibson was not appointed as a regular university professor, perhaps because he was an Episcopalian who might have scrupled at the oaths required of university professors. In 1739, a regular appointment was made. Gibson wrote on '. . . the Nutrition of the Foetus in utero', in *Medical Essays and Observations Revised and Published by a Society in Edinburgh*, ed. Alexander Monro I for The Medical Society [1731–6] (Edinburgh: Thomas Ruddiman, 1733), no. XIV.

24.   John D. Comrie, *History of Scottish Medicine*, 2 vols (London: Wellcome Historical Medical Museum, 1932), I, p. 299; II, pp. 435–7.

25.   *Manuscript Minutes of the Faculty of Physicians and Surgeons of Glasgow*, Vol. II, entry for 3 December 1739. The Faculty also pensioned some midwives. See also Helen M. Dingwall, 'A Famous and Flourishing Society': *The History of the Royal College of Surgeons of Edinburgh, 1505–2005* (Edinburgh: Edinburgh University Press, 2005), p. 115.

26.   These courses are mentioned by Anne Cameron in 'Female Birthing Customs and Beliefs', in Katie Barclay and Deborah Simonton (eds), *Women in Eighteenth-Century Scotland: Intimate, Intellectual and Public Lives* (Farnham: Ashgate, 2013), pp. 17–35, at 31–3. The policing of midwives, as she notes, was not strict, which is one of the reasons doctors tried to do more deliveries themselves.

27.   William Smellie used such dummies in his well-attended London school and was quickly followed in this by others in Scotland. When he retired, his dummies went to Glasgow University. Two 'babies' are still preserved at the Royal College of Physicians, Edinburgh.

28.   Ian A. Porter, *Alexander Gordon, M.D. of Aberdeen*, University of Aberdeen Studies 139 (Edinburgh: Oliver and Boyd, 1958), pp. 57–86.

29. See the Appendix to ch. 4 of Emerson, *Neglected Scots*.
30. Some papers show that doctors like George Young were doing autopsies on women (*EOPL* II, no. 18) and noticing out-of-the-way deliveries (from my reconstructed but unpublished record of the clubs papers – hereafter PSE list, 22\11\38; *EOPL* II, nos. 24 and 25.
31. *EOPL* II, Nos. 34 and 35 (PSE list, 1 May 1755).
32. PSE list, 1 May 1755, ?/?/1757; ?/?/1762; ? August 1764 and 6 September 1764, *EOPL* III, no. 6 (pp. 116–19); *Medical Commentaries* III (1775), pp. 394–410. The last reports on work done in Vienna, Holland, Scotland, and England between 1752 and 1772. In 1763, Dr John Stedman (or Steedman), an Edinburgh physician, produced a book, *Theory of the Menses*, in which he argued that women had more and more slowly circulating blood which needed periodic discharge. Portions of that book are likely to have been read to the PSE. There were other papers on this topic, e.g. *EOPL* II, no. 39. Indeed, the subject had occupied Scots doctors from at least 1720 when Thomas Simson had written a Glasgow medical thesis on it. He expanded that into *A System of the Womb* (London, 1729). It had several editions.
33. This went through about seventy editions by 1805; Richard B. Sher, 'William Buchan's Domestic Medicine: Laying Book History Open', in Peter Isaac and Barry McKay (eds), *The Human Face of the Book Trade: Print Culture and Its Creators* (New Castle, DE, and Winchester, Hamps.: St. Paul's Bibliographies and Oak Knoll Press, 1999), pp. 45–64.
34. *EOPL* I, no. 22.
35. Robert Houston (c. 1682–1734) was an extraordinarily daring surgeon whose account of the operation is in the *Philosophical Transactions of the Royal Society of London*, XXXII, no. 257 (1725). His career is briefly related in *Memorial of the Faculty of Physicians and Surgeons of Glasgow, 1555–1855* (Glasgow, 1896), pp. 248–9.
36. *EME* V (1742), no. 31.
37. E.g. *Edinburgh Medical Commentaries*, V (1778), p. 211; *EOPL* II, no. 34.
38. E.g., Ebenezer Gilchrist, 'Observations on the Catarrhal Epidemic of 1762', *EOPL* III, no. 18.
39. See the 'Preface' to the *EME* I. Among those PSE members who kept such journals were the Earl of Bute and his brother, some of which survive at Mount Stuart House. Andrew Pringle, Lord Alemore and his sometime assistant James Lind (1736–1812) recorded weather observations at the observatory at Hawk Hill, near Edinburgh. So did an hitherto unlisted member of the PSE, Dr James Badenach. He farmed three small estates near Stonehaven; see Mowbray Pearson (ed.), *Flitting the Flakes: The Diary of J. Badenach a Stonehaven Farmer 1789–1797* (Edinburgh: Aberdeen University Press and the National Museums of Scotland, 1992). His membership in the PSE is noted on p. 3. His daily entries included the weather. Both the *Medical Essays* and the PSE's *EOPL* published weather reports (1764–76). See also Jan Golinski, *British Weather and the Climate of Enlightenment* (Chicago: University of Chicago Press, 2007). This has a miscellany of information on this

topic, as does Paul B. Wood's brief, 'The Science of Man', in N. Jardine, J. A. Secord and E. C. Spary (eds), *Cultures of Natural History* (Cambridge: Cambridge University Press, 1996), pp. 197–210. Wood points to the Baconian prehistory of this concept and to some explorations of it by Aberdonians.

40. For the Glasgow Literary Society's concern with meteorology and weather, see the list of the Society's known papers in Emerson, *Neglected Scots*. A similar list for the Aberdeen Philosophical Society exists, but in Aberdeen only a few dealt with climate and meteorology, usually in papers on natural history and mankind.

41. For a discussion of malaria in Scotland, see Guenter B. Risse, *New Medical Challenges during the Scottish Enlightenment*, Wellcome Series in the History of Medicine (Amsterdam and New York: Editions Rodopi, 2005), ch. 5, 'Ague in Eighteenth-century Scotland?: The Shifting Ecology of a Disease', pp. 171–97. Other chapters are also relevant to this essay.

42. John Butt, *John Anderson's Legacy: The University of Strathclyde and Its Antecedents, 1796–1966* (East Linton: Tuckwell Press and Strathclyde University, 1996), pp. 28–9.

43. Butt, *John Anderson's Legacy*, pp. 36, 38, 54.

44. This is the main subject of the book mentioned above, *Character, Self and Sociability in the Scottish Enlightenment*; see, in particular, the essay by Silvia Sebastiani, 'National Characters and Race: A Scottish Enlightenment Debate', pp. 187–205.

45. For thinkers like Cicero, there was always a form of deism which Hume did not see as changing much. See Emerson, 'Hume's Histories', in *Essays on David Hume*, pp. 132–40

46. That was also the view of others; see David Spadafora, *The Idea of Progress in Eighteenth-Century Britain* (New Haven and London: Yale University Press, 1990). See, esp., ch. 7, 'The Progress of Human Culture: Scotland' (pp. 253–320). There he finds Scots noting changes but often uncertain of improvement and betterment over time.

47. These questions have been mulled over in rather different ways by Iain McDaniel in *Adam Ferguson in the Scottish Enlightenment* (Cambridge, MA: Harvard University Press, 2013).

48. The citations to papers come from my unpublished notes on the PSE taken so I could write the articles which I published on it. Some material has been added to them since the 1980s. Those entries were not available when I wrote my PSE essays.

49. This topic and many others are touched on by Stuart Piggot in 'The Ancestors of Jonathan Oldbuck', ch. VII in his *Ruins in a Landscape: Essays in Antiquarianism* (Edinburgh: Edinburgh University Press, 1976), pp. 133–59.

50. Alexander Fraser Tytler, in *Transactions of the Royal Society of Edinburgh*, II (1790), pp. 3–32.

51. Efforts to civilise Highlanders in the 1500s centred on breaking the clans, enforcing a unified national law, building towns, and promoting trade, better agriculture and schools. Some roots of the Enlightenment go back a long

way. See W. Croft Dickinson and Gordon Donaldson (eds), *A Source Book of Scottish History*, 3 vols (Edinburgh: Thomas Nelson & Sons, 1954), III, pp. 261–74. For the controversies, see the brilliant book by Fredrik Albritton Jonsson, *Enlightenment's Frontier: The Scottish Highlands and the Origins of Environmentalism* (New Haven and London: Yale University Press, 2013). Jonsson has an interesting and original critique of the basic principles of the social thinking of the prominent enlightened Scots, such as Hume and Smith.

52. A copy of this later published paper exists at Edinburgh University Library, Laing Manuscript II.96.3.

53. Hume by then was a Secretary of the PSE but is unlikely to have read this paper there.

54. *EOPL* III, no. 9.

55. The PSE at the beginning of 1756 began to collect information on quakes and the high water levels caused by them. The first indication of that is found in the *Philosophical Transactions of the RSL* 49: part II: no. lxxii: letters xxi, xxii, lxvii. Those include a letter to Dr John Pringle from Edinburgh. There were later letters and more discussion in the PSE in April which led to *EOPL* II, no. 36.

56. Some of the canals and waterways are discussed by me in *An Enlightened Duke: Archibald Campbell, Earl of Ilay, 3rd Duke of Argyll 1682–1762* (Glasgow: Humming Earth Press, 2013), pp. 212–13, 318, 454 n. 34. See also David Wark's PSE paper, 'An Account of the Use of Furze in Fencing the Banks of Rivers . . .', *Philosophical Transactions of the Royal Society of London* 52 (1761), pp. 1–3. This related to the deepening the Clyde River below Glasgow.

57. This relies on material published in my essay on the GLS in *Neglected Scots*.

58. At Aberdeen, Linnaeus found a correspondent in Dr David Skene, at Edinburgh in Prof. John Walker, DD. I know of no correspondent at Glasgow, but Linnaeus's work was discussed in the GLS, which also noticed Lord Kames's views on race.

59. Berlin made this argument in several places where he tried to distinguish the Enlightenment from Romanticism. One place was in 'The Decline of Utopian Ideas in the West', in J. M. Porter and Richard Vernon (eds), *Unity, Plurality and Politics: Essays in Honour of F. M. Barnard* (London and Sydney: Croom Helm, 1986), pp. 120–42. Similar ideas lie behind J. L. Talmon's *The Origins of Totalitarian Democracy* (New York: Praeger, 1960) and works by the Frankfurt School, which tended to view the Enlightenment from the Left but found it equally nightmarish.

60. For a perceptive treatment of this subject, see Elie Kedourie, *Nationalism*, rev. edn (New York: Praeger, 1961).

61. I have discussed this in *Neglected Scots* since some of John Anderson's friends supported it.

2

The 'Almost Wilfully Perverse' Lord Monboddo and the Scottish Enlightenment's Science of Human Nature

R. J. W. Mills

Introduction

In celebration of Chris Berry's important account of the Scottish Enlightenment's 'science of human nature', this chapter explores the neglected contribution to that science by James Burnett, Lord Monboddo (1714–99). The following analyses Monboddo's understanding of his philosophical project, articulated in both *Origin and Progress of Language* (6 vols, 1773–92) and *Antient Metaphysics* (6 vols, 1779–99), as developing a comprehensive 'History of Man'.[1] For good reason – he believed in mermaids, kraken, men with tails, ancient daemon kings and so on – Monboddo is often placed at one step's remove from mainstream Scottish Enlightenment thought. An exploration of his 'History of Man', however, shows Monboddo to be a scientist of human nature keenly aware of issues of evidence and method, even if in his natural philosophy and his metaphysics he was out of step with his times. If we focus less on Monboddo's eccentric beliefs and instead examine the methods by which he reached such beliefs, a picture emerges of Monboddo as a studious, proactive and reflective natural historian of humanity. His account of human nature was predicated on evidence stemming from his own pioneering personal researches into wild children and the orangutan, as well as evidence flowing in from his extensive network of contacts and researchers that brought back knowledge from the furthest extremities of the British Empire. The cause of Monboddo's eccentric worldview stemmed both from his worldview being built on ancient Greek and not Newtonian natural philosophy and because he had a particularly credulous lawyer's faith in testimonial evidence.

Monboddo deserves more attention in Scottish Enlightenment scholarship.[2] He has been the subject of extensive discussion by historians of linguistics,[3] as well as by researchers exploring the man–beast distinction

in Enlightenment thought.[4] But he has a reputation for being an outlier –
'almost wilfully perverse' in Berry's phrase – who need not be prominent
in accounts of the age.[5] The below provides a wide-ranging exploration
of Monboddo's methodology as a natural historian of human nature and
society. This involves approaching Monboddo from another starting point
than his conjectural history of the origin and development of language, and
undertaking a more sustained engagement with the *Antient Metaphysics*
than is usually found in the literature.[6] Monboddo's approach contains
both elements characteristic of the Scottish 'science of human nature' and
elements strikingly different. The resultant picture is one of Monboddo as
an interesting and original thinker who was an active scientist of man –
undertaking his own research, utilising a large research network and applying legalistic standards of evidence – but an anti-modernist proponent of a
return to ancient Greek thought. He is neither purely Christian humanist
nor enlightened scientist of man.

   Monboddo was unusually credulous yet fervently believed he was being
stringently empirical and rational when studying human nature. This position can be explained by emphasising two aspects to his approach. Firstly,
Monboddo placed research and utilisation of facts about oddities, curiosi-
ties and highly unusual occurrences at the very centre of his philosophical
project. In comparison, the leading practitioners of the science of human
nature concerned with the history of man – Hume, Kames, Smith, Ferguson, Robertson, Millar and Dunbar – rejected unusual claims as the result
of false or inaccurate reporting or as irrelevant exceptions to the general
tendencies of human development. When it came to natural philosophy
and metaphysics, Monboddo believed that the answers to the central
questions of the 'science of human nature' were to be founded upon Platonic and Aristotelian thought. To understand man, and avoid the failings
of eighteenth-century materialism, we must adopt the philosophy of the
ancient Greeks.[7] Monboddo was a fundamentally paradoxical figure who
combined 'enlightened' methods and concepts with discredited ancient
natural philosophy.

Monboddo's 'History of Man'

To situate Monboddo's approach to studying man, we first need to
recap some of Berry's central claims about the Scottish Enlightenment's
'science of human nature'. At its core, this science was built on the idea
that human nature had inherent operating principles which were constant
and uniform in function. Hume summarised this point neatly in his *Enquiry
concerning the Principles of Human Understanding* (1748) when claiming

that 'it is universally acknowledged that there is a great uniformity among the actions of men, in all nations and ages, and that human nature remains still the same in its principles and operations'.[8] This fact about the universally held qualities of human nature was discerned from the accumulation of facts about human behaviour in societies past and present. The accumulation of facts was justified by the belief that investigation into human nature must be based solely on experience and observation.

The enlightened Scots were keen to state their inspiration and methodological inheritance as involving the application of earlier natural philosophy to the newly naturalised human sciences. From study of Francis Bacon came both the process of accumulating facts from which arguments were induced and the focus on the utility of knowledge. From Isaac Newton came an emphasis on reducing the complexity of phenomena to a few simple and generalisable explanatory principles. Less explicit was the engagement with John Locke's *Essay concerning Humane Understanding* (1690). The literati adopted Locke's account of the human mind as something that develops through experience, education and habit-formation, but historicised the account by placing the development of the human mind in the context of the long transition from pre-social savagery through to contemporary civil society. From Montesquieu's *Spirit of the Laws* (1748) came an imitable method of sociological taxonomy and a sense of the interlocking development of institutions and human behaviours.

The Scots put together natural histories of mankind that explained human behaviours and institutions as developing over long periods of time and as a largely unintended result of human action. This separated them from theological accounts, which utilised the explanatory factor of providence, and from civil history, which charted the succession of events. Instead, the Scots disentangled the immense anthropological testimony present in travel literature and historical works and replotted it on a trajectory of socio-economic and political progress. The 'science of human nature' organised human experience into useful heuristic models of expected social change. The most famous model was that of the 'four stages' of development from savage, through pastoral and agricultural, to commercial society. The model, associated most with Adam Smith and John Millar, explained changes in social, economic and political structures, as well as human behaviour, as occurring during the largely unintentional consequences of human activities to cope with the natural and human environments.

At first blush, Monboddo's description of his 'History of Man' aligned his project with that of the Scottish Enlightenment's 'science of human nature'. The subject of the 'History of Man' was not the 'history of any particular nation' but that of 'the whole species' through 'the various stages of his progression'.[9] Monboddo adhered to the enlightened mantra that he was 'discovering the nature of man from fact and experience', rejected unempirical philosophical systematising and claimed he collected facts 'in the same manner as we collect the history of any other animal'.[10] Monboddo's subject matter was the formation of humanity's 'character, sentiments, manners, customs, and institutions' through the maturation into 'actuality' of the intellectual aspects of human nature.[11] Regardless of his emphasis on ancient Greek philosophy, Monboddo had clearly imbibed and adopted many of the concepts and language of enlightened social theory – we surely mischaracterise him if we accept his bald assertions of his anti-modernism.[12]

Yet despite these striking conceptual and linguistic similarities with his contemporaries, Monboddo maintained that his methodology was taken from the ancients not the moderns.[13] The 'science of human nature' was not a new study dated from the mid-seventeenth century and which involved the extension of the methods of experimental natural philosophy into the study of human nature and society. It had its origins, and reached its apogee, in ancient Greek thought. Monboddo ignored sustained public engagement with works by his fellow literati – aside from repeatedly attacking Hume as a dangerous materialist. He made no published comment on his fellow judge and sparring partner Henry Home, Lord Kames, whose *Sketches of the History of Man* (3 vols, 1774) covered very similar territory.[14] He did, by contrast, engage with enlightened French thought. One major, if negative, inspiration for Monboddo's work was the earlier volumes of Buffon's *Histoire naturelle, générale et particulière* (1749–1804); while an interest in Buffon was common among the literati, Monboddo's engagement was of a higher order of intensity.[15] The two eighteenth-century natural historians of man Monboddo praised were both members of the French Enlightenment. Monboddo was impressed by Joseph-François Lafitau's *Mœurs des sauvages amériquains comparées aux mœurs des premiers* (1724), while Rousseau was 'an author of so much genius, and original thought, as well as learning'.[16] Monboddo praised Rousseau as the only contemporary philosopher who had inquired whether 'by the improvement of our faculties, we have mended our condition, and become happier as well as wiser'.[17] Rousseau received Monboddo's praise, then, because did not accept the Enlightenment's complacent belief in progress.

Aristotle was the natural historian who inspired Monboddo the most. The study of the operation of man's intellectual faculty was not, as it was for most Scots, a Baconian position but one Aristotelian in inspiration. Monboddo's methodological manual was Aristotle's *Historia animalium*, and he praised its investigations into the 'affections and dispositions' of animals. By applying Aristotle's methods to man we should be able to learn 'what sort of animal we ourselves are'.[18] Imitating Aristotelian natural history was an unfashionable step, Monboddo averred, but it was the best method for authoring an accurate history of the human species.[19] Monboddo's willingness to accept tales about fabulous creatures may stem from his immersion in Aristotelian natural history. The *Historia animalium* does not use a rigid system of biological classification in a manner akin to Linnaeus or Buffon, but arranges its material in a capacious fashion, avoiding essentialist definitions and willing to comprehend difference.

Monboddo used a modified version of the Aristotelian definition of 'man'. Man was indeed a biped and a 'rational animal, mortal, capable of intellect and science'.[20] Rational here was understood to mean possessing a 'comparative faculty, by which [humans] compare things together, deliberate and resolve'. This feature was shared with other animals. The specific differences defining the human species was their morality – which distinguished them for immaterial beings – and the fact they were capable of intellect and science. The intellect referred to the 'faculty of forming perfect ideas', whereas 'science' was knowledge about those 'perfect ideas'.[21] Perfect ideas are those found described in Plato's doctrine of the Forms.[22] So far Monboddo was in line with the Aristotelians, supplemented by Platonic ideas. But he added to the definition, however, the other specific differences of man's 'mild, humane, docile, tractable disposition, capable of love and friendship, and the strongest attachments, with a sense of decency, honour, and justice'.[23] While adding an emphasis on man's moral sentiments and affections might appear like a characteristically enlightened Scottish position to take, it was also a clear extension of Aristotle's methods in the *Historia animalium* to humans.

Ancient Greek metaphysics – Platonic and Aristotelian – underpinned Monboddo's 'History of Man'. This point is absolutely key to understanding Monboddo's paradoxical place in eighteenth-century Scottish intellectual life. Following his Greek teachers, Monboddo believed in 'mind': an immaterial substance equated with reason, vitality and able to produce motion in passive matter.[24] Monboddo rejected the Newtonian position that movement in the universe was, after an initial act of providence, the 'operation of matter and mechanism merely'.[25] Greek philosophy taught that mind acted constantly in the universe, but that this took the form of a great chain of being consisting of gradations of mind. This belief lead to Monboddo's acceptance of the existence of intermediary intelligences between man and God.[26] Monboddo believed he was 'following the philosophy of Aristotle' in believing that 'everything exists which is possible to exist' – and the abundance of nature suggested these possibilities far exceeded what most natural historians of man were willing to accept.[27] But he framed this is theistic terms: a benevolent and omnipotent supreme being would create 'every sentient being that is capable of pleasure [and] whose existence is possible' – otherwise 'there would be something wanting in the system of nature'.[28] Monboddo's universe and its potential contents, then, were very different from mainstream enlightened Scottish thought.

Monboddo did not remain an enlightened scientist of man: he went through an 'antiquarian turn' in the final decades of his life. From the mid-1780s, Monboddo mixed his 'enlightened' approach to the natural history of man with increased enthusiasm for philological and mythological studies. This strange mixture can be best illustrated by listing the religious topics that came to enthral Monboddo: allegorical interpretations of scripture; decoding the etymology of pagan gods; the possible *prisca theologia* contained within ancient Egyptian wisdom; the transfer of such wisdom from one society to another by specific kings and philosophers; the existence of the doctrine of the Trinity as an aspect both of ancient wisdom but also natural religion; and the relationship between Egyptian mysticism and Christianity. At the same time, his approach to these topics distinguished Monboddo from contemporary mythographers. He did not study ancient Egyptian 'fable' or 'myth', but the naturalistic category of 'religion'. He did not do so to understand the corruption of an original Noahite religion, but to understand the origin and progress of religion from savage man onwards. He did not situate his account within biblical time (which he did not believe in) nor, indeed, did he use scripture as historical evidence, but through the heuristic prism of long-term social development. Unlike most contemporary mythographers, he was not interested in proving the historical truth of Christianity but to understand man.[29] Even as the balance in his work tipped towards Christian humanism in the final years of his life, Monboddo remained committed to the concepts and methods – despite his dispute over their origins – of the 'science of human nature'.

Monboddo on Evidence

The natural history of man relies upon experience – the natural historian's and the testimony of others – to establish its claims. Monboddo discussed the empirical elements of his account of man as much as any other literatus. Monboddo explained his approach to establishing matters of fact in the second volume of *Antient Metaphysics*. He took 'facts as I find them': 'if the author is credible, I believe them without supposing them to be exaggerated.'[30] To modify the material found in another's testimony, to lop off any elements thought exaggerated or to interpret the material according to extraneous principles, is not to find facts but 'to make them' yourself. This process of fact-creation, with its resultant distancing of the natural historian's claim from reality, occurs when a philosopher applies their preconceived philosophical system to testimony. But there was no reliable way of knowing whether one's extraction of perceived truth out of testimony was done accurately: it was far safer to just believe the testimony to be true.

Monboddo explained that his method for establishing the credibility of testimony involved four steps. Firstly, he assessed whether the witness was well informed about what they described. Secondly, he assessed whether they were a credible or suspectable individual. Thirdly, he judged whether their testimony was contradicted by others more credible than them. Finally, he judged whether the testimony made contained claims that were 'by the nature of things, impossible to be true'.[31] At each stage, however, Monboddo was not very strict. He utilised hearsay evidence. He was unsuspicious about the motives or the capabilities of explorers to accurately recorded facts about foreign lands. He valued certain authorities, especially Herodotus, to the extent that they were effectively gospel. His Greek understanding of 'the nature of things' was such that, what was impossible for the moderns around him, was very much plausible for Monboddo. Perhaps most importantly in explaining his credulity, Monboddo failed to distinguish between what eyewitnesses of purported animal and humanoid cryptids saw and what they thought they saw. Accounts of mythical creatures or behaviour are built on such failure to separate observations and conclusions.

Also setting Monboddo apart from his fellow literati was his reliance upon the extensive citation of authorities. He viewed citing authorities as an act of authorial good practice – 'I do not think it below me to give the reader the satisfaction of knowing my authorities for the facts I advance' – and implied his contemporaries hid their own.[32] Indeed, Monboddo utilised arguments from authority with a frequency and confidence uncharacteristic of his fellow literati. The latter occasionally utilised the appeal to the *consensus sapientium* but they professedly did not rely upon or cite authorities – or, indeed, sources. Monboddo's appeal to authority – even when the authority's reported fact was *prima facie* ridiculous – is one of the reasons why he has been frequently placed within the tradition of Christian humanism.

Monboddo's position on evidence can be helpfully illustrated by recounting the wider debate within the Scottish Enlightenment over testimony. Leading the charge for judicious scepticism towards testimony was David Hume. In the *Treatise of Human Nature* (1739–40) Hume discussed credulity or the 'too easy faith in the testimony of others' in terms of the workings of the mind, which was 'very naturally account for from the influence of resemblance'.[33] When we read an account testifying to the existence of a mythical creature, a mermaid, we conflate our mind's ability to conceive of a mermaid with the real-world existence of the imagined mermaid. Hume developed this position further in the *Enquiry concerning the Principles of Human Understanding* (1748) by emphasising the human propensity to believe in tales of the marvellous. When we received testimony containing 'utterly absurd and miraculous' claims, our nature is primed to believe such accounts precisely because they are absurd.[34]

Hume encouraged his readers to be aware of the natural processes at work when judging unusual claims. In the *Treatise* Hume also outlined the appropriate method for assessing the truth of testimony. We must correct our initial credulous judgement by taking a reflective moment and engage our understanding. We will be reminded of our accumulated experience – whether personal or derived from others – which we then need apply in judgement of the testimony. This judgement involves the 'opposition of experiments and observations' for and against the claim.[35] We then dismiss as false the claim with less evidence. Hume developed his account of credulity in the *Enquiry*'s 'Of Miracles'. Belief in the testimony of miracles could only ever be an act of faith, and never of reasoned judgement. Hume did claim that we should consider the standing, morals and motivations of any witness – not least, because the witness of an outlandish claim is more likely to have an ulterior motive. Yet Hume's recommended method of assessing testimony concentrated, regardless of the witness's personal reliability, on the point that we should reject claims if they go against our experience of the overwhelming evidence of the usual course of nature.

Hume's account of testimony did not deny that extraordinary things could be true, only that it is the correct philosophical position to await considerably larger volumes of supporting testimony before assenting. From a Humean perspective, Monboddo was a credulous historian of man whose easy assent to witness reports resulted from a palpably inadequate degree of scepticism bound up with a mystical view of the abundant diversity of the natural order. Hume's standard of evidence for accepting a claim as likely is very high, with unusual claims battling against all accumulated experience of a universe characterised by regularity and order. The Humean strand of the 'science of human nature', to which we might add Kames, Smith, Ferguson and Robertson, did not rely upon the claims of individuals, especially travel literature, in their social theory.

Monboddo's approach to testimonial evidence was more in tune with the Aberdonian response to Hume's arguments against miracles. In his

Dissertation on Miracles (1762), George Campbell agreed with Hume that human nature contained an innate disposition to give credence to testimony – in a way comparable to how we immediately give credence to memory. Campbell accepted Hume's point that claims about highly unusual events were more likely to be believed precisely because they were unusual and did not deny that 'the uncommonness of an event related is a presumption against its reality'.[36] But, Campbell claimed, testimony of specific events should often be assumed to be true until proved false. As suggested by Campbell's example of reports of a ferryboat sinking, this depended on the circumstance. The burden of proof lies on the individual wishing to reject the testimony. In his *Inquiry into the Human Mind* (1764) Thomas Reid went so far as to hold that human testimony was analogous to perception. Underpinned by his providential naturalism, Reid argued that God had framed human nature with two propensities that ensured that the vast extent of our knowledge comes from the testimony of others. These were the 'principle of veracity' or our 'propensity to speak truth' and the 'principle of credulity' which is our innate 'disposition to confide in the veracity of others, and believe what they tell us'.[37] That said, Reid did stress that testimonial evidence became irresistible when the witnesses were trustworthy, large in number, not personally invested in the matter, and had not been able to liaise prior to giving their testimony.

To both, Hume's stance was impracticable. While waiting for testimony to be assessed, Campbell's ferry would have sunk with all lives lost or, in Reid's argument, social life would have disintegrated because everyone's time would be spent checking the validity of even the most banal statements from others. Key also to the Aberdonian critique of Hume's position on credulity was the accusation that Hume had begged the question. In stressing that we need to judge individual testimony against the weight of experience, Hume had understated the fact that the latter was made up of aggregated instances of individual testimony – we have to believe such testimony to get to a position where we can talk about the weight of evidence. From the perspective of Campbell and Reid, Monboddo's belief in the existence of men with tails, based as it was on testimonial evidence, was legitimate – or, at least, should not be rejected out of hand. In this very subtle debate, however, the difference is primarily one of emphasis. While Monboddo also claimed to judge testimonial evidence against the course of nature, he both weighted the standing of the witness highly and believed in a more variable universe than either Hume or his critics.

John Millar directly addressed the issue of how to judge *prima facie* unbelievable claims in his *Origin of the Distinction of Ranks* (1773) in a way that went beyond the issue of witness credibility. Millar's recommendations came

in the context of discussing the accumulation of evidence of the early stages
of humankind. Here the historian of man is dependent on comparison with
travel accounts describing current 'rude parts of the world'. The authors
of such accounts are subject to the suspicion of being easily deceived or of
endeavouring to deceive their readers – certainly their accounts contain
hard-to-believe details. But through the act of comparing and contrasting
many unbelievable descriptions, such claims as appear frequently gain a
'degree of authority, upon which we may depend with security'. Indeed, the
act of accumulation and comparison renders the issue of the standing of a
specific witness 'very much out of the question'. If several witnesses agree,
separately, in relating a highly unlikely event, then we can take that event
as true. Millar believed his method enabled him to be 'convinced of the
truth of extraordinary facts, as well as of those that are more agreeable to
our own experience'.[38] As we will see below when discussing his research
into 'wild' humans, Monboddo believed he could provide such evidence for
many of his more outlandish claims.

Monboddo's legal training and professional expertise influenced his
approach to testimony. Both Monboddo and his rival historian of man and
fellow legal literatus Henry Home, Lord Kames, relied heavily upon the
witnesses and testimonies of ancient history and travel literature. This may
be attributed to the fact they were natural historians writing in imitation
of Buffon's *Histoire naturelle*, but it also stemmed from their profession's use
of testimony and its associated standards of judging content and validity.
Where possible, Monboddo would apply legal methods in his accumulation
of evidence. Among his papers are extensive notes on and correspondence
with eyewitnesses who believed that they had sighted supposedly mythical
creatures.[39] This included signed affidavits by Robert Jamieson, a fishing
boat captain, and his crew testifying to their sighting of a kraken.[40] Monboddo was mocked for his claims in the first edition of the first volume of
OPL that humans are occasionally born with tails. In the second edition,
he added a passage in which he emphasised that he could 'produce legal
evidence, by witnesses yet living' of a man in Inverness who had a tail.[41]
That he didn't is a little telling, but Monboddo's appeal to sworn testimony
from several witnesses is seen as the 'gold standard' of cryptozoology.[42] Yet
just as frequently Monboddo was willing to cite the hearsay evidence of his
sources – he included claims by his Bristol merchant that the latter had
heard that orangutans had kings or governors, or that his Liverpool slave-
ship captain had heard that orangutans buried their dead.[43]

For all his apparent credulity, Monboddo believed he was striding out
on a moderate path between the two extremes of pure fact and pure sys-
tematisation. He criticised natural historians of man who 'have attended

so much to facts, and dealt so much in experiment' that they reject all evidence other than that of the senses.[44] Reason played no role in their accounts of man. Monboddo did not name his materialists, but it is most likely that he is referring to Hume given the extensive criticism of Hume elsewhere in his writings. Monboddo was equally critical of those who 'have gone to a contrary extreme' and adjusted or ignored any fact that 'prejudicated' their systems.[45] The most prominent culprit was Buffon.[46] An authoritative account of human nature that escaped these competing methodological simplifications needed to rely on a combination of rational deductions, experimental inductions and appeals to claims from authority. Monboddo would offer two differing descriptions of his middle path. One was framed in Aristotelian natural philosophical language. The historian of man first starts with the 'method of investigation' – the accumulation of facts from which a theory can be deduced. He then uses the 'method of science': the application of his theory to comprehend a particular fact. The actual difference between this position and the standard one of the 'science of man' is negligible. Monboddo also discussed his middle path as involving the conclusions drawn from of 'fact', or experiential evidence, and from 'theory', drawn from investigating the thing-in-itself. In the case of whether marriage is a natural or artificial institution, the facts of travel literature show that it is instituted by governments upon the first formation of civil society. The 'theoretical' take confirmed this: early humans would necessarily have settled first in areas of natural abundance in which primitive woman would have been self-sufficient in raising children and would not need marriage.

Monboddo the Anthropologist

Monboddo was committed to 'enlightened' standards of evidence and spent considerable intellectual energy contemplating the methodological issues at the heart of the Scots' 'science of human nature'. Yet his anthropological theories were often downright weird and based on a striking credulity. But the out-of-place quality of Monboddo's thought is often cursorily, indeed tautologically, explained by reference to his eccentricity. Or, worse still, by pseudo-psychological explanations that his aggressively different anthropology stemmed from an inferiority complex resulting from his diminutive height and his Graecophilia stemmed from his embarrassing, to English ears at least, Scottish pronunciation of Latin.[47] If we explore his approach to accumulating facts on the issues that intrigued him the most, we see Monboddo in a far more sympathetic light: as an inquisitive collector of first-hand reports of faraway cultures and unusual humans, and arguably the most proactive enlightened Scottish anthropologist. The Scottish 'science of man' is increasingly criticised by global intellectual historians as little more than the 'armchair' activity of urban-dwelling professionals framing models based on piecing together facts derived from their book learning.[48] The real anthropological 'work' of the Enlightenment was being undertaken by travellers and colonial officials at the frontiers of empire.[49] Yet the extent and variety of Monboddo's research precludes any easy accusation of him being stuck behind his writing desk.

Most famously, Monboddo was fascinated in observing 'with mine own eyes' supposed wild humans: Peter the Wild Boy, the 'Ourang Outang' and Mademoiselle Marie Leblanc, the 'Savage Girl'. Each case study Monboddo viewed as a 'stage' in the 'several steps of the human progression from the Brute to the Man'.[50] Peter the Wild Boy, when discovered, existed as the 'original state of men upon this earth'. The Ourang Outang lived in the 'herding state', which was the 'first step in the progression of man towards the civil life'. The 'Savage Girl' had lived in the 'very first state of civil society' and, as part of this process, learned to 'speak a language the most rude and imperfect that can be imagined'.[51]

Monboddo was at the forefront of the utilisation of observations of wild children in the formation of the naturalised human sciences and played a leading role in the accumulation of information on his two wild children. While the dominant response among the British and French intellectual elites to the two had been keen interest quickly followed by indifference, for Monboddo, Peter and Marie were privileged objects of knowledge.[52] In the case of Peter this was because he was, to Monboddo, essentially still a pre-social human. In the case of Marie-Angélique it was because, since she subsequently learned French, she could provide direct testimony about her experience as a 'savage'.

In June 1782, Monboddo visited Peter the Wild Boy, then living in Hertfordshire. Peter had been captured in 1724 in a forest near Hameln, Hanover, walking on all fours, climbing trees, unable to speak and feeding on acorns. It was guessed that he was about fifteen years old. The following year he was sent to London to the care and also experiment of Dr John Arbuthnot (1667–1735). Once Arbuthnot abandoned the project, Peter lived with several farmers in Hertfordshire until his death in 1785. Following his visit, Monboddo used his observations of Peter, and conversations with his carers and neighbours, to draw up a dissertation on 'The Difference between Man and Brute' included in the third volume of *Antient Metaphysics*.[53] Monboddo believed that Peter the Wild Boy's limited speech was supporting evidence for his position that the orangutan was a pre-social man. Everyone agreed that Peter was a man, despite his limited speech. His humanity was not doubted, Monboddo's contacts informed him, even immediately after Peter's capture in the Hanoverian wood-lands. The fact he had limited speech, Monboddo averred, was because 'he has not been accustomed from his infancy' to speak. [54] This was as much a physiological claim – that the organs of speech are moulded in early years – as a claim about the limited development of Peter's intel-lective faculty. The leap Monboddo made, and which his contemporaries were unwilling to follow, was that 'the case of the Orang Outang . . . is impossible to distinguish from the case of Peter the Wild Boy'. [55]

Monboddo's argument that orangutans were pre-social humans formed one of the central planks upon his whole theory about the artificiality of language was built. [56] Here we see Monboddo's credulity in fullest effect. The orangutan's humanity was demonstrated by its reported ability to reproduce with humans; its use of human children as servants; its senti-ments of gentleness, decency, modesty and honour; the fact it is a biped; and the fact it uses weapons, fire and builds dwellings. Monboddo's evi-dence came partly from Buffon's *Histoire naturelle*, following up the travel literature cited by Buffon, and Rousseau's famous footnote in the *Discourse on the Origin of Inequality* (1755). [57] Yet Monboddo also sought out informa-tion from other means. Monboddo visited the stuffed 'orang-outang' held in the Cabinet du Roi, under the directorship of Buffon. He was guided by Bernard de Jussieu (1699–1777), one of Buffon's subordinates and who, Monboddo would later complain to Sir John Pringle, had given him a false account of the creature's speech organs. [58] Monboddo observed two alive 'Ourang Outangs' in London – and debated buying one of them for £50, but decided against it on the grounds of poverty. He had solicited infor-mation from various shipowners and sea captains with direct experience of the creatures, as well as using hearsay evidence about the orangutan in Sir Ashton Lever's collection in London who reportedly could speak a few words. [59] On the basis of this varied evidence, Monboddo claimed that the reason why Buffon's orangutan did not speak was not, as Buffon had argued, because the creature was not human, but because it was too young and had received no education.

Monboddo also pursued active research into the 'Wild Girl of Cham-pagne', Marie-Angélique Memmie Le Blanc (1712–75). The wild girl, probably around the age of eighteen or younger, was captured in September 1731 in Songy near Chalôns-en-Champagne and was subsequently chris-tened as Marie-Angélique Memmie and then became known as Mademoi-selle Leblanc. Where she had come from was unclear, but contemporary observers accepted as plausible the story that she was part of an Eskimo tribe, who had been taken into slavery, was then sold again disguised as an African, probably in the French Antilles, before being transported to France where she escaped.[60] Attempts to 'civilise' her, as well as convert her to Catholicism, were more successful than attempts with Peter and she eventually moved to a convent in Sainte-Menehould.

Monboddo had met Leblanc during his time in France in the mid-1760s, visiting her in March 1765 while she was in Paris but also visiting her village of Songy in Champagne, recording their interactions as well as the observations of her carers and neighbours.[61] Upon his return to Britain, Monboddo organised a translation of Marie-Catherine Homassel Hecquet's *Histoire d'une jeune fille sauvage trouvée dans les bois à l'âge de dix ans* (Paris, 1755). This appeared as *An Account of a Savage Girl, Caught Wild in the Woods of Champagne* (1768) and was undertaken by Monboddo's clerk John Hunter, who later became Professor of Humanity at University of St Andrews. The work contained a Preface by Monboddo which explained Leblanc's story, its significance and his motivation for publishing. Monboddo printed Leblanc's address so that any incredulous readers could contact her to verify his claims.

Monboddo's researches into the Savage Girl case formed a major part of his thought. He would repeatedly 'quote myself as a traveller', as he put it in the third volume of *Antient Metaphysics*, using his direct interaction with Leblanc to inform his ideas.[62] In the fourth volume he included a transcript of his detailed notes of one of their conversations from when they had met in Paris.[63] Monboddo's questions to Leblanc focused not on her life story but on what she could tell him about the condition of her people. Monboddo's lawyerly interrogation lead to the recording of more details about her life than any previous account. Monboddo used Leblanc's recollection of her early life to explore the formation of language as an artificial development, treating the guttural language of her early society as evidence that the 'first sounds articulated were the natural cries of men' rather than articulated words.[64] Monboddo also took Leblanc's recollection of imitating birds as proof of Lucretius' claim that music began with the imitation of birdsong.[65] Leblanc's body also served Monboddo's philosophy well. Her superior agility and animal-like physical qualities, such as her deformed nails or her ravenous way of eating, as well as the negative consequences of her subsequent modern living such as her teeth decaying, were cited on several occasions in *OPL* and *AM* as evidence of the physical superiority of unsocialised humans.[66] Monboddo believed that Leblanc offered him direct access to, and therefore conclusive evidence about, early socialised humans.

Monboddo claimed that one major conclusion to be derived from studying 'wild humans' was that the 'original' of human nature could not be understood through examining purportedly primordial societies detailed in ancient history and recent travel literature. For Monboddo, as for Rousseau, descriptions of societies detailed humans who were already far advanced from man in the state of nature. Monboddo believed that the orangutan demonstrated for him that 'the natural state of man . . . is not a mere hypothesis, but a state which at present actually exists'.[67] Unlike any of the other Scottish scientists of human nature, this central tenet of Monboddo's theory of the origin and development of society and language was built upon his own anthropological researches.

When making his more extravagant claims, Monboddo combined as many forms of evidence as possible. His observations on the anthropological significance of the 'extraordinary phenomenon'[68] of Peter the Wild Boy were founded on personal observation of Peter, reports from Peter's carers and acquaintances, previously published accounts including newspaper articles spanning several decades, and two reports commissioned by Monboddo undertaken by Sir Joseph Banks and Fellow of Corpus Christi College, Oxford, Thomas Burgess.[69] As we have seen, this was characteristic of his general practice. Monboddo was very active in seeking out the testimony of his contemporaries beyond what could be found in printed travel literature.

Monboddo's evidence base for his 'History of Man' contained many facts gained from conversations with a network of predominantly London-based contacts who provided him with a wealth of anthropological testimony about the extra-European world. Monboddo would frequently make claims based on 'my information' stemming from numerous respectable but unnamed sources. But just as often he was explicit about who he had been talking to and what he had learned from them. When possible, Monboddo stressed the individual's professional or social standing, their life experience or their character. Monboddo was far more likely to praise contemporary explorers and travellers than he was to praise contemporary philosophers. He described one unnamed British traveller to the Pacific Islands – possibly Joseph Banks, given their strong ties – as 'one of those gentlemen, to whom the learned world, and indeed all mankind, is so much obliged for the toils and dangers they have gone through in search of knowledge'.[70]

Monboddo treated the observations he gained from these conversations as being on a par with published travel accounts and ancient texts. The issue of informative conversation had troubled other Scots. For example, Adam Ferguson, in his *Essay on the History of Civil Society* (1767), averred that it was 'necessary . . . for the sake of those [readers] who may not have conversed' with 'living witnesses, to refer to printed authorities'.[71] Monboddo had no such scruple and cited information gained from conversation, often citing conversation with an influential author rather than the author's book itself. Among his papers in the National Library of Scotland are numerous letters from travellers and colonial officials, as well as extensive notes on non-European cultures stemming from Monboddo's conversation. The best example of this latter practice is the set of notes which Monboddo took in 1769 following conservation with Joseph-Marie Roubaud (1735–97), a Jesuit missionary who had worked among the Abenaki in North America.[72] Monboddo would incorporate the material he gained from Roubaud into several volumes of both *OPL* and *AM*. Implicit in such evidence accumulation is Monboddo's confidence in himself as a reliable recorder of facts – something that would have stemmed from his professional standing.

The names of individuals Monboddo discoursed or corresponded with and utilised the observations of reads like a who's who of late eighteenth-century British exploration. He had struck up a correspondence with Sir Joseph Banks following a meeting in Edinburgh in 1772. Banks supplied Monboddo with information about Pacific Islanders – though, disappointingly for the Scottish judge, Banks could not supply him with any evidence of men with tails.[73] Monboddo kept up requests for empirical information from Banks throughout their correspondence. Monboddo also used information learned during conversations with Daniel Solander soon after the latter's return from the Pacific – Solander, like Banks, had to disappoint Monboddo with lack of evidence of tail-possessing humans.[74] Conversations with Charles Wilkins, the translator of the Bhagavad Gita and leading Sanskrit scholar, had proved to Monboddo the resemblance between Sanskrit and Greek.[75] William Hastings, governor of India, informed Monboddo that he believed the Indians to be the happiest people he ever knew due to Indian's highly socially stratified society.[76] Monboddo quickly developed an acquaintance with the African explorer James Bruce upon the latter's return from Abyssinia – though, again, Monboddo was disappointed in his hopes for news of men with tails. Monboddo's high standing in British cultural, legal and commercial life enabled him to develop the network of contacts, cultivated especially during his annual summer trips to London, to bring to him the experience of the British Empire's explorers and officials. It is unclear, however, whether his correspondents and interlocutors knew that their words were going to be treated as evidence.

Conclusions

By exploring in depth Monboddo's methods we can confirm the validity of Antonio Verri's defining assessment that, in his metaphysics, Monboddo was 'l'antimoderno' but in his anthropology he offered a naturalised and secularised account of man – that is, he was, perhaps despite himself, a modern.[77] The fact that Monboddo can be plausibly situated as a participant of the Enlightenment's 'science of man', however, has been lost in more recent literature. This is understandable: at the centre of Monboddo's social thought is a paradoxical mixture of ancient philosophy, enlightened methodology and mockable credulity. But Monboddo does warrant greater inclusion in our picture of the Scottish Enlightenment. His inclusion hints at the diversity of approaches to the science of man: alongside the dominant thinking framed by Hume, Ferguson and Smith, there is a legally inflected version reliant on the accumulation and presentation of testimony. He suggests the potential merging of ancient philosophy with modern proto-social scientific methods, and the continued relevance of Aristotle to the Scottish Enlightenment.[78]

While he is obviously a participant in Scottish studies of conjectural histories of society, Monboddo's thought has a far greater emphasis on the 'natural history of man' – the sort of study undertaken in Buffon's *Histoire naturelle* – than Hume, Smith and Ferguson did. Indeed, and perhaps to Monboddo's chagrin, he has more in common methodologically with his rival, Kames. But Monboddo is arguably unique among literati for his proactive researches into the natural history of man. Monboddo believed that he was undertaking sustained and original research. He believed that the claims he was making about human nature and the conjectural history of society were built upon a very solid base of evidence. And his information stemmed from sustained contact with a variety of officials, merchants and travellers associated with the British Empire, whom he was keen to cite.

What appears to us like Monboddo's eccentricity seems to have been a combination of his legal training, an unusual personal level of credulity and his grounding in Greek philosophy. Monboddo's legalism exhibited itself through his use of testimony and his interrogation of sources, epitomised by his notes of his gentle interrogation of Mademoiselle Leblanc. His belief in the Great Chain of Being informed his sense that the natural world was a far more varied place than someone like Hume could accept and encouraged him to believe accounts and theories that seemed incredible to his contemporaries. As Loxton and Prothero have shown, the Enlightenment's application of the methods of the natural history of man to the study of cryptids confused and beguiled many an educated individual.[79] Indeed, the attempted explanation of marvellous creatures and their incorporation into the enlightened sciences of man was a normal activity among many 'enlightened' Europeans and Monboddo was characteristic of this development.[80] Many of the eccentric things Monboddo reported do have some truth to them. It is rare, but humans sometimes are born with tails – both in the sense of abnormal growths and in the sense of atavism or vestigial tails from an earlier evolutionary stage. Giant squid could be confused for mythical kraken, especially among observers expecting to see such beasts. Humans and orangutans are very similar creatures, and the mockery of Monboddo, arguably, speaks to European Christian pre-Darwinian anthropocentricism. His dietary advice sits well alongside current medical opinion: scotch broth is very good for your health.[81] But he did not separate conclusions and observations when dealing with testimonial evidence; rather, he accepted the standing of the witness as the determining criterion of acceptance. The example of Monboddo also (re)emphasises the centrality of the significance, as Berry has shown, for most enlightened Scots, of the regularity of human nature and the natural world. The mainstream Scottish Enlightenment emphasised the constancy and uniformity of the principles of human action but claimed that the specific balance of these varied according to the circumstances of the society. Monboddo's position was similar to the extent that he believed that human nature usually developed in a certain direction, and this development involved the actualisation of certain inherent principles. But while his fellow literati strove towards understanding uniformity in context and providing heuristic models of social change, Monboddo directed as much of his attention towards the unusual and the extraordinary. He was directed, then, more to the marvellous than the mundane and to exploring what was on the fringes of eighteenth-century natural historical knowledge about man. Despite this or, even, *because of this*, he deserves greater space within our histories of the Scottish Enlightenment's 'science of human nature'.

Notes

1. Major works on Monboddo are: E. L. Cloyd, *James Burnett: Lord Monboddo* (Oxford: Clarendon Press, 1972); Nicolao Merker and Lia Formigari (eds), *Herder–Monboddo. Linguaggio e società* (Rome: Editori Laterza, 1973); Antonio Verri, *Lord Monboddo dalla metafisica all'antropologia* (Ravenna: Longo, 1975); and Nadja Noldin, *Lord Monboddo im Kontext der Sprachursprungsdebatte und Naturgeschichte des Menschen im 18. Jahrundert* (Würzburg: Königshausen & Neumann, 2013). For Monboddo's biography, see also William Knight, *Lord Monboddo and His Contemporaries* (London: John Murray, 1900).

2. On the state of the field, see Roger L. Emerson, 'What is to be Done about the Scottish Enlightenment?', in his *Essays on David Hume, Medical Men and the Scottish Enlightenment: 'Industry, Knowledge and Humanity'* (Farnham: Ashgate, 2009), pp. 225–48; Christopher J. Berry, 'The Study of the Scottish Enlightenment: An Autobiographical Journey', in his *Essays on Hume, Smith and the Scottish Enlightenment* (Edinburgh: Edinburgh University Press, 2018), pp. 1–27; Paul Wood, 'Postscript: On Writing the History of Scottish

Philosophy in the Age of Enlightenment', in James Harris and Aaron Garrett (eds), *Scottish Philosophy in the Eighteenth Century*, 2 vols (Oxford: Oxford University Press, 2015–), I, pp. 454–65.

3. The literature is extensive. On top of the items in fn. 1, I have used Thomas Frank, 'Lord Monboddo e l'origine del linguaggio', *Belfagor* 43:4 (1988), pp. 440–51; Patrice Bergheaud, 'Autour de l'œuvre de Monboddo: Réflexions sur les tensions dans le théories de l'origine du langage en Grande Bretagne dans le dernier tiers du 18e siècle', in Joachim Gessinger and Wolfert von Rahden (eds), *Theorien vom Ursprung der Sprache* (Berlin: de Gruyter, 1989), pp. 241–86; Lia Formigari, 'Language and Society in the Late Eighteenth Century', *Journal of the History of Ideas* 35:2 (1974), pp. 275–92; Emma Vorlat, 'The Origin and Development of Language according to Monboddo', in P. Schmitter (ed.), *Essays towards a History of Semantics* (Münster: Nodus 1990), pp. 83–103; and Patrick Chézauc, 'James Burnett, Lord Monboddo et le débat autour de l'origine du langage dans l'Écosse du XVIIIe siècle', in Pierre Morère (ed.), *Écosse des Lumières. Le XVIIIe siècle autrement* (1997), pp. 285–318.

4. Robert Wokler, 'Apes and Races in the Scottish Enlightenment: Monboddo and Kames on the Nature of Man', in Peter Jones (ed.), *Philosophy and Science in the Scottish Enlightenment* (Edinburgh: John Donald Publishers, 1988), pp. 145–68; Silvia Sebastiani, 'Challenging Boundaries: Apes and Savages in Enlightenment', in Wulf D. Hund, Charles W. Mills and Silvia Sebastiani (eds), *Simianization: Apes, Gender, Class, and Race* (Zürich: LIT, 2015), pp. 105–37; Alan Barnard, '*Orang Outang* and the Definition of Man: The Legacy of Lord Monboddo', in Arturo Alvarez Roldan and Han Vermeulen (eds), *Fieldwork and Footnotes: Studies in the History of European Anthropology* (London: Routledge, 1995), pp. 95–112. For a more sceptical view about the purported 'eccentricity' of Monboddo's position, see Laura Brown, *Homeless Dogs & Melancholy Apes: Humans and Other Animals in the Modern Literary Imagination* (Ithaca: Cornell University Press, 2010), pp. 53–8.

5. Christopher J. Berry, *The Idea of Commercial Society in the Scottish Enlightenment* (Edinburgh: Edinburgh University Press, 2012), p. 126.

6. But for a recent treatment of *Antient Metaphysics* work, see Francesco Bottin, 'The Scottish Enlightenment and "Philosophical History"', in Gregorio Piaia and Giovanni Santinello (eds), *Models of the History of Philosophy: Vol. III: The Second Enlightenment and the Kantian Age* (Dordrecht: Springer, 2015), pp. 428–37.

7. Chézauc, *James Burnett*, pp. 285–6.

8. David Hume, *Enquiry concerning the Principles of Understanding* (Edinburgh, 1748), §8 pt 1 para. 65.

9. James Burnett, Lord Monboddo, *Antient Metaphysics*, 6 vols (Edinburgh: Balfour, 1779–99), III, pp. ii, 2. Hereafter AM. See also James Burnett, Lord Monboddo, *The Origin and Progress of Language*, 6 vols (Edinburgh, 1773–93), I, pp. 144–6; IV, p. 397. Hereafter OPL, and National Library of Scotland (NLS) MS 24501 Monboddo to James Harris, 26 March 1766.

10. *OPL* I, pp. 144, 444; AM III, pp. ii–iii.

11. AM IV, p. 401; IV, p. 350. See also AM III, p. 2.
12. Compare, for example, with Catherine L. Hobbs, *Rhetorics on the Margins of Modernity: Vico, Condillac, Monboddo* (Carbondale, IL: Southern Illinois University, 2002), pp. 127–59.
13. NLS MS 24501 Monboddo to John Pringle, 21 June 1776.
14. Kames's very brief methodological considerations emphasised the necessity of using 'probable reasoning' and 'conjectural arguments' when studying the natural history of man, and the easiness by which such studies could detach themselves from firm empirical foundations. See Henry Home, Lord Kames, *Sketches of the History of Man*, 3 vols (Edinburgh, 1774), I, p. vi.
15. On the Scots' reception of Buffon, see Wood, 'Natural History of Man', pp. 99–100, and Paul B. Wood, 'Buffon's Reception in Scotland: The Aberdeen Connection', *Annals of Science*, xliv (1987), pp. 169–90.
16. *OPL* I, p. 141. On Monboddo's engagement with Rousseau, see the still-useful Arthur O. Lovejoy, 'Monboddo and Rousseau', *Modern Philology* 30:3 (1933), pp. 275–96.
17. James Burnett, Lord Monboddo, 'Preface', in *An Account of a Savage Girl*, trans. [John Hunter] (Edinburgh, 1768), p. xviii.
18. AM IV, p. 81.
19. *OPL* I, p. iv; AM IV, pp. i–ii, AM IV, p. 8.
20. *OPL* I, p. 338.
21. *OPL* I, p. 109.
22. *OPL* I, pp. 96–109.
23. *OPL* I, p. 343.
24. NLS MS 24501 Monboddo to John Pringle, 21 June 1776.
25. AM I, p. i.
26. AM IV, pp. 160–1. See also AM IV, pp. 18–19 and AM IV, p. 162.
27. AM III, p. 261, citing Aristotle's *Physics*.
28. AM III, p. 262. See also Bergheaud, *Autour de l'œuvre de Monboddo*, pp. 266–7.
29. On Enlightenment-era British mythography, see Colin Kidd, *The World of Mr Casaubon: Britain's Wars of Mythography, 1700–1870* (Cambridge: Cambridge University Press, 2016).
30. AM II, p. 132.
31. AM II, p. 133.
32. AM IV, p. 131.
33. David Hume, *A Treatise of Human Nature*, 3 vols (Edinburgh, 1739), 1.3.9.12.
34. Hume, *Enquiry*, 10.17.
35. Hume, *Enquiry*, 10.4.
36. George Campbell, *Dissertation on Miracles* (Edinburgh, 1762), p. 19.
37. Thomas Reid, *Inquiry into the Human Mind*, 2nd edn (Edinburgh, 1765), pp. 336, 338.
38. John Millar, *Observations concerning the Origin of the Distinction of Ranks* (Edinburgh, 1771), pp. xii–xv.
39. For example, NLS MS 24537 Miscellaneous Papers of James Burnett, Lord Monboddo, esp. fol. 15.

40. NLS MS 24537 signed affidavit by Robert Jamieson, pp. i–vi, 12–24.
41. *OPL* I, p. 262.
42. See the intriguing Daniel Loxton and Donald R. Prothero, *Abominable Science: Origins of the Yeti, Nessie, and Other Famous Cryptids* (Columbia, NY: Columbia University Press, 2013), quote at p. 253.
43. *AM* IV, p. 30.
44. *OPL* I, p. 292.
45. *OPL* I p. 292.
46. For the centrality of Buffon for Monboddo's 'History of Man', see the discussion in Iain Maxwell Hammett, 'Lord Monboddo's *Of the Origin and Progress of Languages*: Its sources, Genesis and Background, with Special Attention to the Advocates' Library', PhD Thesis (University of Edinburgh, 1985), esp. pp. 212–14.
47. Cf. Hobbs, *Margins of Modernity*.
48. See a fascinating account of this accusation against William Robertson's *History of America* in Caroline Winterer, *American Enlightenments: Pursuing Happiness in the Age of Reason* (London: Yale University Press, 2016), pp. 73–109.
49. Winterer, *American Enlightenments*; Jürgen Osterhammel, *Unfabling the East: The Enlightenment's Encounter with Asia*, trans. Robert Savage (London: Princeton University Press, 2018), pp. 37–253.
50. *AM* IV, pp. 25–34; quote at p. 25.
51. *AM* VI, pp. 164–5.
52. For accounts of contemporary responses, see Adriana S. Benzaquén, *Encounters with Wild Children: Temptation and Disappointment in the Study of Human Nature* (Montreal: McGill-Queen's University Press, 2006).
53. See also *AM* III, pp. 57–70.
54. *AM* III, p. 366.
55. *AM* III, p. 367.
56. *OPL* I, pp. 270–361. On this debate more generally, see Silvia Sebastiani, 'A "monster with human visage": The Orangutan, Savagery, and the Borders of Humanity in the Global Enlightenment', *History of the Human Sciences* 32:4 (2019), pp. 80–99.
57. See Hammett, *Origin and Progress of Language*, pp. 212–14.
58. Hammett, *Origin and Progress of Language*, p. 212; NLS MS 24501 to Sir John Pringle, 16 June 1773.
59. NLS MS 24537 Miscellaneous Papers fol. 15 Letter from Bristol Merchant; *AM* IV, pp. 28–30. For Sir Ashton Lever's Collection, see *AM* III, p. 40.
60. See Julia Douthwaite, *The Wild Girl, Natural Man, and the Monster: Dangerous Experiments in the Age of Enlightenment* (Chicago: University of Chicago Press, 2002).
61. NLS MS 24589 Notebook of James Burnett, Lord Monboddo, containing contents lists, notes and fragments. Monboddo's Index lists the contents of Folio Volume 12 – which is recorded by the NLS as now being lost – as containing notes on Leblanc. This is the same folio volume that contains the first

plan for the *OPL*, suggesting that Leblanc was on his mind during the first composition of the work. See also AM IV, pp. 33–4.

62. AM III, p. 38.
63. AM IV, pp. 403–8.
64. E.g. *OPL* I, pp. 193–4, 475–6, 480–1.
65. *OPL* I, pp. 208, 493–4; *OPL* VI, pp. 136–7.
66. See, e.g., *OPL* I, pp. 242–3, 389, 394–5; AM III, pp. 73, 164, 176, 198.
67. *OPL* I, p. 360.
68. AM III, p. 367.
69. Burgess's account was reproduced in AM III, pp. 368–73. The Monboddo–Burgess correspondence can be found at University of Oxford Bodleian Library MS Eng. Letters C. 133, fols 136–89. For Monboddo's correspondence with Banks, see the items in vol. 1 of *Scientific Correspondence of Sir Joseph Banks, 1765–1820*, ed. Neil Chambers, 6 vols (London: Pickering & Chatto, 2007) from summer 1782.
70. *OPL* I, p. 513.
71. Adam Ferguson, *Essay on the History of Civil Society*, 2nd edn (London, 1768), p. 125.
72. NLS MS 24536, "Of the Indians in North America', 1769, based on an account by the Jesuit missionary, P J A Roubaud', fols 36–55.
73. For a summary, see John Gascoigne, *Joseph Banks and the English Enlightenment: Useful Knowledge and Polite Culture* (Cambridge: Cambridge University Press, 1994), pp. 172–5.
74. Boswell recorded the exchange: "'Have they tails, Dr Solander?" "No, my Lord, they have not tails."' James Boswell, *Boswell for the Defence, 1769–1774*, ed. K. Wimsatt and F. K. Pottle (London: Yale University Press, 1960), p. 146.
75. AM IV, p. 323. See also IV, pp. 329–32 and *OPL* VI, p. 149.
76. AM IV, pp. 242–3.
77. Verri, *Lord Monboddo*, pp. 9, 59.
78. See, from a French perspective, Dan Edelstein, 'The Aristotelian Enlightenment', in Dan Edelstein and Anton Matytsin (eds), *Let There be Enlightenment* (Baltimore, MA: John Hopkins University Press, 2018), pp. 187–201.
79. Loxton and Prothero, *Abominable Science*.
80. E.g., Vaughn Scribner, '"Such Monsters Do Exist in Nature": Mermaids, Tritons, and the Science of Wonder in Eighteenth-Century Europe', *Itinerario* 41:3 (2017), pp. 507–38.
81. AM VI, p. 306.

3

The Rough Edges of Civilisation in the Scottish Enlightenment

Craig Smith

The thinkers of the Scottish Enlightenment were fascinated by the ideas of progress, improvement and civilisation. The historiography of the period has underlined the importance of the division between, and changing nature of, Highland and Lowland Scotland as an impetus to this desire to understand society. The Enlightened Scots' practical concerns with the 'backward' Highlands and the new commercial society of the Lowlands led them to develop a way of doing social theory that has deeply influenced the development of the social sciences. Four stage theory and conjectural history both depend on a conscious desire to generalise from specific historical examples to understand how different kinds of society work. One underlying theme of this is the move from simple to complex that seems to accompany the Scots' theory of the difference between savage and commercial societies.

In his *Social Theory of the Scottish Enlightenment* and elsewhere in his work Christopher Berry has developed what he calls the 'Berry line'[1] which explores this urge to generalise about the move from simple to complex societies while also noting that such theories were not intended as theories of inevitable historical development. He points out that the Scots are best understood as self-conscious social scientists rather than historians of any particular society.[2] The thinkers of the Scottish Enlightenment produced many detailed histories of particular places and time periods, but these histories were characterised by the urge to place the particular events in a wider explanatory setting. Histories such as the works of Robertson on Scotland and America, Hume on England, and Ferguson on Rome all include meditations on the theme of civilisation in specific places intended to speak to a more universal set of concerns.

In this chapter I aim to toe the Berry line and in so doing to explore another attempt to understand the idea of the development of civilisation drawn from Tobias Smollett's historical writing. Smollett is often missed out of the core group of Scottish historians, marginalised as a figure best considered for his fiction, and a hired hack when it comes to his journalism and historical writing. Yet he shared the Scottish Enlightenment's fascination with different types of society. In what follows I want to make the case that Smollett should be considered among the mainstream social theorists of the Scottish Enlightenment. But unlike his peers he was deeply interested in the points at which one stage of society rubbed up against another. As a result Smollett considers an element of stadial theory, the coexistence of societies at different stages, that is comparatively underexamined by his fellow Scottish historians. Smollett's preferred way of examining this is found in his suggestion that the edge of civilisation, the boundary where Lowland commerce and agriculture came up against Highland pasturage, lay near his home town of Dumbarton.

The Berry Line

The main features of the social theory developed by the Scottish conjectural historians are well known. They use history as the empirical data for the development of a science of society that traces the differences between stages or types of society, most famously the four stages of Smith and Millar (hunter, shepherd, agricultural, commercial), but also the three of Ferguson (savage, barbarian, civilised). Christopher J. Berry has developed an analysis of this general approach that stresses the move from simple to complex, from concrete to abstract, that characterises these accounts. As he puts it: 'Their contribution to the history of social sciences, we can say, is twofold. It lies in understanding society in general as an interrelated set of institutions and behaviours that varies over time. It also lies, more particularly, in their recognition that commercial society represented something new.'[3] Along with this science is a very particular normative commitment: 'They are committed to amelioration and to the judgement that the basic institutions of their own society are an improvement on what has gone before; some ways of life are better than others.'[4] This is not to say, as Berry stresses, that they are unqualified cheerleaders for commercial society.

The Scots recognise that commercial modernity, and the modern sense of liberty that comes with it, are better ways of life.[5] They are also aware that they come with potential pitfalls that must be avoided. But at no point does avoiding those pitfalls lead them to nostalgia. Commerce represents progress, with the new conception of freedom under the rule of law and private opulence replacing the virtuous political participation of the civic republican tradition. In Berry's work this pivotal role of the Scots is nowhere clearer than in their reconfiguration of the concept of luxury in an attempt to 'de-moralise' it.

Social and economic historians of the period have dwelt on the Enlightened Scots' attitudes to their own society. We might point to the bloody aftermath of the Battle of Culloden, or to deliberate attempts to assimilate the Highlands to the Lowlands through agricultural reform and planned towns and villages,[6] where the aim was to extend law and deliberately to 'civilise' the Highlands. But the very different types of society were also an abundant source of illustrations. For example, in *The Wealth of Nations* Adam Smith uses the Highlands and Lowlands to illustrate the division of labour being limited by the extent of the market.[7] Or in his *Lectures on Jurisprudence* where 'naked unarmed Highlanders' threaten civilisation during the 1745 Rebellion.[8]

The Highland/Lowland divide seems tailor-made as an explanation for why the Scottish Enlightenment was interested in social change and, at the same time, the contrast between commerce and shepherdry provides a temptingly neat account for the descriptive content of the stadial theories. Christopher Berry notes this, but also interjects a cautionary note:

> This exploitation of their 'economic' environment should not be oversold. The contrast between Highland and Lowland can only play that role if it is asked to do so in the first place. Imputed self-evidence is always a shaky historical assumption. The Scots are not primarily 'merely' theorising their own society.[9]

The four stages is not a generalisation of the Scottish experience. Rather than an inevitable and linear account of development, it represents a rubric or schema that helps us to understand different types of society. For Berry, the Scots' interests were more general, more universal than a parochial attempt to explain themselves and force progress on their Highland neighbours.

In his *Social Theory of the Scottish Enlightenment* Berry underlines this point by noting the difference between the history of a particular place and the social science of a generalised account of different types of society. It is worth quoting him at length on this as his example is particularly apposite given my line-toeing intentions:

> As Stewart said the aim of the conjectural historians was to answer the question: how and in what way has the transition from rude to cultivated nations happened? Even though local histories might have pretensions, the aim is not to give an account of happenings in (say)

Dumbarton from 1630 to 1660. To use Kames' terminology, such an account would be a mere 'geographical' compilation of facts. This history of Dumbarton may tweak antiquarian or purely parochial curiosity but it cannot in isolation be 'interesting' (always a benchmark of 'proper' history for the Scots). What is needed is the general context that a causal enquiry would provide. Not only is it important to know how Dumbarton at this time compares to Stirling (or Rennes or Naples) but also, bereft of some wider explanatory framework, what took place in Dumbarton during those years cannot be truly appreciated. Nor as a consequence, and as Kames also pointed out, can this localised list of facts be instructive. This is the key point. Conjectural history as a way of conducting social science was integral to the Baconian temper of the Scottish Enlightenment.[10]

Dumbarton

A history of the Scottish Enlightenment in Dumbarton, or even Dunbartonshire, would be a slim volume. As Berry points out the history of the events in the town would be of parochial interest to locals or might reach a wider audience as examples of more general phenomena of social change. The town's history, in many respects, represents a case study of the development of a Scottish county town.

The earliest reliable accounts of the town date from AD 142 and refer to a settlement around the Rock in relation to the nearby Antonine Wall that marked the extent of Roman influence in Britain.[11] By 730 Bede refers to Alcluith, 'the rock on the Clyde', and the town becomes known as the capital of the Kingdom of Strathclyde and the Britons. The name of the town derives from this time as it was known as Dun Breatann, the fortress of the Britons. For most of the following centuries the town was remarkable solely on account of the castle whose strategic importance derived from its position in proximity to the Western Highlands. It became, along with Stirling and Edinburgh, one of the three key installations for control of the central belt of Scotland. Control of the castle became a feature of almost all conflicts within Scotland, and as a result the town became a bit player in the history of the country.[12]

Dumbarton became a royal burgh in 1222, and its school is first mentioned in 1485. The town developed as a naval and shipbuilding centre and was a gateway to France in the Middle Ages. James IV (1488–1513) and James V (1513–42) based their navies there and used it as a base for expeditions to the Western Isles.[13] By the seventeenth century the area was completely Presbyterian with Covenanters controlling the town and castle until Cromwell took it in 1652.[14] In the conflicts of the later seventeenth century the town resisted episcopacy and supported William and Mary. It opposed both the 1715 and 1745 Jacobite risings, although it escaped notable violence in either.

In terms of the Enlightenment themes of progress and improvement the town can serve an illustrative purpose, with the first piped municipal water supply in Scotland being established in 1713, and the bridge at Levenford being built by John Brown of Dumbarton in 1765 under the patronage of the 4th Duke of Argyll. After 1746, the county road network developed as part of the wider attempts to open access to the Highlands.[15] The town also has a minor part to play in the story of the growth of Glasgow as a centre of commerce, as in 1668 it rejected the opportunity to become a port for Glasgow, and later, in 1700, the town sold the right to tax ships on the Clyde to Glasgow for 4,000 merks in an attempt to relieve its poor financial situation.[16]

Beyond these token examples of wider social and economic change an Enlightenment history of Dumbarton would mostly consist of the details of visits to the town by various luminaries. Boswell and Johnson passed through in 1766 on the way to Loch Lomond. A similar trip was made by Burke and Smith in April 1784 on their way to Burke's installation as rector at Glasgow University.[17] Loch Lomond also saw one of the classic examples of improvement in the development of the model village of Luss on the Colquhoun family estate. The more permanent enlightened presence within the county was to be found in the ministers and schoolmasters, among them Adam Smith's student John Stuart who went on to become minister of Luss and first translator of the New Testament into Gaelic.[18]

Joseph Black spent a holiday in the 'romantic Vale of Leven' in July 1763, and Robert Burns visited Dumbarton in 1787 and was made an honorary burgess. Several such visits are connected to the 3rd Duke of Argyll who served as the town's provost and had an estate at nearby Rosneath (held by the family from 1489 to 1945).[19] Hume passed through the town going to visit Argyll at Rosneath. John Anderson also had connections with Rosneath. He was born there, and his father served as its minister. In 1782 Anderson would return to the county and use Dumbarton Castle as a base for his artillery experiments. So far all of these would fit the Berry description of parochial history or data for comparative analysis.

Yet beyond these fleeting visits the town's strongest connection to the Scottish Enlightenment was as the birthplace of Tobias Smollett. Smollett's connection with the area are memorialised by the Smollett Monument, a Tuscan column erected in 1774 in the village of Renton. With Smollett we move from the realm of parochial history to that of biography.

Smollett's Birth and Education in the 'Scottish Arcadia'[20]

Smollett was born into a family long established in the town. The Smolletts were merchants and shipbuilders in Dumbarton and burgh records
show them as bailies and provosts through the seventeenth century.
Originally based in the town at the estate of Round Reddin, Smollett's
grandfather bought the nearby estate of Bonhill in 1684 and added the
estate of Dalquhurn in 1692.[21] John Smollett was a 'zealous advocate for
union with England' and served as one of the Commissioners for framing the Articles of Union.[22] He served as the town's first MP in the new
British Parliament and was knighted by William III. The Smolletts of
Bonhill, as they were now known, had become one of the leading families
in the county.

Tobias Smollett was born at Dalquhurn in 1721. His father, Archibald,
had married against his father's wishes, and as a result he was maintained
on an allowance of £300 a year on the Dalquhurn estate rather than at
the Bonhill estate or the family seat at Cameron on Loch Lomond. He
was educated at Dumbarton where the burgh school was in the Old Parish
Church. Like other eighteenth-century Scots, Smollett benefitted from the
celebrated Burgh school system. In his case he was taught by the famous
Latin grammarian and 'controversialist' John Love who was schoolmaster
at Dumbarton.[23] Love became the model for the character Mr Syntax the
Schoolmaster in *Roderick Random* who greets the hero's return home with
an elaborately pompous Latin oration. Smollett seems to have excelled at
the school and even at this early age had begun to write satires aimed at
his school fellows.[24]

From Dumbarton, Smollett went on to Glasgow University where he
was a student between 1735 and 1739. This period meant that he was
almost certainly taught by Francis Hutcheson and that among his fellow
students was Adam Smith.[25] Smollett seems to have had fond memories
of his time at Glasgow and later described it as 'the most flourishing university in Scotland'.[26] He left the university to pursue a medical career,
initially in the Navy and then in civilian practice in London.

At first glance, the young Smollett looks like any other talented young
Scot on the make in Georgian Britain. He was educated and well connected but had to make a living for himself. Initially this was through medicine, but later he turned to literature, history and journalism. With this
kind of trajectory, we might assume that he sits comfortably among the
general accounts of the Scottish Enlightenment. His *Complete History of
England* (1757–65) was well received and sat alongside the works of Hume
and Robertson, with Hume jokingly writing to Robertson: "A plague take

you." Here I sit near the historical summit of parnassus, immediately under Dr Smollett: and you have the impudence to squeeze yourself by me, and place yourself directly under his feet.'[27] Smollett jokingly compared their respective styles in a passage from *The History and Adventures of an Atom*, where he noted that the atom would give a plain historical narrative: 'without pretending to philosophize like H—e, or dogmatize like S—tt'.[28]

Despite his social background, career path and literary life as a public intellectual, Smollett is often seen as a marginal figure in discussions of the Scottish Enlightenment. As a historian and political writer he is often excluded from accounts of the mainstream of the Scottish Enlightenment.[29] There are a variety of reasons for this: most of his career was spent outside Scotland, his chief fame lay in literature, an area marginalised in some accounts of the 'core' Scottish Enlightenment, and his politics seem to rub against many of the main tenets associated with the group. Two main issues seem to arise when Smollett is discussed in connection with the other Scots. The first of these is Smollett's alleged Toryism, supposedly apparent from his preoccupation with the symbols of Scottish patriotism, the fascination with William Wallace, and the poem 'The Tears of Scotland' directed at the harshness of the post-Culloden military campaign to pacify the Highlands. The second is his apparent distrust of commercial society and his critique of luxury in his later writings, particularly the novel *Humphrey Clinker*.

The first point need not delay us too long. The consensus among Smollett scholars has largely debunked the crude reading of him as a Tory, and the nationalism of his writing is easily accommodated by the Unionist nationalism that forms the general consensus among the enlightened Scots.[30] His anger after Culloden is better understood as an example of his personal irascibility and frustration at what he saw as bad politics.[31] Smollett was obviously deeply opposed to the violence used in the Highlands as he returns to it again and again in his work.[32] In *The History and Adventures of an Atom* he satirises the response to the rebellion with particular relish. He sympathises with the leading rebels given the death sentence, but sarcastically notes that, instead of giving into blood lust for revenge, the wise Duke of Cumberland 'by dint of clemency and discretion, extinguished the last embers of disaffection'.[33] This is both moral outrage and political frustration and points to his view that a more successful pacification strategy was possible.

Smollett's thrawn response to Culloden was doubtless compounded by the Scottophobia he experienced in London and, more particularly, by his role in the defence of Lord Bute and the opposition to Wilkes.[34] Britishness was just as much of a preoccupation for Smollett as his defence of

the cause of Scotland. Smollett's time in government service as editor of
the *Critical Review* 1756, and then of *The Briton* (1762–3) in opposition to
Wilkes's *North Briton*, raised his prickliness about anti-Scottishness. And
as *The History and Adventures of an Atom* amply demonstrates, Smollett's
satirical wit is aimed at all of the leading politicians of the day. Whig and
Tory, country and court, king and rabble are mercilessly mocked. No one
escapes, even those whom he initially supported, like Pitt, or for whom he
worked, like Bute. [35]

Smollett's politics have been the topic of some debate. J. G. A. Pocock
has argued that he began as a mainstream Scottish Whig and gradually
moved to a position that was more like a Tory. Pocock reads Smollett as
representative of the more sceptical end of the group of Scottish thinkers
trying to analyse their society and provide a historical narrative suitable to
the defence of the Glorious Revolution and the Hanoverian Settlement.
For Pocock, Smollett is an exponent of the 'distinctively Scottish way of
viewing the history of society in general'.[36] In other words, he is within
the mainstream in terms of historical methodology, but the generalisations
that he draws from this history depart from the conclusions of the mainstream of the Scottish Enlightenment.

There is some evidence for this reading of methodological congruence.
When Smollett discusses his own methodology in *A Plan for a New History
of the Human Mind* (1752) the intention is classic 'Berry line' conjectural
history:

> My principal intention is to describe as well as I can, the manners of
> men, and the revolutions of the human mind; to regard the order of
> succession of kings and chronology as the guides, but not as the chief
> aim of my labour; for it would be a very unpleasant work, should I limit
> myself to the sole task of recording the year in which some barbarous
> prince succeeded another who was unworthy to be known.[37]

We see the same themes touched upon in *Humphrey Clinker* where he
refers to 'the science of man'[38] and 'the natural progress of improvement'.[39]

For Pocock, Smollett became the enlightened Scot most sceptical of
the benefits of modernity. His 'Neo-Harringtonian'[40] concerns about commercial society were, Pocock conjectured, a product of his experience of
London and distance from Scotland. As he puts it: 'Smollett's radical Tory
concern with corruption led him to equate civilization with corruption
but freedom with savagery.'[41] This view is based on the standard reading
of *Humphrey Clinker* as a novel that contrasts primitive and pure Scotland
with complex and corrupt England.

The perception that Smollett was sceptical of commercial modernity, particularly the corruption created by luxury, and that he doubted the qualified faith in improvement and progress that typifies the mainstream Scots, seems to distance him from the Enlightenment in Scotland. His writings include a number of satirical critiques of Enlightenment. The criticism seems to extend to the literati themselves. In *Humphrey Clinker* he has one character observe of the new class of public intellectuals that: 'I have no great confidence in the taste and judgment of coffee-house connoisseurs.'[42] Elsewhere in *Humphrey Clinker* he has Lismahago sarcastically observe of his fellow countrymen that: 'The Scots (said he) have a slight tincture of letters, with which they make a parade among people who are more illiterate than themselves; but they may be said to float on the surface of science, and they have made very small advances in the useful arts.'[43]

When these doubts about Enlightenment and commerce are usually discussed in the literature, it is through the well-worn comparison of Adam Ferguson (sceptic) with David Hume and Adam Smith (proponents). I have argued elsewhere that this is the wrong way to read Ferguson and that his doubts are perfectly compatible with support for commercial modernity if they are read as an attempt to diagnose threats to that order.[44] The tendency to paint Ferguson as an outlier is often justified by his status as the only Highlander among the literati. But the same might also be said of Smollett: he was born and raised at the point where the Highlands and Lowlands meet. As he writes in Humphrey Clinker: 'From Dumbarton, the West Highlands appear in the form of huge, dusky mountains, piled one over another.'[45] The liminal nature of his home town seems to have led him to consider what is involved when one stage rubs up against another very different one, and this becomes central to his discussion of commercial society.

The Highland/Lowland divide

Smollett's description of Dumbarton in *The Present State of All Nations* (1768) is as a 'small inconsiderable royal burrough'[46] set in a county that is 'agreeably diversified'.[47] The castle 'commands navigation of the Clyde, and being deemed the key of the Western Highlands, is kept in some repair . . .'.[48] Turning to the town itself he notes 'the grammar school, which has been always in some reputation . . .' and 'some piddling efforts in the way of trade and manufacture'.[49] The description of manufacturing was quickly outdated as by the 1770s the Dixon family's glassworks at Dumbarton, using kelp harvested from the West Highlands, had become a major centre of glass manufacture in Scotland.[50] Dunbartonshire's position as the boundary with the Highlands becomes a running theme in Smollett's work.[51] It is the point at which the Lowlands give way to the Highlands, where two very different ways of life come into contact. Moreover, this is not a new feature of the place. As Smollett relates, Dumbarton has always sat on the edge of something. Historically, it has marked the line between the Romans and Picts, between the Picts and Britons, and between the Highlands and Lowlands. The area has been a geographic, social, cultural, linguistic, agricultural and economic border zone for two millennia. This liminal status seems to fascinate Smollett, and he returns to it again and again in his writing.

When Smollett refers to Dumbarton in the *History* it is almost always in connection with its status as a border zone, for example where he describes how the Romans stop at the Antonine Wall and its strategic connection to the Firths of Clyde and Forth,[52] or when he gives an account of Strathclyde as independent Britons based at Dun Briton.[53] He observes that the castle has been fought over for centuries and 'deemed impregnable'.[54] One way in which this divide impacts on Smollett's thinking is in his recognition that Scotland and Scottishness are complex forms of identity. In the *Critical Review* he dwells on the fact that Dumbarton was the capital of a British kingdom.[55] As Lewis points out this leads Smollett to realise that the Britons had been there longer than the Scots.[56] His prickly sense of his own Scottishness is tempered by the recognition that nationalism, in the sense of Scotland versus England, is a relatively recent phenomenon, while older forms of British identity could be perceived in the history of places like Dumbarton where the boundaries marked in its history were boundaries within present-day Scotland that reflected differences within Scottish identity.

Smollett's discussion of the border zone around Dumbarton caught the attention of J. G. A. Pocock. He observes of Smollett: 'Dumbarton he proposed as the point where Britons fleeing Roman despotism had wisely but precariously stopped short of Gaelic barbarism.'[57] Pocock points out that both Smollett and Thomas Carte, in his *A General History of England* (1747), say it is a boundary between Pictish shepherding and British agriculture.[58] In Carte's discussion of AD 448 he argues Dumbarton is the limit of Britain and that beyond it the lands are not tilled and people live as shepherds or nomads: 'The lands were not tilled; nor had the inhabitants any fixed habitation, but lived like *Nemetes* or *Nomades*, in tents or slight huts; attending their cattle whilst they grazed, and driving them from place to place for the convenience of pasture.'[59] The border zone fascinates Carte who observes that 'The borders of adjoining nations, living always in a state of unsettled peace, or of open war with one another, are never well cultivated, and are for the most part thinly inhabited.'[60] Different modes of agricultural production and different societies sit uneasily next to each other, and this was as true of Dumbarton in the eighteenth century as it had been in fifth century.

In both *The Present State* and *Humphrey Clinker* Smollett offers near-identical descriptions of the point at which the Lowlands meet the Highlands. He describes the differences between the two peoples: 'The Lowlanders are generally cool and circumspect, the Highlanders fiery and ferocious'[61] and 'a natural and rancorous prejudice still pervades between them'.[62] For Smollett this is a sign that the Scots hold multiple layers of identity. They identify with country, with county, with town or village, and with the clan and its chief.[63] The lingering division between Highlanders and Lowlanders seems to invite generalisations. Dumbarton, as a place, marks the point at which two of the Scots' four stages of society face each other in real time.

Smollett was alive to this and notes that 'A remarkable spirit of industry has of late years appeared very visibly in many parts of Scotland.'[64] Smollett's own family had a hand in this process, introducing linen bleaching at Renton[65] – an industry noted by Mathew Bramble in *Humphrey Clinker* who 'conversed with a sensible man of this country, who, from a real spirit of patriotism, had set up a fishery on the coast, and a manufacture of coarse linen, for the employment of poor Highlanders'.[66] Smollett's treatment of economic development in the border region falls squarely in with the mainstream Scottish Enlightenment views on scientific agriculture.[67] Indeed, it could have been Adam Smith or Lord Kames who argued that: 'we must not impute [the lack of economic growth] to the barrenness of the soil, so much as to the sloth and poverty of the tenants, oppressed by rapacious landlords, who refuse to grant such leases as would encourage the husbandman to improve his farm, and make himself better acquainted with the science of agriculture.'[68] The barriers to development in the Highlands were social and political rather than geographic.

The Conflict between Stages

We have reached a point where it is clear that Smollett has his own approach to the generalisation on types of society that characterises the 'Berry line' on the social theory of the period. Smollett, like Carte, was particularly focused on the points and places where stages met each other. As Carte had observed, border areas like Dumbarton are usually areas of conflict. This was particularly true of the border between the Highlands and the Lowlands in the case of Dumbarton. The Lowland agricultural way of life and the gradually developing commercial burgh faced a constant low level threat from their shepherdic neighbours. In the fifteenth century 'Highland brigands' mounted a raid on the town. They were forcibly repelled by the inhabitants, and those captured were torn apart by wild horses and their remains hung in chains to remind the Highlanders of the price of attacking the town. Through the fifteenth and sixteenth centuries the townspeople were permanently armed in preparation for an attack by their Highland neighbours.[69] The main Highland clans in the area were the MacGregors, including the famous outlaw Rob Roy, the Colquhouns, Galbraiths and MacAulays.[70] To these constantly feuding clans we can add the burgesses of Dumbarton and the garrison of the castle into a heavily armed and volatile mix. What we begin to see is a case study in the rise of the rule of law and the violent suppression of predation by the clans, giving us a close-up view of the move from one stage to another as the rule of law is extended.[71]

One particular incident comes to symbolise this for Smollett, the so-called Battle of Glen Fruin, which took place a few miles from his family estate at Bonhill. Smollett's discussion of the event in *Humphrey Clinker* is a reminder that in a very real sense his own family had been on the front line in the conflict between the Highlands and Lowlands. The Battle of Glen Fruin was an armed skirmish that led to the forfeiture of the MacGregor lands to the Duke of Montrose and the development of an armed alliance between the Colquhouns, the burgesses of Dumbarton, the emerging county gentry and the castle garrison. The Colquhouns and the MacGregors lived on opposite sides of Loch Lomond and had been long-term antagonists. In 1603 incidences of cattle theft by the MacGregors against the Colquhouns and the Burgesses came to a head. A force of Colquhouns and townspeople faced the MacGregors on the west side of Loch Lomond. The result of the uneven battle saw 140 Colquhoun and town casualties against two MacGregor casualties. Perhaps even more shocking was that a party of students from the Dumbarton Grammar School became caught up in the violence and several of them were also killed.[72] The MacGregor victory was short-lived. When news of the violence reached Edinburgh, a swift response was enacted to enforce the rule of law in the area. The MacGregors were outlawed, their land forfeited, twenty-five of them were executed and their heads displayed on the tolbooth at Dumbarton Cross. For the next century the town lived with the constant threat of raids from the outlaws. As late as 1715 the burgesses armed the town and held an expedition against the MacGregors whom they suspected of involvement in the rebellion.[73]

Smollett's discussion of the incident in *Humphrey Clinker* takes place in the context of a wider discussion about the spread of the rule of law. It is an almost textbook discussion of the Scottish Enlightenment's views on civilising the Highlands. Matthew Bramble speaks against the influence of Highland chiefs: 'The chieftainship of the Highlanders is a very dangerous influence operating at the extremity of the island, where the eyes and hands of government cannot be supposed to see and act with precision and vigour.'[74] Bramble supports the suppression of the clans, but doubts that violent suppression alone will work.[75] The extension of civilisation and law to Highlands is proceeding on a false prospectus in Bramble's view because the currently fashionable account of the clans as an example of the feudal system is wrong. The tribal nature of the connection between the clan and their chief is such that even attainting the estates of the Jacobite rebels will not on its own be enough to break the link between clan and chief. Smollett has Bramble use the example of Cameron of Lochiel (the same family used by Smith in *The Wealth of Nations* III.iv.8 to discuss the same point) who returns and is immediately hailed as chief even though he has no control of the estate taken from his father.[76] This is a point that Smollett makes elsewhere in his work. In *Roderick Random* he remarks on the extreme loyalty of the Scottish peasants to their masters.[77] As we saw above, it was this loyalty that led Smollett to doubt the wisdom of the oppressive actions following Culloden.

Bramble's prescription is for meaningful economic reform suited to the terrain and the people. As he puts it: 'The most effectual method I know to weaken, and at length destroy this influence, is to employ the commonalty in such a manner as to give them a taste of property and independence.'[78] The discussion of improvement and the forfeited estates in a novel published in 1771 shows that the debate about how to best develop the Highlands was still live among the Scottish literati, and that Smollett was well within the mainstream in his views.

The Spread of Law and the Case for the Union

As we noted above, the substantive case for Smollett as an outlier from the mainstream of the Scottish Enlightenment is based on his critique of luxury and commerce. The scholarly consensus now rejects the Smollett as late convert Tory reading. Indeed, if we look to his discussion of politics in *The Complete History* and *The Briton* we find someone who might more usefully be read as one of Duncan Forbes's 'sceptical Whigs'.[79] In the *History* his accounts of the key steps towards Union are well within the establishment Whig mainstream.[80] In his analysis of the civil war he suggests that it was as much about taxation as religion.[81] Like Hume he expresses sympathy for Charles I on his execution as a 'martyr' and is harsh on

Presbyterians, republicans and extremists.[82] As he puts it: 'Fanaticism, with all its levelling principles, had now overspread the land'[83] and, more tellingly, 'The fanatics in Scotland continued to insult the law, through a misguided zeal for religion.'[84]

In his discussion of the late seventeenth and early eighteenth centuries he identifies three factions – Williamite, Jacobite and Revolutionary. Smollett is clearly more sympathetic to the first of these. But his approval is not unconditional, and he attacks the corruption of politics and the entry of money into management of Parliament.[85] The politics of the era is damned in terms just as polemical as his later journalistic work. He describes the impact of corruption and luxury. 'All principle, and even decency was gradually banished; talent lay uncultivated, and the land was deluged with a tide of ignorance and profligacy.'[86]

When he turns his attention to the Union of Parliaments he provides an account that dwells on the role of the 'projector' William Paterson and the impact of the Darien scheme on the Scottish economy.[87] The discussion of the Union debates,[88] of the Scottish parties,[89] and of the contributions of Andrew Fletcher of Saltoun[90] on the choice between a federal or an incorporating union are generally impartial in tone. The popular dissatisfaction with the Union is described without comment.[91] It is only once all of this has been related that Smollett turns to his pro-Union arguments. These are arguments from hindsight and stress the benefits of a stable legal and political order and modern liberty under the law. None of the bad consequences predicted in the Union debates came to pass.[92] As Smollett puts it: 'Hence we may learn, that many great difficulties are surmounted, because they are not seen by those who direct the operation; and that many schemes which theory deems impracticable, will yet succeed in the experiment.'[93]

As the *History* approaches more contemporary events Smollett's tendency to commentary increases. He is sharply critical of government policy, while at the same time remaining broadly supportive of Parliament and the Whigs.[94] When it comes to Scottish policy, most of his criticism focuses on the crude and heavy-handed nature of some government policies. The restoration of patronage in the Kirk,[95] the malt tax and the response to the subsequent riots,[96] and ultimately the 1715 rising are all a result of missteps by the government. Smollett argues that the 'violent measures'[97] of the Whig administration against Scotland allowed the Old Pretender to exploit grievances and raise his rebellion. Smollett's advice was simple, better management of Scotland could have avoided the 1715 rising.

The analysis of the 1745–6 uprising is very similar. Smollett calls it 'a dangerous convulsion in the Bowels' of Great Britain.[98] The complaints of the Scots, including the continuing malt tax issue, created the space for the rebellion. It was the work of 'dangerous adventurers and vindictive highlanders'.[99] But in 1745 these grievances are far less widely and deeply felt, and this explains the failure of the Lowlands to rise with the Highland clans. Smollett is supportive of the government and glad to see the defeat of the Young Pretender and his Highland army. He shares the common Scottish Enlightenment view that the ease with which the Lowlands and the cities fell to a far from impressive military force was deeply troubling. For Smollett, like Ferguson, and like Hume and Smith for that matter, the events made the case for a Scottish militia and showed the fragility of commercial society.[100]

It is in his discussion of the aftermath of the Battle of Culloden that Smollett returns to his criticism of government policy. As he puts it: 'The glory of the victory was sullied by the barbarity of the soldiers.'[101] On one level his criticism is moral, but on another it is political. His point is not that action to prevent a future rebellion was unnecessary, rather it was the particular violence of the response was likely to be counterproductive from the point of view of securing the area, and pacifying a body of people wedded to their own culture and clan loyalties. Violence breeds grievance, and this would, so Smollett feared, come back to haunt the government. By the time Smollett comes to edit *The Briton* historical distance has lent some hindsight. Smollett changes his tone to stress the loyal service of Scots to the Crown. The subsequent imperial service of the Highlanders and their integration into the British Army are cited as grounds against the anti-Scottish views of *The North Briton*.[102] At no point in these discussions does Smollett consider an end to the Union. Even when the anti-Scottish frenzy was at its height, his politics are those of someone advancing Scotland's (and his own) interests in the new Great Britain.

Like the other figures of the Scottish Enlightenment, Smollett was broadly supportive of the constitutional settlement, but is sceptical about the 'the old hackneyed expressions' of the Whig and Tory positions.[103] Smollett regarded himself as a Whig in 'the true sense of the word'.[104] He contrasted this with the rabble rousers and theoreticians who seemed to plague the politics of London in particular. There was a real danger of a 'mob-ruled commonwealth'. For Smollett the threat lay in mistaking 'the right worshipful mobility of London'[105] for 'The People'.[106] The London mob are not the people. The people are more extensive; they live beyond London and are comprised of many different ranks. As Robert Adams Day points out, Smollett's conception of the People referred to the respectable middle and upper classes.[107] The concentrated rabble of London are easily assembled and moved, but their interest, and the interests of those who seek to ride on their back, are not the interest of 'The People'.[108]

The danger of demagoguery is a continuous target in Smollett's later writings:

> A wise man will scorn alike the censure and applause of the multi-
> tude . . . There are some examples on record, of good men and great
> patriots sacrificed by popular frenzy: but I could fill a whole volume
> with instances, both from antient and modern history, of men without
> real merit, whom the mob, without reason, has raised into idols, wor-
> shipped for a season; and then their adoration changing into disgust,
> abandoned to contempt and oblivion.[109]

Once the mob has been excited by a politician who hopes to rise on their back they soon pass out of his control. This approach to politics is compounded by those philosophical idealists who demand reform in the name of democracy.

Smollett's politics were not less Whiggish as a result of his disdain for populists and democrats. Instead, they were typical of the mainstream of the Scottish Enlightenment's version of Whiggery. If we look at Adam Smith's accounts of the politics of the 1790s, we see almost the same view being taken of 'ignorant quacks and imposters', rabble rousers and men of system.[110] Even the supposedly most 'republican' of the Scots, Adam Ferguson, was no democrat, no republican and an elitist when it came to the danger of the mob and Wilkes.[111] Smollett sums up his view in the following terms:

> True Whiggism is representative government – the 'people' are not a
> separate source of legitimacy. 'If generals, politicians, and preachers,
> according to the true maxims of Whiggism, and they right ones, acquire
> no credit by having the vulgar for them, ought a minister to acquire
> discredit by having them against him?[112]

The true Whig commitment is to the principles of parliamentary government, the rule of law, and the liberties granted by the British constitution. Politicians and radicals who seek to enrage the mob in the name of the people are not true Whigs. Smollett, then, is not so much a Pocockian Neo-Harringtonian as he is a sceptical Whig keen to preserve the 'Berry line' on the benefits of modern liberty.

Luxury

Smollett's critique of populist politics turns to an attempt to understand how the mob can be so manipulated by figures he clearly regarded as charlatans. His answer touches on another Berryian concern: luxury. Smollett argues that the mob, but not 'The People', had become corrupted by luxury. In the hands of a civic humanist or civic republican interpreter of the politics of the period this would be read as a paean to the old politics of virtuous citizens. But, as we have seen, Smollett is a firm advocate of representative and elitist government. There is no Harringtonian concern for citizen participation or admiration for the participatory democracy of the ancients. Quite the reverse in fact:

> Every Kingdom, and every age, for a series of centuries, has produced a set of speculative philosophers, who have endeavoured to refine upon the constitution of their country; and almost all of these projectors, have either affected, or actually felt, an enthusiastic attachment to the democracies of antient Greece.
>
> This, however, I take to be a mistaken philanthropy, which, conceiving every individual to be equally free by nature, draws this erroneous inference, that every individual has an equal right to intermeddle in the administration of public affairs; a principle subversive of all government, magistracy and subordination; a principle destructive to all industry and national quiet, as well as repugnant to every fundamental maxim of society.[113]

This is not civic republicanism, but there is a sharp critique of corruption from luxury and its impact on the character of the people, and once again the Highland/Lowland divide and Dumbarton loom large in Smollett's account.[114]

The clearest version of this comes in *Humphrey Clinker*. The book is a satirical examination of luxury and civilisation which alternates between two accounts of the same incidents; one told from the point of view of the 'natural progress of improvement'[115] (Lydia Melford) and the other from a sceptic of the 'tide of luxury'[116] sweeping the people to corruption (Matthew Bramble). Matthew Bramble's curmudgeonly attacks on the urban settings he visits link urban life, luxury, corruption and the mob in a chain reaction leading the country to anarchy. Commenting on the social life of Bath, he suggests: 'All these absurdities arise from the general tide of luxury, which hath overspread the nation, and swept away all, even the very dregs of the people.'[117] All are corrupted, but the corruption of the 'dregs' leaves them open to political manipulation.

> Woe be to that nation, where the multitude is at liberty to follow their own inclinations: Commerce is undoubtedly a blessing, while restrained

within its proper channels; but a glut of wealth brings along with it a glut of evils: it brings false taste, false appetite, false wants, profusion, venality, contempt of order, engendering a spirit of licentiousness, insolence, and faction, that keeps the community in continual ferment, and in time destroys all the distinctions of civil society; so that universal anarchy and uproar must ensue.[118]

His view is sharply contrasted to that of the Lydia Melford who expresses innocent delight at the 'diversions'[119] of Bath and London and the politeness of society. Melford's comments on the comfort and advantages of urban life contrast a nature that is beautiful, but crude, with the conveniences of civilisation.

The case for reading Smollett as a critic of luxury speaking through the character of Bramble lies at the heart of John Sekora's reading of the work. He argues that Smollett is 'probably the last major English writer to accept wholly the classical conception' of luxury.[120] And that this distances him from the views of the wider Scottish Enlightenment that form the centrepiece of Berry's account of the 'de-moralisation' of luxury.[121] To his credit, Sekora develops a convincing interpretation, citing Smollett's self-description: 'A perfect man I am not, but assuredly I will not countenance luxury in any of its forms.'[122] It becomes the central preoccupation of Smollett's political thinking – 'For Smollett luxury is a hanging matter. From 1756 through 1771 he treated it as a capital crime against British civilization and as the unresolved issue upon which the future of that civilization depended'[123] – and proves, for Sekora, the explanation for why he moves from a Whig position to a Tory position.[124]

Sekora contrasts Smollett's analysis of luxury with that of his fellow Scots. He points out that Hume, Smith and Ferguson all argue that luxury is relative and that it is not necessarily a source of corruption. Describing Ferguson's *Essay*, Sekora argues that 'He [Ferguson] largely reduces the question of visible luxury to one of mere changing tastes; Smollett four years later was reducing visible changes in taste to a question of dangerous luxury.'[125] Smollett, then, is out of step with even the most 'republican' of the Scots. Hume shows the way to the modern conception of luxury and does so by showing how the political interests of the few have been served by an attack on luxury. He is followed by 'Ferguson and Smith, who together delivered the intellectual coup de grace to the more blatant political purposes to which the idea of luxury had been put.'[126]

As influential as Sekora's reading has been, it stands in contrast to Goldberg's. On Goldberg's reading, Smollett is closest to Ferguson on luxury; indeed, luxury does not necessarily equal corruption and can happen in any age – luxury is relative and a state of mind.[127] I have argued elsewhere that the scepticism of luxury in Ferguson has been exaggerated by those who wish to read him into a debate with Hume and Smith.[128] But if Goldberg is right, Smollett, like Ferguson, might well have been read by us into a position more sceptical of luxury than he ought. This position is also not a million miles from that of Hume, who cautions against vicious luxury, and Smith who is caustically aware of the 'deception' that material goods bring happiness.

Arcadia

One of the interesting features of the discussion of luxury in *Humphrey Clinker* is that Smollett appears to draw a direct contrast between the complexity, luxury and corruption of London and Bath and the simplicity, rusticity and virtue of the 'Scottish Arcadia'. Once again, Smollett's home ground sits on the edge of a divide. The contrast between civilisation and barbarism, between Lowland and Highland, is also implicated in the moralised discussion of luxury. The divide between the urban, luxurious and corrupt South and the rural, poor and virtuous North is magnified by the idyllic descriptions of the Vale of Leven.[129] This reaches its high point in *Humphrey Clinker* with the inclusion of the 'Ode to Leven Water',[130] though it is humorously undercut by the observation that 'This county is justly styled the Arcadia of Scotland; and I don't doubt but it may vie with Arcadia in every thing but climate.'[131]

What Smollett called the 'tide of luxury' lapped up to Dumbarton and, so it seems, petered out against the shores of Loch Lomond. The literary contrast is no doubt deliberate, but it does raise some questions. As we saw above, the borderland of Dunbartonshire was already developing, and this was no less true of the Smollett's themselves who would soon play a part in turning the Vale of Leven into an major industrial centre. Moreover, there is a certain irony in both Smollett's characters, and the man himself, ruminating on a rural idyll from the comfort of Cameron House. The 'ragged Highlanders'[132] acting as ghillies to the visitors are no doubt picturesque when compared to the increasingly comfortable and complacent burgesses, but is Smollett really making quite so sweeping and crude a generalisation?

Part of Sekora's account of luxury in Smollett is based on this contrast between Scotland and England. He points out that, in addition to Bramble, the other main anti-corruption voice in *Humphrey Clinker* is the 'the disputaceous caledonian'[133] Lismahago. Murtz agrees and sees the exchanges between the two as an attempt by Smollett to contrast England and Scotland and favour Scotland.[134]

A simple glance at the accounts of Edinburgh as the 'hot-bed of genius'[135] or Glasgow as 'the pride of Scotland', which might very well pass for an elegant and flourishing city in any part of Christendom',[136] suggests that this is not a Scotland and England contrast. It can only really be read as such if one goes looking for it. This becomes even more apparent when we consider the characters of Bramble and Lismahago. They are both clearly drawn for comic effect. Bramble's attacks on luxury and Lismahago's perversely argumentative national pride, which is as much raised by compliments as by insults, are humorous exaggerations.[137] Lismahago's chippiness is part of the humour on display in his scenes. This is particularly true of the debate about the 'improvement' that Bramble observes in Scotland since the Union. What follows is a satire of Scottish defensiveness as Lismahago argues that there were economic downsides to the Union which have been overcome by 'the natural progress of improvement'[138] and would likely have occurred without the Union. The point of the passage is to satirise both English complacency and Scottish defensiveness. Lismahago can start an argument in an empty room and is clearly meant as an exaggeration, just as the bovine and complacent Bramble is meant as a satire on a certain type of English gentleman.

In his assessment of *Humphrey Clinker* Goldberg claims that the book is indeed designed to allow a contrast between primitive and simple Scotland and complex and refined England. A crude reading would see this as virtuous Scotland being compared to corrupted England, but as Goldberg points out:

> Although degeneration is most perceptible in England and primitivism is most perceptible in Scotland, the dualism was never absolute. Distinctions are constantly being drawn in both countries between improvements that result in real progress, and improvements without regard for taste or convenience that result in degeneration.[139]

Even at his most nationalistic and defensive, so Goldberg argues, Lismahago is never crudely clear on the divide between Scotland and England.[140] Following a similar thought Sekora suggests that Smollett is favourable to English institutions but not Englishmen, and favourable to Scotsmen, but not Scottish institutions.[141] But again, this seems too clear cut a distinction to make: Smollett's defence of the constitution and his vicious attacks on contemporary politics in London suggest a more complex view of English institutions, just as his obvious pride in the accomplishments of Edinburgh and Glasgow suggest at least some attachment to the institutions that made them possible. For Sekora, Matthew Bramble's ruminations on Edinburgh and Glasgow suggest that 'In Scotland the pursuit of wealth is restrained by reason and virtue.'[142] Had the Scots then managed to pursue luxury without corruption, or were they simply less far along the road to debauchery?

Conclusion

We have reached a point where Smollett has come closer to the main-stream of the Scottish Enlightenment in terms of his historical method, his social theorising, and his whiggish politics, but where his views on luxury continue to see him, as Pocock argued, among the most sceptical of the Scots. But sceptical, not because of Pocock's suggested Neo-Harringto-nianism, or because he rejected the benefits of modern liberty and com-merce, but rather because he saw the potential for corruption. In this he represents a particularly strong expression of the Scots' general qualified support for commercial society, but, crucially, not one that departs radi-cally from the 'Berry line'.

As we noted at the start, the history of particular places is significant for the Scots when it forms the basis for wider generalisations about society and social change. For Smollett it turned out that his home town was ideal for just such general reflections. Dumbarton was illustrative of where a complex, commercial, law-governed world met a simple, tribal, clan-based one: it was where law stopped, or where it needed to be imposed with force. In a small space, and over a relatively short historical period, civilisa-tion came to that part of the world. The Scottish Arcadia that stretched north from the town to Loch Lomond also served as a helpful literary illus-tration of the distinction between urban luxury and rural simplicity. It was where two or more stages blurred: society's rough edges were clear to be seen in places like Dumbarton.

Notes

1. Christopher J. Berry, *Essays on Hume, Smith and the Scottish Enlightenment* (Edinburgh: Edinburgh University Press, 2018), p. 23.
2. Berry, *Essays*, p. 24.
3. Berry, *Essays*, p. 26.
4. Berry, *Essays*, p. 25.
5. For Berry, the Scots stand at a pivotal point in the history of the idea of luxury. Christopher J. Berry, *The Idea of Luxury: A Conceptual and Histori-cal Investigation* (Cambridge: Cambridge University Press, 1994), pp. 101, 146–62.
6. Christopher J. Berry, *Social Theory of the Scottish Enlightenment* (Edinburgh: Edinburgh University Press, 1997), pp. 10, 12, and *The Idea of a Commercial Society* (Edinburgh: Edinburgh University Press, 2013), p. 116.

7. Berry, *Commercial Society*, p. 74.
8. Adam Smith, *Lectures on Jurisprudence*, ed. Ronald L. Meek, David Daiches Raphael and Peter Stein (Oxford: Oxford University Press, 1978), p. 541, Berry, *Social Theory*, p. 148.
9. Berry, *Social Theory*, p. 12.
10. Berry, *Social Theory*, p. 68.
11. Iain Murdoch Macleod MacPhail, *Short History of Dumbartonshire* (Dumbarton: Bennett and Thomson, 1962), p. 4.
12. In the period of the wars of independence it also gained notoriety as a prison: William Wallace was held there under governor Sir John Graham of Menteith (MacPhail, *Short History*, p. 19). The area began to develop royal connections. Robert Bruce spent the final years of his life in a grand hunting lodge near the town, and on his death in 1329 his viscera was buried there. The royal connections continued with James VI using the castle as a hunting base. See Donald Macleod, *History of the Castle and Town of Dumbarton*, 2nd edn (Dumbarton: Bennett and Thomson, 1877), p. 19.
13. MacLeod, *History*, p. 56.
14. MacPhail, *Short History*, p. 43.
15. MacLeod, *History*, p. 62.
16. MacLeod, *History*, p. 70.
17. Ian Simpson Ross, *The Life of Adam Smith*, 2nd edn (Oxford: Oxford University Press, 2010), pp. 376–7.
18. Ross, *Life of Smith*, p. 139.
19. See Roger L. Emerson, *An Enlightened Duke: The Life of Archibald Campbell (1692–1762), Earl of Illay, Third Duke of Argyll* (Kilkerran: Humming Earth, 2013).
20. Tobias Smollett, *Humphrey Clinker*, ed. Charles Lee with an introduction by Howard Manford Jones (London: J. M. Dent and sons, 1943), p. 245. The references to Dumbarton and the Vale of Leven in Smollett's fiction and non-fiction writing are fulsome in their praise. As Matthew Bramble declares in Humphrey Clinker: 'Everything here is romantic beyond imagination. This country is justly styled the Arcadia of Scotland . . .' Smollett, *Humphrey Clinker*, p. 237.
21. Macleod, *History*, p. 162.
22. Macleod, *History*, p. 163.
23. Donald MacLeod, *Dumbarton, Vale of Leven, and Loch Lomond: Historical, Legendary, Industrial and Descriptive* (Dumbarton: Bennett and Thomson, 1885), p. 98.
24. MacLeod, *Dumbarton*, p. 98.
25. Milton Allan Goldberg, *Smollett and the Scottish School: Studies in Eighteenth-century Thought* (Albuquerque: University of New Mexico Press, 1959), p. 6.
26. Tobias Smollett, 'The Present State of All Nations (1768–9)', in *The Miscellaneous Writings of Tobias Smollett*, ed. O. M. Brack, Leslie Chilton and Walter H. Keithley (London: Pickering and Chatto, 2015) pp. 293–423, at p. 353.

27. Jeremy Lewis, *Tobias Smollett* (London: Jonathan Cape, 2003), p. 142.

28. Tobias Smollett, *The History and Adventures of an Atom*, ed. Robert Adams Day (Athens: University of Georgia Press, 1989), p. 27.

29. As Adams Day points out, this runs against Smollett's self-image as 'an enlightened Scot, a gentleman, and a satirist'. Robert Adams Day 'Introduction', in Tobias Smollett, *The History and Adventures of an Atom*, ed. Adams Day (Athens: University of Georgia Press, 1989), pp. i–lxxvi; p. xxxviii.

30. See Colin Kidd, *Union and Unionisms: Political Thought in Scotland, 1500–2000* (Cambridge: Cambridge University Press, 2008). As Lewis notes 'Smollett was to embody this combination of a prickly pride in being Scottish with an appreciation of the broader horizons and opportunities offered by the new status of a "Briton".' Lewis, *Tobias Smollett*, p. 7. He also points out that Smollett remained a Unionist and a friend of the Moderate Literati (Lewis, *Tobias Smollett*, p. 69).

31. He seems, by all accounts, to have been the angriest of the polite young Scotsmen making their way into public life. As Goldberg points out, 'his conversation in company was a continual string of epigrammatic sarcasms against one or the other of those present' (Goldberg, *Smollett*, p. 3).

32. Smollett, *Atom*, pp. 20–5.

33. Smollett, *Atom*, p. 25.

34. Lewis, *Tobias Smollett*, p. 70.

35. Goldberg, *Smollett*, p. 3. For Goldberg (*Smollett*, p. 15), this apparent tension in Smollett's politics is an indication that he does indeed fit in the mainstream of the Scottish intellectual life of the period. According to Goldberg, Smollett, like the others, can look contradictory because he takes part in the general Scottish attempt to reconcile: sensibility/rationalism, art/nature, reason/feeling, primitivism/progress, benevolence/self-love. Goldberg uses these dichotomies as a way to structure his study of Smollett's novels. But he might have added another dimension – the move from reform to reaction generated by the bedding in of the Whig settlement. Smollett, like the other literati and especially like the Moderates in the Kirk, was closely associated with an increasingly secure establishment that grew more conservative as the century progressed. Lewis observed that Smollett seems to be a contradictory character who is 'an autocratic Tory, but simultaneously a plebeian Whig' (Lewis, *Tobias Smollett*, p. 201), and has challenged the reading of Smollett as a bifurcated Whig–Tory. He suggests that Smollett probably had most in common with the country Whigs, and that his ambiguous politics are likely in part an inevitable feature of the complicated factional positions of the period. He does not seem to have been a party man, despite his service as one of Bute's 'rhymsters' and 'dirt-casters' (Smollett, *Atom*, p. 120). Indeed, the passages in *The Adventures of Peregrine Pickle* which satirise the public and political career of a man of letters were clearly drawn from Smollett's own view of eighteenth-century politics. Tobias Smollett, *The Adventures of Peregrine Pickle*, ed. James L. Clifford, revised Paul-Gabriel Boucé (Oxford: World's Classics, 1983 [1751]), pp. 632, 666–76.

36. J. G. A. Pocock, *Virtue, Commerce, and History: Essays on Political Thought and History, Chiefly in the Eighteenth Century* (Cambridge: Cambridge University Press, 1985), p. 250.

37. Tobias Smollett, 'A Plan for a New History of the Human Mind 1752', in *The Miscellaneous Writings of Tobias Smollett*, ed. O. M. Brack, Leslie Chilton and Walter H. Keithley (London: Pickering and Chatto, 2015), pp. 141–86, at p. 141.

38. Smollett, *Humphrey Clinker*, p. 307.

39. Smollett, *Humphrey Clinker*, p. 263.

40. Pocock, *Virtue, Commerce*, p. 251.

41. Pocock, *Virtue, Commerce*, p. 254.

42. Smollett, *Humphrey Clinker*, p. 72.

43. Smollett, *Humphrey Clinker*, p. 193.

44. Craig Smith, *Adam Ferguson and the Idea of Civil Society: Moral Science in the Scottish Enlightenment* (Edinburgh: Edinburgh University Press, 2019), pp. 167–74.

45. Smollett, *Humphrey Clinker*, p. 227.

46. Smollett, *Present State*, p. 348.

47. Smollett, *Present State*, p. 347. MacPhail (*Short History*, p. 71) suggests a town population of 1,480 in 1755 growing to 2,541 by 1801.

48. Smollett, *Present State*, p. 349.

49. Smollett, *Present State*, p. 349.

50. MacPhail, *Short History*, p. 67.

51. Smollett, *Present State*, p. 295.

52. Tobias Smollett, *A Complete History of England from the Descent of Julius Caesar to the Treaty of Aix-la-Chapelle*, 2nd edn, 11 vols (London: James Rivington and James Fletcher, 1758), I, p. 75.

53. Smollett, *Complete History* I, p. 118.

54. Smollett, *Complete History* II, p. 341.

55. Tobias Smollett, 'Review of Hugh Blair A critical dissertation on the Poems of Ossian, February 1763', in 'Selected Reviews for the Critical Review', in *The Miscellaneous Writings of Tobias Smollett*, ed. O. M. Brack, Leslie Chilton and Walter H. Keithley (London: Pickering and Chatto, 2015) pp. 280–5, at p. 283.

56. Lewis, *Tobias Smollett*, p. 8.

57. Pocock, *Virtue Commerce*, p. 253.

58. Thomas Carte, *A General History of England* (London: J. Hodge, 1747), pp. 130, 175.

59. Carte, *General History*, p. 175.

60. Carte, *General History*, p. 175.

61. Smollett, *Humphrey Clinker*, p. 241.

62. Smollett, *Present State*, p. 295.

63. Smollett, *Present State*, p. 296.

64. Smollett, *Present State*, p. 307.

65. MacPhail, *Short History*, p. 64.

66. Smollett, *Humphrey Clinker*, pp. 243–4.

67. See Brian Bonnyman, *The Third Duke of Buccleuch and Adam Smith: Estate Management and Improvement in Enlightenment Scotland* (Edinburgh: Edinburgh University Press, 2014).

68. Smollett, *Present State*, p. 298.

69. MacLeod, *History*, p. 34.

70. MacPhail, *Short History*, p. 57.

71. MacPhail, *Short History*, p. 37.

72. MacPhail, *Short History*, pp. 38–9.

73. MacLeod, *History*, p. 57.

74. Smollett, *Humphrey Clinker*, p. 242.

75. Smollett, *Humphrey Clinker*, p. 242.

76. Adam Smith, *An Inquiry into the Nature and Causes of the Wealth of Nations*, ed. Roy Hutcheson Campbell, Andrew S. Skinner and W. B. Todd (Oxford: Oxford University Press, 1976 [1776]), p. 416.

77. Tobias Smollett, *Roderick Random* (London: Everyman's Library, 1964 [1748]), p. 426.

78. Smollett, *Humphrey Clinker*, p. 243.

79. Duncan Forbes, 'Sceptical Whiggism, Commerce and Liberty', in Andrew S. Skinner and Thomas Wilson (eds), *Essays on Adam Smith* (Oxford: Clarendon Press, 1975), pp. 179–95.

80. See Smollett, *Complete History* VI, p. 164, for his discussion of the origins of terms 'Whig' and 'Tory' in abuse.

81. Smollett, *Complete History* VII, p. 134.

82. Smollett, *Complete History* VII, p. 374.

83. Smollett, *Complete History* VII, p. 169.

84. Smollett, *Complete History* VIII, p. 186.

85. Smollett, *Complete History* VII, p. 464.

86. Smollett, *Complete History* VII, pp. 463–4.

87. Smollett, *Complete History* IX, pp. 65, 178.

88. Smollett, *Complete History* IX, pp. 258–76.

89. Smollett, *Complete History* IX, pp. 309, 383.

90. Smollett, *Complete History* IX, p. 411.

91. Smollett, *Complete History* IX, p. 430.

92. Smollett, *Complete History* IX, p. 437.

93. Smollett, *Complete History* IX, p. 437.

94. Smollett, *Complete History* IX, p. 446.

95. Smollett, *Complete History* X, p. 90.

96. Smollett, *Complete History* X, pp. 182, 308.

97. Smollett, *Complete History* X, p. 196.

98. Smollett, *Complete History* XI, p. 211.

99. Smollett, *Complete History* XI, p. 213.

100. Smollett, *Complete History* XI, p. 220.

101. Smollett, *Complete History* XI, p. 237.
102. Tobias Smollett, *The Briton*, in *The Works of Tobias Smollett: Poems, Plays, and The Briton*, ed. O. M. Brack (Athens: University of Georgia Press, 1993), pp. 219–432, at p. 238.
103. Smollett, *The Briton*, no. 5, p. 261.
104. Smollett, *The Briton*, no. 36, p. 415.
105. Smollett, *The Briton*, no. 25, p. 364.
106. Smollett, *The Briton*, no. 6, p. 266.
107. Adams Day, 'Introduction', pp. xxix–xxx.
108. A point that Smollett puts to satirical effect in *The History and Adventures of an Atom*, where the House of Commons becomes the 'self-constituted college of the mob' (*Atom*, p. 37).
109. Smollett, *The Briton*, no. 11, p. 292.
110. Adam Smith *The Theory of Moral Sentiments*, ed. David Daiches Raphael and Alec Lawrence Macfie (Oxford: Oxford University Press, 1976), VI. ii. 2. 17, p. 233 and VI. iii. 27, p. 249.
111. Smith, *Adam Ferguson*, pp. 224–6.
112. Smollett, *The Briton*, no. 31, p. 393.
113. Smollett, *The Briton*, no. 16, pp. 316–17.
114. The critique of luxury is also apparent in the *Complete History* where he writes of the accession of George II, 'The vice, luxury, and prostitution of the Age, the almost total extinction of sentiment, honour, and public spirit, had prepared the minds of men for slavery and corruption', and refers to the ministry as bribing the people with places and pensions (*Complete History* X, p. 326).
115. Smollett, *Humphrey Clinker*, p. 263.
116. Smollett, *Humphrey Clinker*, p. 83.
117. Smollett, *Humphrey Clinker*, p. 35.
118. Smollett, *Humphrey Clinker*, p. 267.
119. Smollett, *Humphrey Clinker*, p. 40.
120. John Sekora, *Luxury: The Concept in Western Thought, Eden to Smollett* (Baltimore: The Johns Hopkins University Press, 1977), p. x.
121. Berry, *Luxury*, p. 138.
122. Sekora, *Luxury*, p. 51.
123. Sekora, *Luxury*, p. 136.
124. Sekora, *Luxury*, p. 138.
125. Sekora, *Luxury*, p. 104.
126. Sekora, *Luxury*, p. 105.
127. Goldberg, *Smollett*, p. 149.
128. Smith, *Adam Ferguson*, pp. 182–6.
129. Lewis (*Tobias Smollett*, p. 3) describes Smollett's account of the Leven valley as 'a green and uncorrupted idyll far removed from the noisy, dirty, pestiferous, luxury-loving London in which he spent his adult life'.
130. Smollett, *Humphrey Clinker*, pp. 237–8.

131. Smollett, *Humphrey Clinker*, p. 237.

132. Smollett, *Humphrey Clinker*, p. 231.

133. Smollett, *Humphrey Clinker*, p. 266.

134. Louis L. Murtz, *The Later Career of Tobias Smollett* (New Haven: Yale University Press, 1942), p. 170.

135. Smollett, *Humphrey Clinker*, p. 221.

136. Smollett, *Humphrey Clinker*, p. 225.

137. Such as when Lismahago argues against the view that the Scots are particularly educated as a people (Smollett, *Humphrey Clinker*, p. 193).

138. Smollett, *Humphrey Clinker*, pp. 262–3.

139. Goldberg, *Smollett*, p. 163.

140. Goldberg, *Smollett*, p. 168.

141. Sekora, *Luxury*, p. 153.

142. Sekora, *Luxury*, p. 233.

4

The Stickiness of Manners? The Progress of Middling Rank Manners in David Hume, Adam Smith and John Millar

Spyridon Tegos

During my encounter with Christopher Berry's multi-layered and subtle oeuvre, I was particularly struck early on by his recurrent reference to the 'stickiness of institutions'[1] that pervades the Scottish Enlightenment. I thought that this captures nicely one of the landmarks of the Scots, their capacity to provide multi-causal explanations of natural and social phenomena while nurturing a critical spirit: the 'stickiness of institutions' paves the way to a robust moral criticism of manners, practices and beliefs embedded in institutions that have outlived their usefulness. In other words, institutional inertia plays a major explanatory role in how we criticise outdated customs and practices. In this context, manners, Christopher Berry claims, and especially the change in manners, gain prominence. In the aftermath of Montesquieu's *Spirit of Laws*, the Scots cultivate epistemic prudence and even scepticism regarding the historicity of manners and their subsequent, often much desired, reform. The genre of conjectural or stadial history offers a vantage point from which to sketch such a history. Despite the much debated natural history of civil society and its legacy, there is one omnipresent aspect of the Scottish Enlightenment that escapes scholarly attention: the socio-economic and moral outlook of the 'middling rank' and its manners.

Political thinking since Aristotle is convinced that democracy, in order to survive, has to be rooted in 'the middle' (*to meson* [*Politics* 1296a]), and that this middle is most importantly defined in socio-economic terms. This 'middling rank', however, also entails a set of cultural values and norms that Scottish Enlightenment thinkers have referred to as 'civility' or 'manners'. By 'manners' I refer to customarily and often unconsciously or uncritically accepted codes and norms of behaviour and speech in any given society or social group. The category of manners covers an array of notions bearing family resemblance such as politeness, civility or gallantry, and it is often juxtaposed to morality along the lines of the opposition between external behaviour and internal motives.

While the definition of 'middling rank', sitting uncomfortably between the 'neither too wealthy nor too poor', is controversial, the vantage point of manners seems more promising, in between upper-class pretentiousness and vanity on the one hand and servility towards superiors on the other. Suggesting an alternative to the broadly conceived Marxian legacy on 'bourgeois' manners does not lead to a downright dismissal of the socio-economic perspective – valuable per se – but to an alternative, liberal scenario regarding the interaction between social and mental dimensions of selfhood in modernity. From the emergence of the 'middling rank' in the eighteenth century until today, talking in terms of the middle class means alerting society that these very middle classes are threatened. The history of middle-class manners constitutes a privileged perspective in order to capture the subtle, evolving nature of unspotted or unspoken inclusions and exclusions incompatible with liberty.

In this chapter, I first explore David Hume's focus on ceremonial French courtly politeness that deviates from the Enlightenment paradigm of urban manners. Oddly enough, Hume's idiosyncratic Francophile emphasis on courtly politeness goes against the grain of standard conjectural history. Hume focuses on the irreducible ritualistic stickiness that undermines even sophisticated doctrines of progress.[2] To what extent is the middling rank's meritocratic ethos compatible with Humean ceremonial manners? I then turn to Adam Smith's subtle approach which considers middling rank manners as dangerously inclined towards imitation of aristocratic politeness. As a result, he gives priority to middling rank virtues instead of manners. Smith discusses the affective responses to the antagonism between meritocratic ideals and hereditary status at length. Finally, John Millar insists on the unintended consequences of the antagonism between the spirit of independence qua desire of non-domination and the status-seeking ethos. In his view, modern liberty is due to the self-destructive mentality of feudal lords, enamoured by 'trinkets and baubles' introduced through foreign commerce by merchants and manufacturers. Yet modern liberty is preserved by the suicidal behaviour of the latter who, in their turn, undermine their recently acquired status by self-destructive conspicuous consumption. Stickiness of manners seems to have unintended consequences that go beyond the most profound irony and self-sarcasm ever exercised by the Scots.

Hume's Account of Politeness within Political Constitutions

The 'Shaftesburian' paradigm lays emphasis on the 'politeness of the heart' to capture 'true' –that is, natural, authentic and sincere – polite behaviour.[3] By contrast, Mandeville conflates the terms 'manners' and 'politeness'; he incessantly satirises the masking of pride at the heart of all motives of polite behaviour. Manners and politeness are considered artificial, conventions that unfold and evolve through long periods of time. However, those contrasting traditions of thought share the same concern to construct a new model of commercial and increasingly urban manners. While integrating elements from the Shaftesburian tradition, in the *Treatise*, Hume asserts that 'we establish the rules of good breeding, in order to prevent the opposition of men's pride'.[4] Incorporating Mandeville's account of pride into his naturalistic programme, Hume also emphasises the need of solid social identity in order to conform to customs proper to one's rank and display due pride.[5] In the essay 'Of the Rise and Progress of the Arts and Sciences', he characteristically affirms that 'as we are commonly proud and selfish, and apt to assume the preference above others, a polite man learns to behave with deference towards his companions, and to yield the superiority to them in all the common incidents of society.'[6] In this chapter I shift the emphasis from the link between manners and civil society to the connection between manners and political constitutions.

Hume's crucial step is to contextualise the treatment of politeness by inserting it into his regime typology. He takes his cues from Montesquieu. Montesquieu's core argument is that manners constitute status-seeking activities firmly embedded into the core of political regimes. He writes: 'In monarchies, politeness is naturalized at court. One excessively great man makes all others small.'[7] In the *Spirit of Laws*, the balance is markedly tipped towards civility because of the inveterate courtly element deeply rooted in politeness, and this turns manners into 'imitations of virtue'. Despite the lack of interior sincerity, civility turns out to be more reliable: 'Civility is, in this respect, of more value than politeness. Politeness flatters the vices of others, and civility keeps us from displaying our own.'[8] Thus practices of politeness increase integration across ranks fostering stability within hierarchical social relations.[9] In the essay 'Of the Rise and Progress of the Arts and Sciences', Hume follows a similar pattern and contrasts between 'civilized monarchies' on the one hand, mainly France, and republics on the other. Although Hume acknowledges a background of shared standards of modern civilization – that is, common security of property and rule of law – he draws a sharp contrast between civilised monarchies and republics regarding the nature of ambition and distinction of ranks.[10]

Put bluntly, in monarchies politeness is an art of social distinction while in republics people distinguish themselves through their merit in economic life or their successful participation in politics. As Hume puts it, political authority:

excites the ambition and avarice of mankind. The only difference is that, in a republic, the candidates for office must look downwards, to gain the suffrages of the people; in a monarchy, they must turn their attention upwards, to court the good graces and the favour of the great. To be successful in the former way, it is necessary for a man to make himself useful, by his industry, capacity, or knowledge: To be prosperous in the latter way, it is requisite for him to render himself agreeable, by his wit, complaisance, or civility.[11]

This line of reasoning leads to the conclusion that 'strong genius', and more generally science, find a more appropriate ground in republics while 'refined taste' and 'polite arts' chiefly flourish in civilised monarchies.[12]

Hume continued to argue that 'politeness of manners, therefore, arises most naturally in monarchies and courts, and where that flourishes, none of the liberal arts will be altogether neglected and despised'.[13] A point noted by Charles de Saint-Évremond who explains in his own humorous way the total lack of industriousness in courts and the thriving spirit of it in commercial republics:

> The only study in the courts of princes is how to please, because a man make his fortune there by being agreeable. This is the reason why courtiers are so polite. On the contrary, in towns and Republicks where men are forced to take pains to get their living, the last of their cares is to please, and this is what it makes them so clownish.[14]

Thus Hume pauses on a far-reaching antithesis of the grounds of social distinction in European societies: the art of pleasing versus the art of being useful, favours accorded by socially superiors versus co-optation by peers, rent seeking versus meritocracy; put bluntly, status versus merit.

French Politeness and the Middle Stations of Life's Manners in Hume

At this point we reach the crux of the matter. To what extent is Hume ready to admit a certain amount of social servility as a necessary cost for diffusing 'French' softness of manners? We should remain cautious. In a letter dated 5 September 1765, Hume asked Adam Smith, his closest friend, who was in France but had not yet reached Paris, for his 'judgment' about where he should settle. He was inclined to remain in Paris, but worried that 'Offers' that would make his life 'agreeable' there would cost him his 'Independence' by 'entering [him] into engagements with great Lords and

Ladies'. In other words, a social distinction based on generalised politeness creates an atmosphere of elegance and polishes manners yet it can also lead to social servility.[15]

Hume considers differently given republican regimes such as modern Holland and 'republican manners' of liberty. The latter are always tied with the liberating spirit from oppressing nobility, and Hume seems to stand against Montesquieu's *thèse nobiliaire* in the context of political constitutions:[16] the engine of stability resides in the 'middle stations of life', in no case in the titled nobility. Indeed, the post-feudally established 'middle stations of life'[17] reach a state of mind beyond the condescension of the 'great' and the obsequiousness of the popular strands. In the essay 'Of Refinements in the Arts' the language of politeness serves to reject the civic humanist critique of luxury and defend commercial civilisation. Hume's analysis sheds light on the economic basis and virtues of those middle social strata that become the 'firmest basis of public liberty'.[18]

In the essay 'Of the Middle Station of Life', the image of the rich and powerful is traditionally tainted by the stain of fake esteem. The middling rank's social status simply renders obsolete any reason for obsequiousness in the face of the rich and for pretentiousness towards those of lower status. In this context he distinguishes between the merely instrumental friendships of 'the Great' and the real friendships – friendships built on and fostering independence – in the middle station. Indeed, Hume contextualises his assessment of the 'middling rank of men' along the lines of his political regime typology. Therefore, the 'middling sort' can defy 'monarchical as well as aristocratical tyranny' and cultivate the virtues of friendship.[19]

Regardless of the removal of this essay from the subsequent editions, the status of the 'middling rank' in the British mixed constitution remains enigmatic in Hume's thought. Albeit in his *Essays*, and the *History*, he endeavours to create a new political culture that informs citizens about the nature and history of the British constitution, Hume's assessment of French politeness seems mostly enthusiastic.[20] Is it compatible with the polite manners of the 'middle station of life'? This 'elegant part of mankind' undoubtedly composed his audience. To be sure, from a 'skeptical whiggish' point of view, civil and political liberties are divorced.[21] Thus Hume makes it clear that, in a civilised monarchy, there is a long train of dependence, which is not great enough to render property precarious, or depress the mind of the people; but is sufficient to beget in every one an inclination to please his superiors, and *to force himself upon those models*, which are most acceptable to people of condition and education. Yet, without an interest to please social superiors, citizens are somehow rustic in manners. In 'Of the Rise of the Progress of the Arts and Sciences', Hume unambiguously

asserts that 'the good manners of a Swiss civilized in Holland' is the pro-
verbial expression of rusticity, the English falling to a certain extent 'under
the same censure' in direct proportion to their republicanism. Here is the
stunning conclusion of an idiosyncratic Francophile: the British are somehow rude, or the British politeness is a second-order politeness; in other
terms the British are depicted as *bourgeois gentilhommes* à la Molière.

In the essay 'Of the Rise of the Progress of the Arts and Sciences',
Hume introduces the somehow paradoxical notion of 'mutual deference':[22]
the virtue of civility is natural but the Ancien Régime's structure crucially
reinforces this natural tendency that can plainly come into fruition only
within the hierarchical structure of French society. However, the point
regarding the status of politeness in the British 'Ancient Regime' remains
unclear. It is needless to insist on the ubiquitous references throughout
Hume's work on the progress of *urban* and *commercial* polite manners in
Britain.[23] In the essay 'Refinement in the Arts', Hume defends modern
politeness without any reference to courts and civilised monarchies.[24] On
balance, one might wonder how Hume, a staunch defender of middle stations of life, reconciles their moral, cultural or socio-political outlook with
the clearly aristocratic timbre of French politeness.

Adam Smith on the Middling Rank's Independent and Servile Manners

It has to be recalled that Adam Smith opens the *Theory of Moral Sentiments*
by construing propriety as behaviour that is considered proper in different
social and cultural contexts by a real or imagined impartial spectator. The
Smithian notion of propriety – or 'the sense of propriety', according to the
title of the first part of the *Theory of Moral Sentiments* – paves the ground
for the Smithian conception of sympathy. Smithian sympathy denotes the
ability to put yourself in the shoes of others and simultaneously imagine how
your fellow citizens are seeing you. Hence, he reserves an important role for
the faculty of imagination and judgement in order to properly contextualise the complexity determining the standard of propriety. Given a certain
degree of social and psychological development, the figure of the impartial
spectator emerges as a personification of moral conscience bypassing and
rectifying conformism, unchallenged moral customs, and context-insensi-
tive general moral rules, his theory of propriety goes beyond manners.[25]

Within this frame, Smith accounts for manners as a subset of custom
in the *Theory of Moral Sentiments*. Smith pulls no punches: he claims that
standards of politeness and civility conceal class, race and cultural domination.[26] Echoing the important early modern reception of Ciceronian

decorum, Smith introduces the notion of propriety instead of politeness or civility used interchangeably.[27] In his vernacular, he offers a novel account of manners and morals, and anticipates Norbert Elias's insights regarding the civilising process in Europe within which courtly etiquette gradually yielded to new codes of civility from the emerging civil society.[28] This line of reasoning is diametrically opposed to Hume's conventionalism revolving around the social function of secular rituals of politeness. Duncan Forbes shrewdly notes that: 'Progress for the school of Adam Smith was a law of history and not an article in a new religion . . . the progress of society is both science and propaganda.'[29] The progress from rude to refined manners constitutes a key moment. Despite his sardonic critique of courtly and bourgeois manners, Smith acknowledges that aristocratic behaviour within proper social class constraints is tolerable for a moderate social hierarchy to be respected.[30] However, aristocratic shallowness and social servility are treated with cynicism and irony. The satire of courtly manners and their imitation in the context of eighteenth-century upward social mobility foregrounds a problem: is an education in manners possible without imitation? Smith's response lies within his theory of moral sentiments.

In section V.ii he essentially explores the tensions between manners and morals, making nuanced terminological and conceptual distinctions.[31] Cultural relativism and diversity based on age, status and historical period allow for certain variation in manners, fashion and customs up to a certain point beyond which core moral requirements trump them. The threshold appears to be quite clear given that 'the sentiments of approbation and disapprobation' are founded on 'the most vigorous passions of human nature'. In this sense, Smith lays out a core distinction between an array of soft virtues, such as humanity and civility on the one hand, proper to 'polite ages', and inflexible self-command and self-denial, proper to a savage mentality and rude ethos, on the other. The tone is clearly descriptive: 'The general security and happiness which prevail in ages of civility and politeness, afford little exercise to the contempt of danger.'[32] This stays in tune with the basic tenets of the Scottish Enlightenment. Smith claims: 'The peculiar character and manners which we are led by custom to appropriate to each rank and profession, have sometimes perhaps a *propriety independent of custom*.'[33] Proper manners seem to further buttress moral sentiments, while corrupted manners undermine sound moral intuitions:

When custom and fashion coincide with the natural principles of right and wrong, they heighten the delicacy of our sentiments, and increase our abhorrence for every thing which approaches to evil. Those who have been educated in what is really good company, not in what is commonly called such, who have been accustomed to see nothing in the persons whom they esteemed and lived with, but justice, modesty, humanity, and good order.[34]

In the sections regarding the origins of distinctions of ranks and the corruption of moral sentiments through the admiration of wealth, Smith seemingly endorses the commonplace of 'bourgeois resentment' against titled aristocracy and hereditary status. While scrutinising aristocratic manners and royal prestige, he repeatedly argues that Louis XIV and other noble celebrities have few 'talents and virtues' above mediocrity. The 'man of rank and distinction' distinguish himself by a 'propriety of his ordinary behavior': 'His air, his manner, his deportment, all mark the elegant and graceful sense of his own superiority, which those who are born to inferior stations can hardly even arrive at.'[35] Put bluntly, royalty and aristocrats have no virtue or talents; they simply manage the code of manners that is 'frivolous accomplishments' or eccentricities serving to distinguish themselves from the upwardly mobile middling rank. The young noble '. . . shudders with horror at the thought of any situation which demands the continual and long exertion of patience, industry, fortitude and application of thought'.[36]

It is rarely observed that throughout those lines Smith does not reason in terms of middling rank but of 'middle *and* inferior ranks of life'.[37] Therefore, he worries less about middling rank than about upward social mobility excluding hereditary wealth or status. On one occasion, he juxtaposes aristocratic nothingness to the 'the greatest talents and virtues' required for the 'man of spirit and ambition' to distinguish himself. The 'man of spirit and ambition' whose moderate and uncertain social climbing renders him 'depressed by his situation' is greatly tempted by opportunism. Depression is only matched by tolerance to vexations and sense of injustice suffered when self-made men relying on merit gain positions of power. They are mistreated with envy, resentment and contempt by 'those born their superiors'. By contrast, in all governments, even in monarchies, 'the highest offices are generally possessed, and the whole detail of the administration is conducted by men who were educated in the middle and inferior ranks of life, who have been carried forward by their own industry and abilities.'[38]

Smith's narrative reads as if he is inclined to think that 'middle and inferior ranks of life' have virtues and talents but no manners except bitterness against hereditary status; the latter gains admiration and approval with no effort or merit while commoners are treated with contempt. Finally, while middling rank resentment seems justified, it nurtures corrupted manners, especially those based on servile imitation of the aristocratic lifestyle. After a desperate fight against class prejudice, loaded with bitterness and resentment, the middling rank hero cracks and a tragic fall ensues. The middling sort who imitates the politeness of the great 'is rewarded by a double share of contempt for his folly and presumption'.[39] He turns himself into a coxcomb, a petty bourgeois, as the story has gone ever since. For Smith, the ridicule attributed to the 'inferior and middling rank of life' who imitate noble behaviour, 'the disinterested admirers and worshippers of wealth and greatness', is ultimately suicidal. Middling rank manners are insignificant, eventually bending towards self-destructive conspicuous consumption while their virtues are solid and admirable:

> Many a poor man places his glory in being thought rich, without considering that the duties (if one may call such follies by so very venerable a name) which that reputation imposes upon him, must soon reduce him to beggary, and render his situation still more unlike that of those whom he admires and imitates, than it has been originally.[40]

As we shall see below, John Millar agrees with this critique but draws a radically different lesson from this self-destructive erosion of the socioeconomic basis of the *nouveau riche*.

John Millar's Machiavellian Moment

To what extent is the spirit of liberty and independence co-substantial with the middling rank outlook? In Book III of *The Wealth of Nations* Smith famously endorses the standard narrative about the decline of feudal servility.[41] The gradual introduction of commerce and manufactures brought about a slow and silent change in feudal manners, liberty and prosperity. In the post-feudal British constitutional balance, citizens that defer to monarchical authority are not necessarily servile. Smith endorses Hume's distinction between 'lovers of liberty' and 'lovers of monarchy'[42] and develops it further: Tories seem to follow the principle of authority, while the Whigs tend to follow the utility principle. He reinterprets the conventional categorisation of the forms of government by focusing on the fact that 'the principle of authority is that which chiefly prevails in a monarchy'[43] while the principle of utility prevails more in a republican government or in a democracy. The supporters of the utility principle follow the Whig party and they are described as 'bustling, spirited, active folks', because they think that the authority of the government derives exclusively from the people and that the benefit of the rulers should not be taken into account;

any resistance to the abuse of authority by the magistrates has to be considered as legitimate. The Tories' supporters, who are 'calm, contented folks',[44] are 'pleased with a tame submission to superiority', and moreover belong among the wealthier citizens, who do not want to disturb or be disturbed. To what extent are the middling rank manners bent towards the Tories or the Whigs? Both principles coexist in free constitutions. To be sure, Smith vindicates the meritocratic ethos of the middling rank as symptom of their independent spirit. However, the above-mentioned middling rank's resentment towards hereditary aristocracy betrays a lack of independence. Besides, Smith pauses in length at the widespread obsequiousness towards royalty and social eminence.[45]

Smith often expresses doubts about reaching social harmony in commercial society.[46] However, he rarely gets as close to the Machiavellian spirit of irreducible social antagonism as in the above-mentioned passage regarding the conflicting yet legitimate desires to preserve either social order or independence. In sketching the portraits of those contrasting characters, he portrays the tension between peaceful and conformist citizens on the one hand, iconoclastic and irreverent to cherished idols on the other. The lucidity of Smith qua social and political theorist paves the way to his student John Millar who elaborates further on this Machiavellian praise of social antagonism as a crucial component for preserving liberty. First, Millar focuses on the progress of 'arts and commerce' and then on the diffusion of knowledge as reasons for 'a gradual progress of opinions', According to him, the Tory principle of authority historically recedes while 'The fashion of scrutinizing public measures, according to the standard of their utility, has now become very universal; it pervades the literary circles together with a great part of the middling ranks, and is visibly descending to the lower order of people.'[47]

According to Donald Winch, the effect of commerce is solidly associated with the emergence of the middling rank in John Millar's oeuvre in order to play a major role in modern political constitutionalism. Elaborating on Smith's concerns, John Millar's *The Origin of Distinction of Ranks* (1771)[48] sketches a 'Machiavellian' moment within the Smithian frame of a 'theory and history of law and government'. In Winch's view, Millar's narrative basically runs as follows. Commerce and manufactures, we recall, gradually eliminate feudal dependence and servile *ethos*.[49] The pursuit of luxury undermines hereditary wealth and allows estates to fall into the hands of industrious merchants who then adopt the profligate habits of the landed aristocracy and in their turn undermine their own social status. Such 'fluctuations of property' limit the influence of established wealth and therefore tend 'to introduce democratical government'.[50]

In Millar's view, small states like ancient or modern Italian democracies where the people are able to unite against encroachments on their liberty sustain such regimes. In large commercial monarchies, however, where the sovereign is able to raise large revenues and hence create a loyal standing army, despotism is the outcome to be feared. Smith has dismissed this analysis beforehand:

> Many of the persons of chief rank and station in the army have also large estates of their own, and are members of the House of Commons. They have in this manner an influence and power altogether independent of the King. It would never be their interest to join with the king in any design to enslave the nation.[51]

The balance between popular liberty and royal influence is one of the main themes of *An Historical View of the English Government* (1787). According to Millar: 'the clamour and tumultuary proceedings of the populace in the great town' is one of the most effective means of preserving the 'spirit of liberty'.[52] At this juncture, the structure of the argument changes and Millar follows a different line of thought. We move clearly beyond Smithian worries towards more republican concerns. Middling rank manners lead to a 'democratical' government because of self-defeating conspicuous consumption of recently acquired wealth. The feudal nobility lost ground but the newly emerged commercial middling rank cannot take total advantage because it turns out to be equally suicidal and hence an unstable equilibrium between different classes and social groups emerges.

Millar refers twice in *An Historical View of the English Government* to the 'democratical form' of government, or republic, that is a government in which there is no king, or hereditary chief magistrate'.[53] However, he also refers to the 'democratical part of government', evoking the popular element in the constitution balance. At this juncture, he anticipates the future use of the category of populism to denote insurrectional desire of common, unprivileged people to redress grievances or hinder perceived domination by the 'rich and the great'.[54] The spirit of independence in big cities is due to the urban environment: it is the cradle of ancient and modern democracies. Millar praises populous cities and their intensive commercial sociability despite popular leaders taking advantage of the promiscuity that reigns and uniting the people in discontent. In this context, merchants, manufacturers and artificers simultaneously acquire class consciousness and fall victim to mass psychology:

In all those places of resort, there arises large bands of labourers and artificers, who, by following the same employment and by constant intercourse, are enabled, with great rapidity, to communicate all their sentiments and passions. Among these, there spring up leaders, who give a tone and direction to their companion. The strong encourage the feeble . . . and the movements of the whole mass proceed with the uniformity of a machine, and with a force that is often irresistible . . . The least ground of complaint in a town, becomes the occasion of a riot.[55]

In this context, Millar locates the spirit of independence in the desire not to be dominated and in the seditious spirit in so far as the political expression of popular discontent through populist leaders can be formidable in big cities if not taken seriously or downplayed. Popular indignation and resentment can find privileged expression in populous cities and is akin to the love of liberty once 'artificers and tradesmen were led by degree to shake off their ancient slavish habits' by the progress of improvement. The ease to denounce oppression is a novel element due to the 'extreme facility' in urban environments for communicating 'sentiments and opinions'.

The urban setting is known for the promotion of polite manners, gallantry and humanity, all hallmarks of the Scottish Enlightenment. By contrast, this 'allergy' to oppression introduces middling and lower-class solidarity beyond medieval corporatism, against oppression and injury, organised by 'bold and enterprising' leaders.[56] The legacy of plebeian solidarity in Republican Rome looms large. 'The independence and the influence of this order of people', enhanced by a great deal of mass contagiousness in populous cities, turns the Whig principle of utility into a Machiavellian *virtu* and marks the end of the moderate, mainly socio-cultural self-determination of the middling rank. Republican manners of independence are promoted through political activism and social unrest.[57]

Conclusion

Hume's functionalism regarding secular rituals of politeness embedded into the structure of French civilised monarchy challenges the Enlightenment narrative of progress. Rituals are stationary and evoke socio-cultural immobilism. Within this frame, the civilising effects of French politeness rest on its highly ceremonial nature. However, it is highly unlikely that eminently ritualised politeness can be compatible with a meritocratic, 'middling rank' ethos. In Smith's narrative, the compatibility between meritocracy and uncompromising independence remains a matter for speculation provided that the threat of servility looms large regarding the moderate rise of commoners. Is the middling rank's servility as alarming as Smith suggests? John Millar, though a militant Whig, was 'as much of a social scientist as a reformer'.[58] His approach of 'middling rank' manners shifts the emphasis to the positive side-effects of middling rank imitation of aristocrats, so severely dismissed by Smith. He scrutinises the fluctuation of property and manners in commercial society; the middling rank's virtues heralded by Smith give way to servile imitation of aristocratic whimsies and finally irrational conspicuous consumption, leading to self-destructive behaviours. The spirit of independence is preserved unwittingly thanks to the erosion of the hereditary basis of property or capital accumulation. Within the 'natural history of European civility', manners gain prominence as instances of institutional stickiness thanks to their gradual, often imperceptible change that goes under the radar. This stadial process is slow and uncertain, involving regressions and unintended consequences, and requires a poly-causal lens; the genealogy of manners simultaneously conceal and reveal social antagonisms and unprecedented violence that would remain invisible otherwise. The stickiness of manners within conjectural history gains prominence as an explanatory tool in order to account for atavism, regression, justified or ungrounded moral criticism, and allegedly irrational behaviour.

Notes

1. Christopher J. Berry, 'Sociality and Socialisation', in Alexander Broadie (ed.), *The Cambridge Companion to the Scottish Enlightenment* (Cambridge: Cambridge University Press, 2003), pp. 243–57, at pp. 250–1; *Essays on Hume, Smith and the Scottish Enlightenment* (Edinburgh: Edinburgh University Press, 2018), pp. 78–83, 193.

2. Antoine Lilti, *L'Héritage des Lumières. Ambivalences de la modernité* (Paris: EHESS/Gallimard/Seuil, 2019), pp. 20–1.

3. Lawrence E. Klein, *Shaftesbury and the Culture of Politeness: Moral Discourse and Cultural Politics in Early Eighteenth-Century England* (Cambridge: Cambridge University Press, 1994). Spiros Tegos, 'Adam Smith on the Addisonian and Courtly Origins of Politeness', *Revue internationale de philosophie* 3 (2014), pp. 317–42.

4. David Hume, *A Treatise of Human Nature*, ed. David Fate Norton and Mary Norton (Oxford: Oxford University Press, 2007 [1739]), 3.3.2.10, p. 381.

5. Mikko Tolonen, *Mandeville and Hume: Anatomists of Civil Society* (Oxford: Voltaire Foundation SVEC, 2013). Hume, *Treatise* 3.3.2.11, p. 382: 'There

are certain deferences and mutual submissions, which custom requires of the different ranks of men towards each others and whoever exceeds in this particular, if thro' interest, is accus'd of meanness; if thro' ignorance, of simplicity. 'Tis necessary, therefore, to know our rank and station in the world, whether it be fix'd by our birth, fortune, employments, talents or reputation.'

6. David Hume, *Essays Moral, Political and Literary*, ed. Eugene F. Miller (Indianapolis: Liberty Fund, 1987 [1741–52]), p. 126.

7. Charles de Secondat, Baron de Montesquieu, *The Spirit of the Laws*, ed. Anne M. Cohler, Basia Carolyn Miller and Harold Samuel Stone (Cambridge: Cambridge University Press, 1989 [1748]), p. 32.

8. Montesquieu, *Spirit of the Laws*, p. 317. Montesquieu, *Spirit of the Laws*, ch. 4, p. 28: '[Politeness] . . . rises form a desire of distinguishing ourselves. It is pride that renders us polite: we are flattered with being taken notice of for a behaviour that shows we are not of a mean condition . . . Politeness, in monarchies, is naturalised at court. One man excessively great renders everybody else little . . . hence that politeness, equally pleasing to those by whom, as to those towards whom, it is practiced; because it gives people to understand that a person belongs, or at least deserves to belong, to the court.'

9. Adam Smith shares this assumption. Ancient post-republican Rome was notoriously remarkable for the exchange of deferential civilities among unequals, as the juxtaposition of Plato's – with a conspicuous absence of polite formalities in the democratic context – and Cicero's dialogues testify. See Adam Smith, *Lectures on Rhetoric and Belles Lettres*, ed. J. C. Bryce (Indianapolis: Liberty Fund, 1985 [1762–3]), ii. 158, p. 156; ii. 163–4, p. 158.

10. Hume, *Essays*, p. 126.

11. Hume, *Essays*, p. 126.

12. Hume, *Essays*, p. 126.

13. Hume, *Essays*, p. 127.

14. Charles de Saint-Évremond, *Works*, ed. Pierre Desmaizeaux, II (London, 1728), p. 426.

15. Hume to Adam Smith, 5 September 1765 in *The Correspondence of Adam Smith*, ed. E. C. Mossner and I. S. Ross (Indianapolis: Liberty Press, 1987), pp. 106–7.

16. Duncan Forbes, 'Sceptical Whiggism, Commerce and Liberty', in Andrew S. Skinner and Thomas Wilson (eds), *Essays on Adam Smith* (Oxford: Clarendon Press, 1975), pp. 179–201, at p. 196. Céline Spector, *Montesquieu. Pouvoirs, richesses, société* (Paris: Presses universitaires de France, 2004), Ch. 4.

17. Within a large literature on the status of the 'middling stations of life' or middling rank, see for the larger context, Nicholas Phillipson, 'Propriety, Property and Prudence: David Hume's Defense of the Revolution', in Nicholas Phillipson and Quentin Skinner (eds), *Political Discourse in Early Modern Britain* (Cambridge: Cambridge University Press, 1993), pp. 302–20; a study focusing almost exclusively on the composition of middle and inferior social

strata in Hume is Harvey Chiswick, 'David Hume and the Common People', in Peter Jones (ed.), *The Science of Man in the Scottish Enlightenment: Hume, Reid and Their Contemporaries* (Edinburgh: Edinburgh University Press, 1989), pp. 5–32: 'A nexus of wealth, status, office and power identifies a composite elite of landowners, financiers, legal and administrative functionaries and wholesale merchants which, by its economic and political power, as well as by its social prestige, dominated eighteenth-century society. The people stood against this complex elite, inferior, subordinate, dependent. Between the dominant few and the common people come Goubert's independent groups – well-off farmers, comfortable artisans and merchants, members of the liberal professions, *rentiers* – groups which have variously been called the bourgeoisie, bourgeois of the old-regime type, and "middling sort" or "'middling ranks."'

18. Hume, *Essays*, p. 277: 'But where luxury nourishes commerce and industry, the peasants, by a proper cultivation of land, become rich and independent; while the tradesmen and merchants acquire a share of the property and draw authority and consideration to that middling rank of men, who are the best and firmest basis of public liberty. These submit not to slavery, like the peasants from poverty and meanness of spirit; and having no hopes of tyrannising over others, like the barons, they are not tempted, for the sake of that gratification, to submit to the tyranny of their sovereign. They covet equal laws, which may secure their property, and preserve them.

19. Hume, *Essays*, pp. 546–7.

20. Nicholas Phillipson, *David Hume: The Philosopher as Historian* (New Haven: Yale University Press, 2011), pp. 24–7, 52.

21. Forbes, *Sceptical Whiggism*, p. 191: 'As has been rightly suggested, the point that Hume was trying to make did not concern the superiority of the English constitution in the face of the French absolute monarchy, but the marks of civilised society that Britain and France have in common; a high degree of liberty, although it is not the political liberty secured by the British political system, plus a highly developed division of labour, opulence and, most importantly, ranks'.

22. Hume, *Essays*, p. 127: 'Among the arts of conversation, no one pleases more than mutual deference or civility, which leads us to resign our inclination to those of our companion, and to curb and conceal that presumption and arrogance, so natural to the human mind. A good-natured man, who is well educated, practices this civility to every mortal, without premeditation or interest. But in order to render this valuable quality general among people, it seems necessary to assist the natural disposition by some general motive.' For helpful insights on the idea of mutual deference in Hume, see the remarkable study of Richard Boyd 'Manners and Morals: David Hume on Civility, Commerce and the Social Construction of Difference', in Carl Wennerlind and Margaret Schabas (eds), *David Hume's Political Economy* (London: Routledge, 2008), pp. 65–85, esp. pp. 70–76.

23. See John Christian Laursen, *The Politics of Scepticism in the Ancients, Montaigne, Hume and Kant* (Leiden: E. J. Brill, 1992) for a helpful account of the vocabulary and status of politeness in Hume.

24. Hume, *Essays*, p. 178.

25. Adam Smith, *The Theory of Moral Sentiments*, ed. David Daiches Raphael and Alec Lawrence Macfie (Indianapolis: Liberty Fund, 1982 [1759/1790]).

26. Smith, *Moral Sentiments*, pp. 62, 54, 205–6; Keith Thomas, *In Pursuit of Civility: Civilization and Manners in Early Modern England* (New Haven: Yale University Press, 2018).

27. E.g. Smith, *Moral Sentiments*, p. 202.

28. Eiko Ikegami, *Bonds of Civility: Aesthetic Networks and the Political Origins of Japanese Culture* (Cambridge: Cambridge University Press, 2005), p. 22.

29. Duncan Forbes , '"Scientific" Whiggism: Adam Smith and John Millar', *The Cambridge Journal* 7 (1954), pp. 643–70, at p. 652.

30. Smith, *Moral Sentiments*, p. 226.

31. Smith, *Moral Sentiments*, pp. 200–11.

32. Smith, *Moral Sentiments*, p. 205.

33. Smith, *Moral Sentiments*, p. 202.

34. Smith, *Moral Sentiments*, p. 200.

35. Smith, *Moral Sentiments*, p. 55.

36. Smith, *Moral Sentiments*, p. 56.

37. Smith, *Moral Sentiments*, p. 56; italics added.

38. Smith, *Moral Sentiments*, p. 56.

39. Smith, *Moral Sentiments*, pp. 54–5.

40. Smith, *Moral Sentiments*, p. 64.

41. Adam Smith, *An Inquiry into the Nature and Causes of the Wealth of Nations*, ed. Roy Hutcheson Campbell, Andrew S. Skinner and W. B. Todd (Indianapolis: Liberty Fund, 1981 [1776]).

42. Hume, *Essays*, p. 71.

43. Adam Smith, *Lectures on Jurisprudence*, ed. Ronald L. Meek, David Daiches Raphael and Peter Stein (Indianapolis: Liberty Fund, 1982 [1762–6]), pp. 123, 319.

44. Smith, *Moral Sentiments*, pp. 124, 320.

45. Smith, *Jurisprudence*, pp. 319–20.

46. Eric Schliesser, *Adam Smith: Systematic Philosopher and Public Thinker* (Oxford: Oxford University Press, 2017), p. 23.

47. John Millar, *An Historical View of the English Government: From the Settlement of the Saxons in Britain to the Revolution in 1688*, ed. M. S. Phillips and D. R. Smith (Indianapolis: Liberty Fund, 2006 [1787]), p. 805.

48. John Millar, *The Origin of Distinction of Ranks, or An Inquiry into the Circumstances which give rise to Influence and Authority in the different Members of Society*, ed. with an introduction A. Garrett (Indianapolis: Liberty Fund, 2006 [1771]).

49. Millar, *Historical View*, p. 760: 'From the diffusion of wealth by commerce and manufactures, there has arisen in some countries, such a regular and plentiful supply of provisions as among people in the higher and even middling ranks, to banish the idea of scarcity, and to produce , in this respect, a total change in manners.'

50. Donald Winch, *Adam Smith's Politics: An Essay in Historiographical Revision* (Cambridge: Cambridge University Press, 1978), p. 200.

51. Smith, *Jurisprudence*, pp. 169–70.

52. Millar, *Ranks*, p. 238, Winch, *Smith's Politics*, p. 102. The relevant sequence in *The Origin of the Distinction of Ranks* is ch. V, 'The changes produced in the government of a people, by their progress in arts and in polished manners': Section I 'Circumstances, in a polished nation, which tend to increase the power of the sovereign'; Section II 'Other circumstances which contribute to advance the privilege of the people'; Section III 'Result of the opposition between these different principles'.

53. Millar, *Historical View*, p. 616: 'Thus in a very small state, a democratical government is necessary, because the king would have too little authority; in a very great, because he would have too much.'

54. Millar, *Historical View*, p. 324.

55. Millar, *Historical View*, p. 727.

56. Millar, *Ranks*, pp. 487–8: 'The independence and the influence of this order of people was further promoted by the circumstances of their being collected in towns, whence they derived an extreme facility in communicating their sentiments and opinions. In a populous city, not only the discoveries and knowledge, but the feelings and passions of each individual are quickly and readily propagated over the whole. If an injury is committed, if an act of oppression is complained of, it immediately spreads an alarm and becomes the subject of clamour and censure, and excites general indignation and resentment. Every one roused by the example of those around him, loses the sense of his own danger in the ardour and impetuosity of his companions. Some bold and enterprising leader acquires an ascendant over their common movement; and while their first impressions are yet warm, finds no difficulty in uniting them to defend their privileges, or to demand redress for their wrongs.'

57. Millar, *Ranks*, p. 487.

58. Forbes, *Scientific Whiggism*, p. 234.

5

'The Happiest and Most Honourable Period of My Life': Adam Smith's Service to the University of Glasgow

Ryan Patrick Hanley

University professors, in both Adam Smith's day and our own, have traditionally been understood to have three responsibilities: research, teaching and administration or service. Many professors tend to gravitate to one of these tasks over the others, and it is a rare scholar indeed who relishes and excels at all three. But Smith himself was just such a scholar, and the years he spent at these tasks at the University of Glasgow held a cherished place in his heart and left him with memories he would carry with him throughout his life.

Adam Smith served the University of Glasgow, his undergraduate alma mater, in a professional capacity for thirteen years.[1] First appointed in 1751 to the Professorship of Logic, Smith transferred in the following year to the Professorship of Moral Philosophy – a post he held until 1764, when he resigned his professorship to take up the duty of serving as the tutor and guide to the Duke of Buccleuch on his tour of France. During his thirteen-year professional term at Glasgow, Smith was extensively engaged in the prosecution of all three duties of the professor. As a researcher, he contributed several book reviews to the new local journal in the mid-1750s, and in 1759 published *The Theory of Moral Sentiments*, which itself grew out of his moral philosophy lectures. As a teacher, he lectured on subjects from ethics to economics to politics to jurisprudence to natural theology to rhetoric.[2] And as an administrator, Smith served Glasgow as Dean of Faculties, Vice-Rector and Library Quaestor. These were posts to which he was dedicated and in which he did valuable work – including purchasing texts that significantly bolstered library holdings, and supporting the college's establishment of a workshop for James Watt's renowned work on the steam engine.[3] Taken altogether these were demanding and likely exhausting duties for a young academic just taking up his first post. Yet, for all this, Smith clearly valued his Glasgow time, evident from the claim that is our focus here: namely, Smith's remembrance of his thirteen years of university service 'as by far the most useful, and therefore, as by far the happiest and most honourable period of my life'.[4]

This retrospective statement is arresting, and deserves pause. Smith, after all, lived an influential if not terribly eventful life, and at least two other periods of his life could also be seen as reasonable candidates for the honorific he bestowed on his years at Glasgow. To stay with the convenient range of thirteen years, one might, for example, have thought that the thinker so often and so widely heralded today as the 'father of economics' might have seen his thirteen years researching and writing The Wealth of Nations from 1763 to 1776 as his most useful.[5] So, too, the approximately thirteen years between the initial publication of The Wealth of Nations and Smith's death in 1790 – years that saw Smith enjoy considerable influence in elite circles of London and Edinburgh as well as public service to the nation as Commissioner of Customs – might also seem a worthy candidate to be regarded as his life's most useful and honourable period.[6] But in the end it is not these but his years of service to Glasgow that Smith chose to celebrate. One naturally wonders: why?

What follows offers a possible explanation for just why Smith regarded his years of professional service to his alma mater as his happiest and most honourable. My particular route to this end is to read Smith's celebration of his Glasgow years against the core claims of his moral philosophy as developed in The Theory of Moral Sentiments. In part, this is out of necessity; a famously reticent correspondent who directed his literary executors to burn all of his unpublished manuscripts on his death, Smith left behind him precious few records of his thoughts and feelings. For guides to his sentiments, we are thus compelled to turn to his published texts, and The Theory of Moral Sentiments in particular. But this approach is especially warranted in the present case, in so far as the terms Smith used to celebrate his Glasgow years are concepts at the core of the moral philosophy set forth in The Theory of Moral Sentiments. Reading Smith's account of this period of his life against the principles of his moral philosophy thus may help us better understand why he so cherished his Glasgow years, and thereby help us better understand the coherence of the principles of his thought and the life he sought to lead.[7]

The Useful Professor

Our source for Smith's claim about the utility and happiness and honour-ableness of his Glasgow years is a surviving piece of correspondence from 1787. On 15 November of that year, Archibald Davidson, then Principal of the university, wrote to Smith to inform him of his election to the three-year post of University Rector. Smith happily accepted, thereby succeeding several illustrious predecessors in the rectorship, including Edmund Burke and Lord Dundas. But it is the substance of Smith's response to Davidson that is our concern here. On 16 November, Smith immediately wrote to Davidson to accept his offer:

> I have this moment received the honour of your Letter of the 15th instt. I accept with Gratitude and Pleasure the very great honour which the University of Glasgow have done me in electing me for the ensuing year to be the Rector of that illustrious body. No preferment could have given me so much real satisfaction. No man can owe greater obligations to a Society than I do to the University of Glasgow. They educated me, they sent me to Oxford, soon after my return to Scotland they elected me one of their own members, and afterwards preferred me to another office, to which the abilities and Virtues of the never to be forgotten Dr Hutcheson had given a superior degree of illustration. The period of thirteen years which I spent as a member of that society I remember as by far the most useful, and, therefore, as by far the happiest and most honourable period of my life; and now, after three and twenty years absence, to be remembered in so very agreeable manner by my old friends and Protectors gives me a heartfelt joy which I cannot easily express to you.[8]

Smith's letter is striking for a variety of reasons that go beyond what might be apparent to a casual reader. Such a reader might be inclined to read his letter as merely the genial response of a gentleman to an honour bestowed upon him. Seen thus, Smith's thanks seem no more than customary: the conventional expression of gratitude one would expect from a polite, sociable man of the world. Smith's response is surely this, but it is also much more. Especially striking is his praise of 'the never to be forgotten' Hutcheson. Hutcheson was both Smith's undergraduate teacher as well as his predecessor in the Moral Philosophy chair, and his letter to Davidson has largely been remembered by scholars principally for this encomium.[9] Very recently, this aspect of the letter has re-emerged as important for Smith scholars, as Dennis Rasmussen has noted that Smith applies 'never to be forgotten' to Hutcheson only first after having applied it to his friend Hume (who in both Smith's day and our own has been seen as committed to a different set of principles than Hutcheson).[10]

Those who also know a bit about Smith's biography may also be aware that Smith, in celebrating his Glasgow years to Davidson, doesn't quite tell him the whole truth about his time there. Smith's years on faculty almost certainly included a few less happy moments – including, especially, faculty meetings. Faculty meetings may never be easy events to love, but they must have been unusually difficult affairs at Smith's Glasgow. Smith's colleagues at the time included, for example, John Anderson, the Chair of Oriental Languages and then Natural Philosophy, who had long nursed a bitter grudge against Smith, and who had been given by his colleagues for his acerbic temper the nickname 'Jolly Jack Phosphorus'.[11] Also on the faculty at this time was James Moor, the Professor of Greek. Moor was a particular headache for Smith. In 1763, in his capacity as Vice-Rector, Smith was compelled to call a series of meetings in light of a set of allegations regarding Moor's abusive conduct towards his students – meetings that set in motion the dismissal proceedings that would lead to Moor's firing in 1774 after he beat one of his students over the head with a wooden candlestick.[12]

For all this, there is another and more substantive side to Smith's remarks about his Glasgow years: a side that becomes evident only when we shift the frame of reference from his biography to his philosophy. Smith's reminiscence to Davidson centres on three terms central to his moral philosophy. Specifically, in insisting that his years at Glasgow were his most 'useful' and thus his 'happiest' and 'most honourable', Smith's reminiscence invokes three of the core concepts of his moral philosophy. This compels us to read his statement on his Glasgow years alongside the extensive treatments of utility, happiness and honour in *The Theory of Moral Sentiments* – a text moreover that Smith was, at the very moment that he wrote to Davidson, about to begin revising for its important sixth (1790) edition.[13]

My main aim in what follows is to provide such a comparative reading. But before we turn directly to this work, it is worth noting that Smith's invocation of these concepts – and especially the concept of utility – to describe his work at Glasgow was not a one-time occurrence; Stewart, in his biography, says that Smith would 'frequently' look back to this as his life's most useful and happy period.[14] But we also have additional testimonies from Smith's own hand. Above it was noted that Smith's extant correspondence is scanty, yet a concern with utility is abundantly evident in the letters that survive from his professional years at Glasgow. It is especially evident in his very first letter regarding his Glasgow post. Smith was first informed of his appointment to the Logic chair in a letter from the Clerk of the Senate of the University that was dated 9 January 1751.[15] As was true of his 1787 letter accepting the rectorship, Smith's letter accepting his professorship was dated the following day.[16] And in his 10 January 1751 response to the Clerk of Senate, then Matthew Simpson (a mathematician who would become a friend of Smith's and would be fulsomely praised in *The Theory of Moral Sentiments*), Smith writes that he must

> begg leave by your hands to return my sincere thanks to the gentle-
> men of your Society for the [favour] they have done me by electing
> me to supply the vacant professor-ship to declare my acceptance of
> their favor, and to assure them that it shall be my chief study to render
> myselfe a useful member of their Society.[17]

The potential utility of his contributions to the university was thus foremost in Smith's mind not only retrospectively in 1787, but also prospec-
tively in 1751. And what is more, a concern for utility also clearly animated
Smith during his actual prosecution of his teaching and supervisory duties,
and provided him with the primary lens through which he came to understand his contributions to the growth and welfare of his students. This
can be seen especially clearly in what is what is almost certainly the best
documented side of Smith's career as a university teacher and supervisor.

In 1759 Thomas Petty-Fitzmaurice matriculated at Glasgow.[18] Petty-
Fitzmaurice was the younger son of John Petty, 1st Earl of Shelburne. Lord
Shelburne, solicitous of offering his son the best possible education, made
arrangements for his son to study under Smith and indeed to lodge with
him so as to be always under the professor's watchful eye. This, one sus-
pects, is not likely to be a task many professors today would wish to concern themselves with; a blissful ignorance of dormitory life will seem to
many today preferable to the tasks of lodging and feeding and surveilling
students on top of teaching them. This is, however, what Smith did for
Shelburne's son, and indeed did diligently and enthusiastically. We know
this from several of Smith's letters to Shelburne regarding the academic
progress and welfare of his son. These letters spare no detail; Smith offers
extensive accounts of his student's spartan dinners ('a roasted apple or
some such trifle'), updates on his student's occasional illnesses (including
reports on the state of his urine and stool), the state of his student's financial accounts (money owed to two different booksellers and a clothier),
and the company his student kept (at one point Smith had 'two or three
lawyers' brought in to entertain his pupil when he could not himself be
present).[19] Smith's care in all these details ultimately paid off handsomely.
In a remarkable letter, Shelburne wrote Smith to tell him he 'can not sufficiently express my satisfaction at the account you give me of my son, now
under your care', insisting that 'every thing confirms that you merit that
Character which made me wish so much that you should take the Charge
of him upon you'.[20] Smith, for his part, made clear how seriously he took

these duties in a letter of his own, in which he first thanked Shelburne for his kind words regarding the just-published *Theory of Moral Sentiments* before commenting on his supervisory duties:

> Your Lordship makes me very vain when you mention the satisfaction you have had in reading the book I lately published, and the engage- ments you think I have come under to the Public. I can, however, assure your Lordship that I have come under no engagements which I look upon as so sacred as those by which I am bound as a member of this University to do every[thing] in my Power to serve the young people who are sent here to study, such especially as are particularly recommended to my care. I shall expect, whenever they are settled, that your Lordships friends will look upon my house as their home, and that they will have recourse to me in every Difficulty that they meet with in the Prosecution of their studies, and that I shall never regard any application of this kind as an interruption of business, but as the most agreeable and useful business in which I can be engaged.[21]

Smith's touching letter reiterates several themes we have seen already, and introduces one we have yet to see. Most importantly, Smith here again emphasises the degree to which he regarded his supervisory duties as 'the most agreeable and useful business' in which he could be engaged. This is all the more significant in so far as Smith is here contrasting this 'agreeable and useful' business of caring for his students' welfare with a presumably less agreeable and almost certainly less useful business of responding to critics of his recently published book. Smith's friend Hume famously pro- claimed his 'love of literary fame' his 'ruling passion'.[22] But for Smith it was less his obligations to his literary reputation than his obligations to 'the young people that are sent to here to study' that he considered his most useful and agreeable – and, strikingly, most 'sacred' – duties.[23] All of this leads us back to our question: just why did Smith consider his professional duties as a teacher and supervisor his most useful, agreeable and sacred? For this we need to turn to *The Theory of Moral Sentiments*.

Utility and Education

We begin with the question of utility. Smith treats utility in several dif- ferent places in *The Theory of Moral Sentiments*.[24] By far the best-known and most thorough treatment is that in Part IV, which as its title indi- cates is explicitly dedicated to a consideration of utility. Now, as specialists know, Part IV treats utility in a very particular way. Smith's unnamed but omnipresent interlocutor there is his friend Hume, who had developed a particular and not uncontroversial theory about the ways in which 'the agreeable and the useful' deserve to be seen as the fundamental grounds of moral approbation.[25] Part IV is also remembered by scholars of Smith's political economy for its treatments of luxury consumption and wealth distribution; it is here that Smith first invoked in print his 'invisible hand'.[26] But there is also another side to Smith's treatment of utility in the two chapters of Part IV, and this side has special relevance to our inquiry into his understanding of his employment as a university professor. But to see this, before turning to Part IV, we need to take a brief look at a related comment on utility in Part VII, as this directly concerns the utility of the subject that Glasgow had hired Smith to teach.

Part VII of *The Theory of Moral Sentiments* is dedicated to a study of the responses that various thinkers in the history of philosophy prior to Smith have given to what Smith himself considered to be the two fundamental questions of moral philosophy: first, what is virtue; and second, and by what power or process do we judge virtue and vice? Smith ends his treatment of these questions with a final chapter dedicated specifically to the ways in which previous thinkers have treated what he calls the 'practical rules' of morality. Here he distinguishes between two different approaches, differentiating that of the moderns – and more specifically, 'those who in this and in the preceding century have treated of what is called natural jurisprudence'[27]– from the approach taken by 'all the ancient moralists'.[28] The key difference is that, whereas the moderns aim to 'lay down exact and precise rules for the direction of every circumstance of our behaviour',[29] the ancients, in contrast, sought to describe 'the sentiment of the heart, upon which each particular virtue is founded' as well as the 'ordinary tone and tenor of conduct to which each of those sentiments would direct us'.[30] We today might say that the aim of the moderns, as described by Smith, stands more in line with how deontologists approach ethics, whereas the aim of the ancients, as he described it, is more aligned with the way in which contemporary virtue ethicists approach the study of morality. But for our purposes what is of particular interest is the specific utility Smith attributes to ancient approaches to ethics.

Ancient works, Smith explains, are principally concerned to describe virtue and to show us what it looks like, in an attempt to encourage us to become more virtuous in our own right. Naming Aristotle and Cicero in particular, Smith goes on to insist that their works

present us with agreeable and lively pictures of manners. By the vivacity of their descriptions they inflame our natural love of virtue, and increase our abhorrence of vice: by the justness as well as delicacy of their observations they may often help both to correct and to ascertain our natural sentiments with regard to the propriety of conduct, and suggesting many nice and delicate attentions, form us to a more exact justness of behaviour, than what, without such instruction, we should have been apt to think of. In treating of the rules of morality, in this manner, consists the science which is properly called Ethics, a science which, though like criticism it does not admit of the most accurate precision, is, however, both highly useful and agreeable.[31]

Here Smith repeats the formulation of 'useful and agreeable' that we have already seen him use in his letter to Shelburne. But where before he used this locution to describe his general duties as a teacher, here the Professor of Moral Philosophy applies this locution to the study of the specific subject that he had been hired to teach. Ethics, prosecuted in this way, thus has a direct utility to students in so far as it shapes their moral habits and their character in salutary and beneficial ways. Thus ethical precepts, when properly 'dressed and adorned' by a skilful expounder, Smith explains,

are capable of producing upon the flexibility of youth, the noblest and most lasting impressions, and as they fall in with the natural magnanimity of that generous age, they are able to inspire, for a time at least, the most heroic resolutions, and thus tend both to establish and confirm the best and most useful habits of which the mind of man is susceptible.[32]

And with this we have at least one explanation for why Smith regarded his years of service as a teacher of ethics as so useful: specifically because of the direct utility of this subject to the lives of those who study it, by inculcating the habits that are 'best and most useful' to them.

That said, we know (and indeed have already had occasion to mention) that ethics was only one among several subjects which the Professor of Moral Philosophy at Glasgow was required to teach – subjects we would today put under the heading of political science and economics and law. But what of these subjects? It is easy enough to understand how Smith might have understood his teaching of ethics to be directly useful to his students in their lives, but is it possible to understand his teaching of these other areas of social science to be useful in the same way that he considered the teaching of ethics to be useful? Smith himself seems to have thought so. This becomes especially clear in the conclusion to the first chapter of Part IV. The key aim of the chapter, as its title suggests, is to elucidate the 'extensive influence' of 'the beauty which the appearance of utility bestows upon all the productions of art'. To this end, Smith develops a well-known account of the unintended beneficial consequences of the 'love of distinction' that he identifies as lying at the core of economic activity. Thus in a series of paragraphs crucial to his political economy, Smith demonstrates how the poor man's son's desire to be well regarded and well esteemed serves to drive his efforts to better his condition. In turn, this desire to better one's condition, even when driven by 'natural selfishness and rapacity', Smith famously explains, generates the universal opulence that the invisible hand in time redistributes to others in society.[33] Now, the economic and moral implications of this argument are immense, and cannot be treated here.[34] Instead, I want to say a brief word about how Smith's claims here can inform our appreciation of his understanding of his academic duties.

In the last paragraph of this chapter, Smith argues that the statesman concerned to promote the well-being of society is often animated by the same principle that drives an ordinary consumer to long for luxury goods. Consumers, Smith argues, are often attracted more by the beauty of intricate systems than by the real utility of their discrete parts, and so too political actors. On these grounds, he argues that those who seek to encourage the politically powerful to undertake a certain course of action will do best not to argue for the utility of a specific policy; rather, as he says, 'you will be more likely to persuade, if you describe the great system of public police which procures these advantages, if you explain the connections and dependencies of his several parts, their mutual subordination to one another, and their general subserviency to the happiness of the society.' And with this in place, Smith brings his argument to its striking conclusion:

> Nothing tends so much to promote public spirit as the study of politics, of the several systems of civil government, their advantages and disadvantages, of the constitution of our own country, its situation, and interest with regard to foreign nations, its commerce, its defence, the disadvantages it labours under, the dangers to which it may be exposed, how to remove the one, and how to guard against the other. Upon this account political disquisitions, if just, and reasonable, and practicable, are of all the works of speculation the most useful. Even the weakest and the worst of them are not altogether without their utility. They serve at least to animate the public passions of men, and rouse them to seek out the means of promoting the happiness of the society.[35]

The key claim here is that there is a specific 'utility' in the study of politics and economics and jurisprudence, and indeed, that disquisitions on this subject, in so far as they can rouse public passions, are the 'most useful' of all works of speculation. And in making this claim, Smith rounds out his understanding of the utility of his subject. For here the Professor of Moral Philosophy suggests that there is utility not simply in the study of ethics, but indeed in the study of the other subjects of his syllabus. For just as the study of ethics has a direct utility to those who study it, the study of political science and economics and jurisprudence – in so far as these serve to 'to promote public spirit' and animate the public passions of men – has, Smith insists a direct utility to the society in which such subjects are taught.

Useful, Therefore Happiest

We have so far seen several reasons why Smith might have regarded his teaching as 'useful'. Teaching ethics has a direct utility to students who study it and teaching political science and economics and law has direct utility to the society in which these subjects are taught. But it remains for us still to explain, on Smith's own principles, what is perhaps the most interesting aspect of his comment about his Glasgow years. His comment, as we saw, isn't simply that his teaching years were useful, but that, in so far as they were 'useful', they were 'therefore' by far his 'happiest and most honourable' years. Smith's claim is not that utility is an end unto itself, but that utility has a necessary connection with both happiness and worthiness of honour. But what exactly did he mean by this?

Understanding Smith's intentions on this front requires us to look closely at what he says about both happiness and honour in *The Theory of Moral Sentiments*, and how they are related to utility. We begin with happiness – a topic about which Smith has a great deal to say in his text. A large portion of Part VII of *The Theory of Moral Sentiments* is dedicated to a review of the different ways various schools in the history of philosophy have defined the concept of happiness; here Smith dutifully walks his students through the Epicurean theory that happiness consists in pleasure, the Stoic theory that happiness consists in tranquillity, the Platonic theory that happiness consists in a just and balanced soul, and the Aristotelian theory that happiness consists in moral action. So, too, in *The Theory of Moral Sentiments* Smith at several points examines the phenomenon of unhappiness, and in passages crucial for his economics, Smith insightfully diagnoses how the desire to better their conditions renders unhappy 'the ambitious man' and the 'poor man's son'.[36] But for us what matters is not

these general definitions of happiness and unhappiness, but Smith's understanding of a specific aspect of happiness: the relationship between public happiness and private happiness, the well-being of the society and the
well-being of the individual.

That Smith believed there to be an intimate and even necessary connection between the happiness of the society and the happiness of the
individual is signalled in the very first line of *The Theory of Moral Sentiments*. Smith in fact begins his book with the observation that 'how selfish
soever man may be supposed, there are evidently some principles in his
nature, which interest him in the fortune of others, and render their happiness necessary to him, though he derives nothing from it except the pleasure of seeing it'.[37] The clear suggestion in this opening line – which Smith
reiterates throughout his book – is that human beings have been made in
such a way that our personal happiness is intimately and indeed necessarily
connected to that of those around us. Smith furthermore presents this not
as a normative claim, but as simply a true and objective statement about
the ways in which human beings have been made. Here and elsewhere he
indeed suggests that to be 'altogether insensible to the happiness or misery
of others' is a sort of defect, an aberration or corruption of what nature
intended us to be.[38]

Smith, as just noted, presents this here and elsewhere as a descriptive observation about how human beings have been made. At the same
time, this descriptive observation does real work in his broader normative moral theory. For if indeed our happiness is in some sense necessarily
connected to the happiness of others around us, then it is also the case
that we have an interest in promoting the happiness of others; quite
simply, to add to the happiness of others is to add to our own. Indeed,
again and again, Smith comes back to the idea that there is not only
a particular praiseworthiness that is due to the man who has been the
'instrument of the happiness of his brethren', but that he himself also
enjoys a particular sort of happiness.[39] In fact, promoting the happiness
of others is the end for which we have been made. Thus Smith's most
striking claim on this front:

> Man was made for action, and to promote by the exertion of his fac-
> ulties such changes in the external circumstances both of himself
> and others, as may seem most favourable to the happiness of all. He
> must not be satisfied with indolent benevolence, nor fancy himself
> the friend of mankind, because in his heart he wishes well to the
> prosperity of the world. That he may call forth the whole vigour of his
> soul, and strain every nerve, in order to produce those ends which it

is the purpose of his being to advance, Nature has taught him, that neither himself nor mankind can be fully satisfied with his conduct, nor bestow upon it the full measure of applause, unless he has actually produced them.[40]

This passage continues to strike me as one of the most significant passages in Smith's corpus.[41] A full appreciation of it would be sufficient to put forever to rest any idea that Smith could be reasonably construed as an apostle of selfishness. But this passage has a special significance for our present inquiry. Here, as elsewhere, Smith insists that there is a necessary connection between public happiness and private happiness, and furthermore suggests that active exertions to contribute to promote public happiness are necessary for the full realisation of private happiness. In this way, efforts to promote public utility are not just commensurate with but productive of private happiness. And in so doing, Smith reveals an important side of what he meant when he said that his Glasgow years were not only 'useful', but in so far as they were useful they were 'therefore' his happiest. As we saw above, Smith understood his work as a teacher as directly promoting both the utility of his students as well as the public utility. And his analysis of the relationship of public utility to personal happiness in *The Theory of Moral Sentiments* helps us see how the consciousness of his efforts to promote public utility through his work would have, on his own principles, been indispensable and necessarily connected to his personal happiness.

Useful, Therefore Most Honourable

Our final task is to determine what Smith might have meant when he described his years at Glasgow as not only his useful and happy but also his 'most honourable'. Smith's invocation of the category of the honourable is once again an instance in which there is more than meets the eye. In using the language of the honourable, Smith of course sounds merely like a gentleman graciously paying homage to an institution to which he was indebted. But as was true of the categories of happiness and utility, honourability is a concept with a very specific meaning in Smith's moral theory, and attending to its treatment in his published work can help us see all that is at stake in his praises of his Glasgow years.

Smith invokes the category of the 'honourable' in a variety of discrete instances in *The Theory of Moral Sentiments*. Especially noteworthy is his frequent joining of the 'noble' and the 'honourable'. Indeed, in frequently invoking this compound concept Smith invokes an excellence that is reminiscent of ancient conceptions of excellence. But our interest lies less in the provenance of this idea than its function in Smith's moral theory. In a variety of different places, Smith invokes the concept of the honourable to contrast it to that which is honoured. The honourable, he thus suggests, is that which deserves honour, whether or not it is honoured in fact. Now, this turns out to be a distinction central to Smith's moral theory and receives related expression in Smith's frequent and likely better-known distinctions between the praised and the praiseworthy. Of course, the questions of what marks a certain act or character as honourable or praiseworthy, and indeed how we come to know with assurance that a given act or character is in fact honourable praiseworthy, are fraught ones. At the same time this distinction does crucial work in his moral theory, and attending to the work it does can help us understand just why Smith so valued his time as a teacher.

Smith's main discussion of the difference between the honoured and the honourable comes in his discussion of Mandeville. Smith's moral theory has often been conflated with Mandeville's on the assumption that both championed the normative primacy of self-love in human action. Smith himself took pains to distance his moral theory from Mandeville's, however. Mandeville, according to Smith, went awry in reducing all human moral activity to expressions of self-love driven by a desire for recognition; in his words, Mandeville saw all ostensibly virtuous activity as motivated merely by desire for praise. In response, Smith argues that there are in fact three dispositions that need to be distinguished. The first and lowest is that of those who in fact act only out of a desire for praise and are indifferent to the worth of their acts. But above these are those who not only desire to be praised, but who want to be praised specifically for having acted well and worthily. And above these, Smith insists, stand those who act solely, as he says, out of a 'love of virtue' – that is, those who act in accord with what they understand to be right, independent of any concern to be recognised or praised or honoured for having acted in that way.[42] Smith thus distinguishes 'three passions': first, 'the desire of rendering ourselves the proper objects of honour and esteem; or of becoming what is honourable and estimable'; second, 'the desire of acquiring honour and esteem by really deserving those sentiments'; and third, 'the frivolous desire of praise at any rate'.[43] Mandeville, however, errs by collapsing all three categories into the lowest; hence Smith's insistence contra Mandeville that 'the desire of doing what is honourable and noble, of rendering ourselves the proper objects of esteem and approbation, cannot with any propriety be called vanity'.[44] But what matters for our purposes is the reverence in which Smith held the individual who acts purely from concern for what is honourable: 'the man who acts solely from a regard to what is right and fit to be done, from a regard to what is the proper object of esteem and appro-bation, though these sentiments should never be bestowed upon him, acts from the most sublime and godlike motive which human nature is even capable of conceiving.'[45] Smith here sets a high bar in describing 'the most sublime and godlike motive' that we can possibly even conceive. But it is clear that he himself admired those that were able to clear this bar, and it seems hardly a stretch to think that Smith might have himself aimed to be such a person. And with this we come back to his activities as a uni-versity professor. Very few people – and university professors perhaps least of all – are likely to describe the professor's life as 'sublime and godlike'. But most of us can readily appreciate that indeed the recondite writings and lectures of university professors are very unlikely, by their very nature, to garner much actual 'esteem and approbation' from the general public. As Smith himself knew as well as any, our commercial world is one that recognises and rewards the rich and the great, not the ones that Smith called 'the wise and virtuous'. But this fact can help us to understand why Smith might have so valued his professorial years. If Smith really wanted to be rich and great, to be admired and esteemed in a commercial society, he chose poorly in choosing the life of the professor. But if in fact what he most cherished was not wealth and fame but the consciousness of having acted well by promoting public utility, it is not clear that he could have chosen any other course of life that would have been nearly so honourable as the professor's life that he lived.

Conclusion

Smith's retrospective assessment of his years as a university professor at Glasgow is framed in terms of concepts that are central to his own moral philosophy. In identifying his Glasgow years as not only his 'most useful' but also his 'happiest' and 'most honourable', Smith invites us to under-stand his encomium to his former employer in the light of the core prin-ciples of his ethics. It is an exercise that is valuable, in part, for how it helps us to better appreciate Smith's deep concern to ensure that the life he led aligned with the principles he defended in his books. But even beyond the insight into Smith that such an inquiry affords, such an inquiry is most valuable for the way in which it can sensitise us to better recognise and appreciate the useful and honourable services of those rare university professors today whose uniform excellence in research and teaching and administration marks them as worthy models for our own emulation, and the deserving objects of our gratitude.

Notes

Author's note: Earlier versions of this essay were presented in February 2019 at Boston College and at the University of Glasgow; I am grateful to the audience members on both occasions for their helpful comments. I am also grateful to Robin Mills for his insightful comments. The following abbreviations are used below in citing Smith's works: CAS = *Correspondence of Adam Smith*, ed. I. S. Ross (Indianapolis: Liberty Fund, 1987); EPS = *Essays on Philosophical Subjects*, ed. W. P. D. Wightman and J. C. Bryce (Indianapolis: Liberty Fund, 1982); and TMS = *Theory of Moral Sentiments*, ed. D. D. Raphael and A. L. Macfie (Indianapolis: Liberty Fund, 1984).

1. Helpful overviews of these years can be found in Dugald Stewart, 'Account of the Life and Writings of Adam Smith, LL.D.', in *EPS* (see esp. 1.14, pp. 273ff.) and Nicholas Phillipson, *Adam Smith: An Enlightened Life* (New Haven: Yale University Press, 2010), chs 6 and 8. The most detailed treatments, which are especially valuable for their incorporation of the relevant archival materials, are William Robert Scott, *Adam Smith as Student and Professor* (Glasgow: Jackson, Son and Co., 1937), chs 6–7; and Ian S. Ross, *The Life of Adam Smith*, 2nd edn (Oxford: Oxford University Press, 2010), chs 8–10.

2. We know of these duties chiefly from the testimony of John Millar, as reported by Stewart; see 'Account of the Life and Writings', in *EPS* 1.16–20, pp. 274–5.

3. Smith's activities are helpfully documented in Phillipson, *Smith: An Enlightened Life*, p. 131; Ross, *Life of Adam Smith*, ch. 10, and Scott, *Smith as Student and Professor*, pp. 66–97; Scott also helpfully includes the complete records of Smith's purchases as Quaestor; see pp. 178–84.

4. CAS 274, p. 309. Smith's striking claim has long captured the attention of scholars; see, most recently, Christopher J. Berry, *Adam Smith: A Very Short Introduction* (Oxford: Oxford University Press, 2019), p. 4.

5. On this period, see Phillipson, *Smith: An Enlightened Life*, ch. 10; and Ross, *Life of Adam Smith*, chs 14–15.

6. On this period, see Phillipson, *Smith: An Enlightened Life*, ch. 13; and Ross, *Life of Adam Smith*, chs 19–25.

7. In seeking to connect the life Smith led with the principles of his thought, what follows extends an approach to Smith that I have taken elsewhere and applies it specifically to his Glasgow years. In this vein, see my *Adam Smith and the Character of Virtue* (Cambridge: Cambridge University Press, 2009), pp. 187–209; and 'Adam Smith on Living a Life', in *Adam Smith: His Life, Thought, and Legacy*, ed. Ryan P. Hanley (Princeton: Princeton University Press, 2016).

8. CAS 274, pp. 308–9.

9. See, esp., Ross, *Life of Adam Smith*, ch. 4.

10. See Rasmussen, *The Infidel and the Professor: David Hume, Adam Smith, and the Friendship That Shaped Modern Thought* (Princeton: Princeton University Press, 2017), p. 37.

11. On Anderson, see the editorial note at CAS 19 n. 4, p. 17; and Scott, *Smith as Student and Professor*, pp. 87–8.

12. See Scott, *Smith as Student and Professor*, pp. 88–9, 196–9; and Ross, *Life of Adam Smith*, p. 149. For all this, Smith is said by Scott to have sincerely 'thought the best of his colleagues' on the whole – a position that Scott attributes to the fact that Smith 'had in his daily life the sympathy which he developed as an ethical principle' (*Smith as Student and Professor*, p. 76). Some sense of this also emerges in Smith's letter announcing his resignation of his post, in which he declared 'I never was more anxious for the Good of the College than at this moment and I sincerely wish that whoever is my Successor may not only do Credit to the Office by his Abilities but be a comfort to the very excellent Men with whom he is likely to spend his life' (CAS 81, pp. 100–1).

13. See Phillipson, *Smith: An Enlightened Life*, p. 268.

14. Stewart, 'Account of the Life and Writings', in *EPS* 1.14, p. 273.

15. See Scott, *Smith as Student and Professor*, pp. 137–8; and CAS 7, pp. 3–4.

16. The fact that Adam Smith's two letters of acceptance of his Glasgow posts were written immediately, and in each case the day after receiving notification, may be mere coincidence. But it is at least worth noting that in this respect they form a significant contrast with his typical habits as a correspondent.

17. CAS 8, p. 4.

18. For helpful overviews, see Phillipson, *Smith: An Enlightened Life*, pp. 166–70; and Ross, *Life of Adam Smith*, pp. 135–7.

19. See, respectively, CAS 29, pp. 29–30; 46, p. 64; 48, p. 66; 51, pp. 69–71; 42, pp. 58–60.

20. CAS 32, pp. 36–8.

21. CAS 37, pp. 44–5.

22. David Hume, 'My Own Life', in *Essays Moral, Political, and Literary*, ed. Eugene F. Miller (Indianapolis: Liberty Fund, 1985), p. xl.

23. And it bears mentioning that Smith's solicitude for his students was hardly limited simply to Shelburne's son; Scott writes that Smith 'took great pains in advising his students in the choice of a career and in the fitting of themselves for it' (*Smith as Student and Professor*, p. 69). So, too, Smith is separately reported to have been 'at great pains to discover and cherish the seeds of genius', and in spending time with his students 'took great pleasure in directing their studies and solving their doubts, adapting his hints to their plans of life' (John Ramsay, as quoted in Phillipson, *Smith: An Enlightened Life*, pp. 135–6).

24. On Smith's theory of utility, see, e.g., Marie A. Martin, 'Utility and Morality: Adam Smith's Critique of Hume', *Hume Studies* 16 (1990), pp. 107–20; and Fred Rosen, 'The Idea of Utility in Adam Smith's *Theory of Moral Sentiments*', *History of European Ideas* 26 (2000), pp. 79–103.

25. See David Hume's 'Enquiry Concerning the Principles of Morals', in *Enquiries Concerning Human Understanding and Concerning the Principles of Morals*, 3rd edn, ed. L. A. Selby-Bigge, rev. P. H. Nidditch (Oxford: Clarendon Press, 1975), esp. 9.1, pp. 268–78.
26. For the context of Smith's theory of luxury, see, esp., Berry, *The Idea of Luxury: A Conceptual and Historical Investigation* (Cambridge: Cambridge University Press, 1994), esp. pp. 153ff.
27. TMS 7.4.7, p. 329.
28. TMS 7.4.3, p. 328.
29. TMS 7.4.7, p. 329.
30. TMS 7.4.3, p. 328.
31. On Smith's understanding of the relationship of science to the study of ethics and of human nature and how this understanding compares to Hume's, see, esp., Christopher J. Berry, 'Adam Smith's "Science of Human Nature', *History of Political Economy* 44 (2012), pp. 471–92.
32. TMS 7.4.6, p. 329.
33. TMS 4.1.8–10, pp. 181–5.
34. On the economic significance of these claims, see, e.g., Samuel Fleischacker, *On Adam Smith's Wealth of Nations: A Philosophical Companion* (Princeton: Princeton University Press, 2004), pp. 104–22; and Christopher J. Berry, 'Adam Smith: Commerce, Liberty, and Modernity', in *Philosophers of the Enlightenment*, ed. Peter Gilmour (Edinburgh: Edinburgh University Press, 1989), pp. 113–32.
35. TMS 4.1.11, p. 186.
36. TMS 1.3.3.8, pp. 64–6; TMS 4.1.8, pp. 181–3.
37. TMS 1.1.1.1, p. 9.
38. TMS 1.1.5.2, p. 24.
39. TMS 2.1.2.4, p. 70.
40. TMS 2.3.3.3, p. 106.
41. I examine the significance of this claim elsewhere; see 'Adam Smith on Living a Life', pp. 129–30; and *Our Great Purpose: Adam Smith on Living a Better Life* (Princeton: Princeton University Press, 2019), ch. 3.
42. I provide a more extensive treatment of these categories and their significance in *Adam Smith and the Character of Virtue*, pp. 92–9.
43. TMS 7.2.4.9, p. 310.
44. TMS 7.2.4.8, pp. 309–10.
45. TMS 7.2.4.10, pp. 310–12.

6

Adam Smith on Political Leadership

Eric Schliesser

In this chapter I present Adam Smith's views on political leadership. I argue that he articulates an account of political leadership that has distinctive, liberal features. In particular, such a leader must embrace policies in which the happiness of all citizens is pursued and to do so in a way that makes possible non-zero-sum outcomes. That is, such a leader must presuppose non-trivial moral commitments. I show that Smith embraces a conception of good governance in which a certain kind of moral improvement of citizens is prioritised. I do not mean to suggest that a Smithian (proper) leader is primarily concerned with soul-craft, that is, an approach to governance that aims to make citizens moral. Rather, she aims to encourage a good society.[1] My analysis of Smith's account is illuminated by his treatment of the nature and causes of bad leadership and a new account of Smith's treatment of the evils of petty bureaucrats and state capacity.

My present aim is mainly exegetical, but the reason for this project is philosophical. Contemporary liberal theory, while moving away from a narrow conception on justice, is still primarily focused on procedures, institutions, the rule of law, public reason, the articulation of different kinds of rights violations. Leadership is largely ignored by recent liberal theorists. I suspect that the very idea of leadership has a non-egalitarian and authoritarian quality to it, best left to those (inspired by Max Weber) with a fascination with charisma[2] or revolution;[3] or left to fascists[4] or management consultants and organisational psychologists.[5]

But this neglect by liberal theorists comes at a cost.[6] Institutions and procedures are run by imperfect human beings and without ongoing maintenance, care and investment they decay. While I do not claim that 'leadership' is a sufficient response to the challenges of institutional decay and renewal, it may well be a necessary one. In addition, with liberalism contested, even in clear retreat now, liberal political leadership and mobilisation, which cannot presuppose implicit universal consent to its values, are an urgent matter. For that reason this chapter is the second in a series of historical recoveries on the character of liberal leadership.[7]

I proceed as follows. In Section 1, I critically discuss some comments by Judith Shklar; these present what I take to be the conventional interpretation of Adam Smith as a fundamentally anti-political thinker.[8] By 'anti-political' I do not mean to suggest that serious scholars (still) treat Smith as merely an economic thinker who does not advance political projects or fails to address political problems.[9] But, rather, there is a general view that Smith is suspicious of politicians, and that he primarily promotes an anti-political conception of politics focused on (constitutional) principles;[10] or that he promotes political ends (e.g., alleviation of poverty) through expansion of markets.[11] While I do not deny that Smith is fond of markets and constitutionalism, I show that these interpretations are too limiting.

By contrast, I argue three claims: first (in Section 2), that Smith's most critical comments on the 'crafty' politician also show that even such a politician has some utility. Second, I show that Smith diagnoses three kinds of bad politician (Section 3). I argue that these have in common the idea that politics is zero-sum and focused on partial interests (or what Madison, Hume and Smith all call 'faction'). From Smith's criticism of bad politicians, one can partially infer what qualities a good political leader must have according to Smith. I do so in Section 4, I look at Smith's positive account of a true statesman, which is surprisingly moralistic: a good leader serves the people and aims to create non-zero-sum and peaceful policies which allow the flourishing of everybody.[12] In Section 5, I show that Smith is committed to the development of national political structures and state capacity, including a national currency, as a response to the arbitrary powers of what (following Judith Butler) I call 'petty sovereigns'. In Section 6, I analyse Smith's treatment of the selection of good leaders. This turns out to be rather disappointing: leaders are selected by way of biased lottery.

1 On Vulgar Politicians and Statesmen

In this section I argue against the once common misperception that Smith's 'system of natural liberty' presupposes the idea that society is inherently harmonious, and government the sole source of corruption.[13] I do so here only in order to illuminate his account of true statesmen.[14] Consider the following representative passage:

> With the exception of monopolists, Adam Smith spoke of no one with greater contempt than of politicians. Beneath his accusation lies the common anarchism of the Enlightenment, which essentially amounts

to the belief that society is inherently good, but that governments, and they alone, prevent it from flourishing.[15]

Shklar, one of the great, historically informed liberal thinkers of the twentieth century,[16] is correct that there is no doubt that Smith is very critical of monopolists and that 'insidious and crafty animal', a politician. For Smith, a 'politician' is somebody 'whose councils are directed by the momentary fluctuations of affairs'.[17] Smith treats 'politicians' as those political leaders who are overly responsive to current affairs. Such *responsive* politicians are, according to Smith, mistakenly called 'statesmen' by the uneducated.[18] In what follows when discussing Smith's views, I treat these as *false* statesmen. In addition, if such a responsive politician is guided by a fallacious system, he can well be the dangerous 'man of system' who imagines 'that he can arrange the different members of a great society with as much ease as the hand arranges the different pieces upon a chess-board'.[19] Smith very explicitly contrasts these (false) statesmen with the (true) statesman who 'deliberates' with 'general principles'. Smith sometimes calls the latter 'legislators'.[20]

In context, the crafty politicians are those that treat trade conflict in terms of tit for tat without regard to the economic and political consequences of their behaviour. A key point Smith makes is that often the logic of retaliation in mercantile trade conflicts ends up hurting those who are purportedly being defended twice over (first by the tariff of another country, then by the home tariff which ends up, perhaps, helping other workers, but not the original victims for whom goods become dearer). As Smith writes,

> When our neighbours prohibit some manufacture of ours, we generally prohibit, not only the same, for that alone would seldom affect them considerably, but some other manufacture of theirs. This may no doubt give encouragement to some particular class of workmen among ourselves, and by excluding some of their rivals, may enable them to raise their price in the home market. Those workmen, however, who suffered by our neighbours' prohibition will not be benefited by ours. On the contrary, they and almost all the other classes of our citizens will thereby be obliged to pay dearer than before for certain goods. Every such law, therefore, imposes a real tax upon the whole country, not in favour of that particular class of workmen who were injured by our neighbours' prohibition, but of some other class.[21]

Smith's underlying aim in the passage (and larger chapter) is to reveal the political and economic contradictions at the heart of mercantilism, which

sees the world in zero-sum terms and is an ideology which leads to glorifi-
cation of state-sponsored monopolies and military conquest for economic
gains and purported national advantage.[22] Smith's economic argument is
impeccable. But his claim that the mercantilist inspired politician is merely
reactive is not entirely fair. It is not, of course, wholly unfair because the
mercantilist politician, the false statesman, is not helping those whom he
claims to be helping (those suffering the effects of foreign tariffs). But that
need not entail that such a politician is acting without principles. After all,
and as Smith's French translator Sophie de Grouchy noted, trade barriers
facilitate the creation of (what we may call) artificial monopolies, which
enrich the well-connected few at the expense of the many.[23] It is quite
possible that some mercantilist politicians know that their trade policies
enrich their connected friends. Mercantilism can be a coherent worldview
when you embrace a non-zero-sum logic.

I return to the crafty politician in the next section. Here I focus on
Smith's insistence that the true statesman acts on principles: this is not
an aberration. He makes a similar claim in *The Theory of Moral Sentiments*
(hereafter *TMS*): that 'some general, and even systematical, idea of the
perfection of policy and law, may no doubt be *necessary* for directing the
views of the statesman'.[24] This passage tends to be ignored by those that
emphasise Smith's concerns with the 'man of system'. Shklar, too, fails to
note that for Smith there can be a good kind of politician.[25]

Now, one may be tempted to say on behalf of Shklar: 'Sure, those true
statesmen are those politicians that recognise that government corrupts
society and stay out of its way.' This is mistaken for two reasons: first,
Smith thinks that the roots of corruption of any society are contained in
the very mechanism that gives it stability:[26]

> This disposition to admire, and almost to worship, the rich and the
> powerful, and to despise, or, at least, to neglect persons of poor and
> mean condition, though necessary both to establish and to maintain
> the distinction of ranks and the order of society, is, at the same time,
> the great and most universal cause of the corruption of our moral
> sentiments.[27]

So, even a wholly anarchist society would not be inherently good because
we naturally (and mistakenly) admire the rich and powerful.[28] In fact,
Smith's depiction of anarchism – the 'savage' state of development characterised by hunters and fishermen – is, while not uniformly negative (he
admires the heroic magnanimity made possible in it),[29] certainly not approv-
ing. Such peoples 'are frequently reduced, or, at least, think themselves

reduced, to the necessity sometimes of directly destroying, and sometimes of abandoning their infants, their old people, and those afflicted with lingering diseases, to perish with hunger, or to be devoured by wild beasts'.[30] This is a passage from the Introduction of The Wealth of Nations. It sets up the key, central argument of the book – one partially directed at people like Rousseau (or at least a caricature of Rousseau) – that developed civilisations can represent a moral improvement over anarchic society.[31]

Second, Smith thinks that government needs to take an active role in providing or helping to facilitate quite a number of public goods (transportation, education, military, public health, even some arts, etc.).[32] In Sections 5–6, I develop this point.

There is a more subtle problem underlying Shklar's analysis. While she is not wrong to think that for Smith society is an important analytic and historical reality,[33] she misses that in many ways government constitutes the orders and ranks which compose society. Smith explicitly makes this claim in TMS:[34]

> Every independent state is divided into many different orders and societies, each of which has its own particular powers, privileges, and immunities. Every individual is naturally more attached to his own particular order or society, than to any other ... Upon the manner in which any state is divided into the different orders and societies which compose it, and upon the particular distribution which has been made of their respective powers, privileges, and immunities, depends, what is called, the constitution of that particular state. Upon the ability of each particular order or society to maintain its own powers, privileges, and immunities, against the encroachments of every other, depends the stability of that particular constitution. That particular constitution is necessarily more or less altered, whenever any of its subordinate parts is either raised above or depressed below whatever had been its former rank and condition. All those different orders and societies are dependent upon the state to which they owe their security and protection. That they are all subordinate to that state, and established only in subserviency to its prosperity and preservation, is a truth acknowledged by the most partial member of every one of them.[35]

In fact, the passage does not merely show that society and its orders are dependent on the state (for 'security and protection'), but this very dependence and 'subordination' is, for Smith, constitutive of a state's constitution (and so there is a mutual constitution of state and society). This point suggests that for Smith a constitution is not so much a political-legal document, but the underlying structure or (he would say, general) order which gives a particular state its stability.[36] For Smith, the identity of the state can stay the same while the relationship between society and state can change.[37]

The quoted passage reveals, with its focus on 'rank', the remnants of feudalism in Smith's thinking: 'powers, privileges, and immunities' are granted from above by a great lord and thereby *constitute* an independent sphere. So, the dependence of the lower orders, and even the great ones, on the state, is also conceptual-legal-historical.[38]

Before I offer a taxonomy of Smith's criticisms of bad political leaders, I want to clarify Smith's attitude towards the 'crafty' politician (i.e., the false statesman) in the next section. For it turns out that even this much maligned animal has some utility according to Smith.

2 The Crafty Politician

Nearly all scholarship on Smith assumes that Smith's comments on the crafty politician are wholly negative.[39] And while there is no doubt that he generally favours the statesman (or true politician), who follows principles, even a system, over the responsive (false) politician, it is a mistake to think Smith sees no utility for the crafty politician. I quote the relevant passage before discussing it:

> There may be good policy in retaliations of this kind, when there is a probability that they will procure the repeal of the high duties or pro-hibitions complained of. The recovery of a great foreign market will generally more than compensate the transitory inconveniency of pay-ing dearer during a short time for some sorts of goods. To judge whether such retaliations are likely to produce such an effect does not, perhaps, belong so much to the science of a legislator, whose deliberations ought to be governed by general principles which are always the same, as to the skill of that insidious and crafty animal, vulgarly called a statesman or politician, whose councils are directed by the momentary fluctua-tions of affairs. When there is no probability that any such repeal can be procured, it seems a bad method of compensating the injury done to certain classes of our people to do another injury ourselves, not only to those classes, but to almost all the other classes of them.[40]

Smith is surely no fan of that 'insidious and crafty animal'. He thinks ordi-nary people are wrong to admire such politicians as statesmen. In context, he associates them with the zero-sum and violent politics of mercantilism and national greatness.[41] In addition, such politicians are tempted to meddle in economic affairs (cf. James Steuart).[42]

But it is a mistake to ignore that Smith also recognises such politicians' talents. In particular, the crafty politician has a 'skill': he or she is good at judging how other countries will react to retaliatory tariffs. That is, a genuinely crafty politician understands how other countries are 'likely' to behave. This presupposes considerable knowledge of human nature, a keen understanding of the domestic politics of foreign states, and a natural appreciation of strategic behaviour. This is not trivial.

And, in fact, there is a *tactical* reason to rely on the judgement of the crafty politician, when 'the recovery of a great foreign market' is 'likely'. Smith relies on a cost–benefit analysis in justifying reliance on the crafty politician's judgement: recovering access to a great foreign market, 'will generally more than compensate the transitory inconveniency of paying dearer during a short time for some sorts of goods'. So, in non-ideal circumstances of international mercantile competition, the crafty politician has *some* utility.[43]

Of course, the crafty politician is useless when the confrontational, tactical policies favoured by him are unlikely to work (or have become unlikely to do so). If he were capable of moderation and public honesty, he would inform the public of the limitations of his tactics and encourage alternatives when opening foreign markets through retaliatory tactics are likely to fail. Part of Smith's general criticism of (the 'spirit' of) mercantilism is that as an intellectual ideology it *always* promotes zero-sum and conflictual tactics (focusing on 'monopoly'[44] and colonial resource extraction promoted by 'mean rapacious merchants').[45]

The underlying criticism here is that because crafty politicians are unidimensional[46] – they are constantly looking to win zero-sum battles – they lack the temperament to be true statesmen. And because such a politician lacks the temperament and interest to grasp scientific principles, he may well do genuine harm, unknowingly, to his own citizens over time. While Smith recognises the partial utility of crafty politicians in the context of trade conflict, he also thinks this type ultimately will do more harm than good. In the next section, I show Smith's views on the crafty politician are not ad hoc, but part of a larger account of bad kinds of politicians.

3 Three Kinds of Bad Leaders

In this section I discuss Smith's account of bad leadership. I argue that according to Smith there are three kinds of bad politicians: (1) a decisionist type; (2) an ideological type; (3) a factional type. These three are intended as ideal types; in practice, the qualities that belong to each can be blended, and all of them are compatible with what he says about the crafty politician. I discuss them in turn and then point to some commonalities.

Consider the following passage:

> To insist upon establishing, and upon establishing all at once, and in spite of all opposition, every thing which that idea may seem to require, must often be the highest degree of arrogance. It is to erect his own judgment into the supreme standard of right and wrong. It is to fancy himself the only wise and worthy man in the commonwealth, and that his fellow-citizens should accommodate themselves to him and not he to them . . . This arrogance is perfectly familiar to them. They entertain no doubt of the immense superiority of their own judgment . . . they seldom see any thing so wrong in it as the obstructions which it may sometimes oppose to the execution of their own will. They . . . consider the state as made for themselves, not themselves for the state.[47]

In context, Smith is describing the dangers of acting from the 'idea of perfecting of policy and law' (that is 'that idea' in the first quoted sentence). But the problem that is diagnosed is not unique to it. Rather, what is being rejected is what we would call 'shock therapy' ('establishing all at once') when it comes to policy and institutional change: Smith is a gradualist.[48] He worries that fast economic changes will generate dislocations that are inhumane and disorderly.[49] But he also thinks that such shock therapy shows an arrogant lack of respect for other people's opinions ('in spite of all opposition'). Such political arrogance generally presupposes a moral arrogance: one's 'own judgment' is turned 'into the supreme standard of right and wrong'.[50] This lack of humility is itself a moral failing, but also an epistemic one: because this standard – the 'idea of exact propriety and perfection'[51]– can only be set by the feelings of the impartial spectator.[52]

The arrogant leader assumes that fellow-citizens will accommodate themselves to him. Smith presupposes here that what I have been calling 'true leaders' are not rulers over *subjects*, but their servants.[53] Such arrogant leaders detest delay ('at once'), constitutional process and compromise; they are fond of unitary authority, which facilitates their decisiveness ('obstructions which it may sometimes oppose to the execution of their own will'). In context, Smith is clear that such arrogance comes naturally to royal princes ('imperial and royal reformers' (TMS 6.2.2.18, 234)) and, perhaps, also those with great inherited wealth.[54]

The second kind of bad leader is one who has excessive fondness for a particular 'system' of thought or ideology. To understand Smith's criticism we need to be clear about the role of aesthetics as a *legitimate* political motive to action in his thought. A key passage is the following:

> The same principle, the same love of system, the same regard to the beauty of order, of art and contrivance, frequently serves to recommend those institutions which tend to promote the public welfare. When a patriot exerts himself for the improvement of any part of the public police, his conduct does not always arise from pure sympathy with the happiness of those who are to reap the benefit of it. It is not commonly from a fellow-feeling with carriers and waggoners that a public-spirited man encourages the mending of high roads . . . The perfection of police, the extension of trade and manufactures, are noble and magnificent objects. The contemplation of them pleases us, and we are interested in whatever can tend to advance them. They make part of the great system of government, and the wheels of the political machine seem to move with more harmony and ease by means of them. We take pleasure in beholding the perfection of so beautiful and grand a system, and we are uneasy till we remove any obstruction that can in the least disturb or encumber the regularity of its motions. All constitutions of government, however, are valued only in proportion as they tend to promote the happiness of those who live under them. This is their sole use and end. From a certain spirit of system, however, from a certain love of art and contrivance, we sometimes seem to value the means more than the end, and to be eager to promote the happiness of our fellow-creatures, rather from a view to perfect and improve a certain beautiful and orderly system, than from any immediate sense or feeling of what they either suffer or enjoy. There have been men of the greatest public spirit, who have shown themselves in other respects not very sensible to the feelings of humanity.[55]

Smith clearly thinks that the love of system can be aesthetic, and this also includes systems about 'those institutions which tend to promote the public welfare'. Aesthetics has motivational pull because it is 'pleasing'. What is notable is that according to Smith such aesthetic judgement can compensate for a lack of (or 'imperfect') sympathy with those intended to be aided by one's institutional reform project. *True* public spirit may, in fact, be more a consequence of such aesthetic motives than concern for the lives of those one claims to be helping; this fact does not undermine the reality of 'public spirit'.[56]

I do not mean to suggest the significance of the passage is only in its focus on the nature of helpful aesthetic motivation (although this tends to get overlooked). The key point is that there is a mismatch between why one may desire to improve the constitution of a state – recall from Section 1 that this refers to the underlying social structures which give a particular state its stability – and the proper *normative* grounds or justification for doing so. For constitutions ought to be 'valued only in proportion as they tend to promote the happiness of those who live under them. This is their sole use and end.'[57] That is, when it comes to social affairs, Smith is an egalitarian consequentialist.[58] Imperfect motives, the aesthetic pull of the harmony or fittingness of intellectual systems, can lead to good outcomes. Notice that Smith also allows that 'the perfection of police [that is, public policy], the extension of trade and manufactures, are noble and magnificent objects'. The aesthetic pull of a system that aims to achieve such ends is not illusory; these really are noble objects worth pursuing.[59] This helps explain the comment quoted above that the 'some general, and even systematical, idea of the perfection of policy and law, may no doubt be necessary for directing the views of the statesman'.[60] Smith thinks policy ought to be governed by an ideal vision of society.[61]

The problem is that the aesthetic pull of such an intellectual system can displace the public spirit it should be animating: 'This spirit of system *commonly* takes the direction of that more gentle public spirit; *always* animates it, and *often* inflames it even to the madness of fanaticism.'[62] Smith thinks that such an aesthetic attachment to an ideology is dangerous.[63] For Smith, fanaticism is always associated with violence.[64] Not all fanaticism is associated with an ideology taken too far, and Smith often treats religion and faction as likely sources of violent fanaticism. Either way, fanaticism enhances readiness to use violence and undermines the working of our moral sentiments: 'Of all the corrupters of moral sentiments, therefore, faction and fanaticism have always been by far the greatest.'[65] So, Smith warns against certain kind of political leaders, of an intellectual kind, who are in the grip of a beautiful ideology and turn violent to achieve their ends.

As the passage reveals, Smith clearly also thinks that the spirit of faction, we would say 'partisanship', is very dangerous. Smith's concern runs through the *Moral Sentiments*, to quote a striking passage:

> The animosity of hostile factions, whether civil or ecclesiastical, is often still more furious than that of hostile nations; and their conduct towards one another is often still more atrocious . . . It is needless to observe, I presume, that both rebels and heretics are those unlucky persons, who, when things have come to a certain degree of violence, have the misfortune to be of the weaker party. In a nation distracted by

faction, there are, no doubt, always a few, though commonly but a very few, who preserve their judgment untainted by the general contagion. They seldom amount to more than, here and there, a solitary individual, without any influence, excluded, by his own candour, from the confidence of either party, and who, though he may be one of the wisest, is necessarily, upon that very account, one of the most insignificant men in the society. All such people are held in contempt and derision, frequently in detestation, by the furious zealots of both parties. A true party-man hates and despises candour; and, in reality, there is no vice which could so effectually disqualify him for the trade of a party-man as that single virtue. The real, revered, and impartial spectator, therefore, is, upon no occasion, at a greater distance than amidst the violence and rage of contending parties . . . Even to the great Judge of the universe, they impute all their own prejudices, and often view that Divine Being as animated by all their own vindictive and implacable passions.[66]

For Smith, factions are cohesive because they are echo chambers of mutual sympathy ('general contagion').[67] And in so doing they create a robust form of *partiality* which does not respect, even comes to loath ('hates and despises') truth and equity.[68] Religious factions are inclined to innovate theologically and create theological justifications for their own otherwise immoral behaviour. Smith notes that it is very difficult and lonely to avoid becoming factional in the midst of other people's fanaticism. A key problem of the existence of polarising partisanship is that a robust unwillingness to remain steadfast in one's independent and impartial judgement itself becomes a matter of suspicion and antagonism:[69] leading to the well-known mindset of 'you are either with us or against us'.

And, in fact, he thinks that partisan leaders may well be less fanatical and partisan than they let on,[70] but that they cannot reveal their true feelings amid great partisanship: 'Even though the leaders should have preserved their own heads, as indeed they commonly do, free from this fanaticism, yet they dare not always disappoint the expectation of their followers; but are often obliged, though contrary to their principle and their conscience, to act as if they were under the common delusion.'[71] So, a factional leader will, if she does not willingly encourage fanaticism, be unwillingly carried along by the zeal and madness ('delusions') of her fellow partisans. That is to say, while an arrogant leader tramples on the opinions of the people, a factional leader must flatter her followers to stay in power.

Before I turn to Smith's account of how one can transform oneself from a factional leader to a true statesman, it is worth noting that these three types of bad leadership have some features in common: (1) they are not impartial (and so fail to promote the general interest and happiness of fellow-creatures); (2) they lack proper public spirit; and, most notably, (3) they facilitate the corruption of moral life.[72] In sum, they see political life as a zero-sum activity and act accordingly. They also (4) fail to find the right balance between respecting people's opinions and *guiding* them through persuasion.[73] It follows from this that Smith thinks public spirited leaders, who are impartial and promote good morals (or mores) as well as promote policies with the grain of society in the service of everybody, are laudable. In the following sections I offer more concrete evidence for these claims.

4 True Statesman

In the previous section we looked at some passages where Smith describes factional or partisan leadership (or failure of leadership). But he also thinks that there are political circumstances in which the partisan leader can be transformed into a true statesman. I have already drawn upon this passage, but now I offer context:

> Foreign war and civil faction are the two situations which afford the most splendid opportunities for the display of public spirit . . . In times of civil discord, the leaders of the contending parties, though they may be admired by one half of their fellow-citizens, are commonly execrated by the other . . .
>
> The leader of the successful party, however, if he has authority enough to prevail upon his own friends to act with proper temper and moderation (which he frequently has not), may sometimes render to his country a service much more essential and important than the greatest victories and the most extensive conquests. He may reestablish and improve the constitution, and from the very doubtful and ambiguous character of the leader of a party, he may assume the greatest and noblest of all characters, that of the reformer and legislator of a great state; and, by the wisdom of his institutions, secure the internal tranquility and happiness of his fellow citizens for many succeeding generations.[74]

In victory, a partisan leader can become a statesman when she shows moderation.[75] A true statesman is somebody who establishes or re-establishes practices and institutions that secure 'tranquility and happiness of his fellow citizens for many succeeding generations'. Rather than rejecting pacific ('tranquility') and welfarist ('happiness') political leadership, Smith glorifies it.[76] This is a rejection of the republican's (and Rousseau's) fondness for, say, Lycurgus, or the fetishisation of conquest by those that admire, say, Alexander the Great.

This passage illuminates my claim that Smithian moral statesmanship is aimed at the good society as distinct from state-craft. Tranquillity and happiness are characteristics of a good society.[77] Smith's commitment to such a good society is familiar from his famous claim that 'no society can surely be flourishing and happy, of which the far greater part of the members are poor and miserable'.[78] While I do not deny that Smith thinks in such circumstances we can expect more probity and truth,[79] Smith does not think (as a republican thinker would) that a good society presupposes good citizens.

Of course, Smith doubts that the transformation from partisan to statesman often happens.[80] But when it does, the previously disunified state has minimal unity.[81] I suspect, but cannot prove, that Smith here is presupposing that in victory the partisan leader has sufficient charismatic authority to prevail on his own followers (when previously he could not).[82]

I do not mean to suggest that for Smith good leadership occurs only at such fraught post-civil-war moments. Throughout his writings we can discern the features that Smith thinks characteristic of more ordinary good leadership. For example, recall that for Smith a legislator deliberates with 'general principles which are always the same'. Here a 'principle' is not what we would call a moral commitment. Rather, in the eighteenth-century sciences, 'principle' is a foundational cause of a system of science. (The term is preserved in the common textbook title 'Principles of Economics.') So, Smith is claiming that a true statesman ought not be merely ad hoc in her policies;[83] rather she ought to be guided by robust knowledge (see also, 'some general, and even systematical, idea of the perfection of policy and law, may no doubt be necessary for directing the views of the statesman'[84]) and a coherent vision that has both good (political, social, economic, etc.) effects on ordinary people as well as reinforces their capacity for moral judgements.[85] This vision involves commitment to political and economic institutions that facilitate non-zero-sum outcomes compatible with human flourishing.[86]

At this point a proponent of the view that I have associated with Shklar may argue that, once there is civil peace, the Smithian legislators will create the conditions of the rule of law and a market economy in order to achieve those non-zero-sum outcomes, and then, after providing for some public goods (transportation networks, education, public health and defence, etc.), paid for by modestly progressive taxes,[87] get out of the way of civil society.[88] While this is obviously not all wrong, it understates what, according to Smith, the tasks of government are:

> [t]he civil magistrate is entrusted with the power not only of preserving the public peace by restraining injustice, but of promoting the prosperity of the commonwealth, by establishing good discipline, and by discouraging every sort of vice and impropriety; he may prescribe rules, therefore, which not only prohibit mutual injuries among fellow-citizens, but command mutual good offices to a certain degree.[89]

We tend to understand a 'magistrate' as a judge, but it is clear that here Smith understands 'civil magistrate' more widely as 'government'.[90] What exactly Smith means by the power to 'command mutual good offices' is subject of controversy, but all the options – from requiring families to care of the elderly/orphans to the development of a welfare state – involve an idea of citizenship in which the government has the power to impose some social solidarity. Again, Smith here is not presupposing soul-craft, but rather focusing on polices that can produce socially desirable ends.

More important here, it is rarely remarked that the magistrate's tasks are decidedly moralistic ('discouraging every sort of vice and impropriety').[91] Presumably 'good discipline' is conductive to martial virtues[92] and public order, but perhaps this also has an economic function (good discipline being conducive to productivity).[93] My view is that, in light of the dangers, even high likelihood, of factions capturing government, Smith is rather cautious here. As he writes (in different context warning against the fascination with greatness), 'the peace and order of society, is of more importance than even the relief of the miserable'.[94]

A key point with which I close this description of the *true* statesman is that according to Smith a good leader must make her vision cohere with the prejudices of ordinary people, so that she can govern along the grain of society's tendencies:[95] 'If those . . . principles coincide and act in the same direction, the game of human society will go on easily and harmoniously, and is very likely to be happy and successful.'[96] This vision is ameliorative in character. As he writes:

> When he cannot conquer the rooted prejudices of the people by reason and persuasion, he will not attempt to subdue them by force . . . He will accommodate, as well as he can, his public arrangements to the confirmed habits and prejudices of the people; and will remedy as well as he can, the inconveniencies which may flow from the want of those regulations which the people are averse to submit to. When he cannot

establish the right, he will not disdain to ameliorate the wrong; but like Solon, when he cannot establish the best system of laws, he will endeavour to establish the best that the people can bear.[97]

We see in this passage Smith's preference for 'reason and persuasion'. A good leader does not rely on force, but on rhetoric and arguments.[98] She will exhibit considerable status quo bias, not from a Burkean impulse to preserve tradition, but from an awareness of the political and moral dangers of sudden reform (recall Smith's attack on shock therapy above). Smith's gradualism is not a rejection of establishing what is right – politics can be a moral project for him – but awareness that the project of public enlightenment need not require (instant) full enlightenment to get off the ground. The true leader recognises that her authority rests on opinion[99] and respects that this prevents the establishment of even Smith's system of natural liberty ('the best system of laws'); but such a leader is simultaneously busy shaping (through persuasion) such opinion to make it conducive to becoming a more equitable polity.[100]

5 On Developing State Capacity

Before I turn to Smith's account of leadership selection, in this section I complete the argument that Smith promotes the development of national political structures and state capacity, including a national currency, as a response the arbitrary powers of petty sovereigns. What follows builds on the work of Ryan Hanley on Smith's interest in Chinese statecraft and connects it to Hume's treatment of French political weaknesses.

I start with a passage once famous in debates over to what degree (according to Smith) there is a limit to economic growth as such or whether (as the second quoted sentence suggests) any such limit would be context (institutions/norms) dependent:[101]

> China seems to have been long stationary, and had probably long ago acquired that full complement of riches which is consistent with the nature of its laws and institutions. But this complement may be much inferior to what, with other laws and institutions, the nature of its soil, climate, and situation might admit of. A country which neglects or despises foreign commerce, and which admits the vessels of foreign nations into one or two of its ports only, cannot transact the same quantity of business which it might do with different laws and institutions. In a country too, where, though the rich or the owners of large capitals enjoy a good deal of security, the poor or the owners of small

capitals enjoy scarce any, but are liable, under the pretence of justice, to be pillaged and plundered at any time by the inferior mandarins, the quantity of stock employed in all the different branches of business transacted within it can never be equal to what the nature and extent of that business might admit. In every different branch, the oppression of the poor must establish the monopoly of the rich, who, by engrossing the whole trade to themselves, will be able to make very large profits. Twelve per cent accordingly is said to be the common interest of money in China, and the ordinary profits of stock must be sufficient to afford this large interest.[102]

As Hanley shows in this passage and related ones, Smith comments on the political economy of China and, simultaneously, holds a complex, concave mirror to European eyes.[103] Smith clearly suggests that allowing more foreign exchange would kick-start Chinese growth.

As an aside, it is also notable that, given the stationary state, interest rates are high in China. According to Smith's theory of interest rates, these should (all things being equal) be low in a wealthy country with negligible economic growth:

in a country which had acquired its full complement of riches, where in every particular branch of business there was the greatest quantity of stock that could be employed in it, as the ordinary rate of clear profit would be very small, so that usual market rate of interest which could be afforded out of it, would be so low as to render it impossible for any but the very wealthiest people to live upon the interest of their money.[104]

Smith's treatment of Chinese political economy is also political in character. What explains the unusual economic conditions of China are its political institutions.[105] It is oligarchic in character: with formal and informal laws favouring the rich. As the emphasised passage reveals, Smith notes two features: (1) property rights are protected unevenly (and biased towards the rich); (2) in practice, this is due to the fact that, for the non-rich, experience of the state bureaucracy consists of encounters with petty sovereigns (cf. 'inferior mandarins').[106]

Smith's remarks on China recall an important subsidiary argument by Hume in his essay 'Of Civil Liberty'. The main point of that essay is:

that civilized monarchies, what was formerly said in praise of republics alone, that *they are a government of Laws, not of Men*. They are found susceptible of order, method, and constancy, to a surprizing degree. Property is there secure; industry encouraged; the arts flourish; and the prince lives secure among his subjects, like a father among his children.[107]

Yet, in the next paragraph, Hume went on to note an important exception to this claim:

> The greatest abuses, which arise in France, the most perfect model of pure monarchy, proceed not from the number or weight of the taxes, beyond what are to be met with in free countries; but from the expensive, unequal, arbitrary, and intricate method of levying them, by which the industry of the poor, especially of the peasants and farmers, is, in a great measure, discouraged, and agriculture rendered a beggarly and slavish employment.[108]

In particular, the root problem is that the French crown sold or leased taxing rights to syndicates or tax farms, who paid the tax and then levied the tax (and surplus) from the population.[109] This system generated oppression and prevented economic growth. Hume goes on to argue that such policies also hurt the rich landowners (the nobility) because agriculture is greatly discouraged and so their landholdings and rents are lower than they would be. It is a bit of shame that Hume, who sounds like a modern economist here, fails to explore the possibility that the nobility actually prefers high inequality, which is a source of their political influence, and more power over more income and loss of relative power/status.

Let me return to Smith. The political structure of China maintains a situation in which the property rights of the rich are better protected than the poor from abuse by petty sovereigns. (Presumably, the rich have better access to the upper reaches of the bureaucracy to get redress against any abuses.) Smith cleverly models the consequence of this as an economic monopoly; because of the insecurity of property rights of the poor, their already bad position to compete economically is discouraged even more.[110] Stagnation entails 'low wages for the labor' of the poor. In addition, the trade barriers prevent competition from abroad. The politically created economic monopoly now has the power to ensure that the status quo reproduces itself; hence China's stability and stagnation.[111]

As Hanley shows, Smith, who grants that his sources are imperfect, explains the underlying cause of the Chinese state of affairs by the perverse incentives created by its tax system.[112] The reason why China grew wealthy is, according to Smith, due to the willingness of Chinese 'executive power [to charge] itself both with the reparation of the high roads, and with the maintenance of the navigable canals'[113] and to the fact that 'the sovereigns of China' have been historically 'extremely attentive to the making and maintaining of good roads and navigable canals, in order to increase, as much as possible, both the quantity and value of every part of the produce of the land, by procuring to every part of it the most extensive market which their own dominions could afford'.[114]

The central government's public works policy is not explained by Smith with reference to concern for public welfare, or to Mencius' philosophy, but (as Hanley notes) to the nature of the tax system:

> the revenue of the sovereign arises almost altogether from a land tax or land rent, which rises or falls with the rise and fall of the annual produce of the land. The great interest of the sovereign, therefore, his revenue, is in such countries necessarily and immediately connected with the cultivation of the land, with the greatness of its produce, and with the value of its produce.[115]

Smith goes on to make clear (and this echoes the Humean point above) that the Chinese example shows that modern European states are quite capable of managing extensive public works that, indirectly, promote their own tax income: 'in some parts of Asia this department of the public police is *very properly managed* by the executive power, there is not the least probability that, during the present state of things, it could be tolerably managed by that power in *any* part of Europe.'[116]

I read Smith here as arguing for the development and, in particular, exercise of state capacity by the national executives of European states.[117] Now, to be sure, Smith's Humean point is that state capacity can misfire when incentives are not properly lined up. For he writes about Chinese tax collection (in a manner echoing Hume's point about French mismanagement of taxes) that:

> a public revenue which was paid in kind would suffer so much from the mismanagement of the collectors that a very small part of what was levied upon the people would ever arrive at the treasury of the prince. Some part of the public revenue of China, however, is said to be paid in this manner. The mandarins and other tax-gatherers will, no doubt, find their advantage in continuing the practice of a payment which is so much more liable to abuse than any payment in money.[118]

The absence of money as a means to pay taxes facilitates abuse. Smith is quite aware of money's functional role in taxation.[119] Smith is clear that money makes standardisation in taxation possible, and that the effect of this, which enhances the power of the executive, is to reduce the room for the arbitrary power of petty sovereigns against the poor. Smith, thus, advocates policies and instruments that enhance the state's capacity to create a rule-following, impartial bureaucracy, which will be fairer to the poor and enhance economic growth. This seems to be a task for the statesman that has been largely overlooked.

6 The Qualities and Selection of Leaders

Despite Smith's reputation of timidity when it comes to advancing Hume's career or religious views, he was remarkably bold in articulating, say, a fierce attack on mercantilism and drawing up an ambitious project for an Atlantic parliament in which representatives of the American colonies, Ireland and Great Britain would sit on equal footing. And so it comes as no surprise that he does not ignore the origin of the desire to lead:

> But as from admiring other people we come to wish to be admired ourselves; so from being led and directed by other people we learn to wish to become ourselves leaders and directors. And as we cannot always be satisfied merely with being admired, unless we can at the same time persuade ourselves that we are in some degree really worthy of admiration; so we cannot always be satisfied merely with being believed, unless we are at the same time conscious that we are really worthy of belief. As the desire of praise and that of praise-worthiness, though very much a-kin, are yet distinct and separate desires; so the desire of being believed and that of being worthy of belief, though very much a-kin too, are equally distinct and separate desires.[120]

Even so, Smith is remarkably uninterested in articulating a *means* to *selecting* good leaders. In this section I scrutinise the grounds for his reserve.

He recognises four natural causes – and by natural he explicitly means 'antecedent to any civil institution', that is, in the state of nature – of 'subordination' to another:[121] (1) superiority of personal qualifications (which can involve 'strength, beauty, and agility of body; of wisdom and virtue, of prudence, justice, fortitude, and moderation of mind'); (2) 'superiority of age'; (3) superiority of wealth/riches, which Smith notable associates with 'fortune' (not merit)[122] and thinks nearly impossible in state of nature; (4) 'superiority of birth'.[123]

Smith quite clearly prefers the first ground of subordination, but claims that, with the exception of the superficial bodily characteristics, these involve 'invisible qualities'. And he claims that 'no society, whether barbarous or civilised, has ever found it convenient to settle the rules of precedency of rank and subordination according to those invisible qualities'. Smith fails to say what the sources of inconvenience are, but he clearly implies that no future society will find a way to overcome them and opt for Platonic philosopher-kings. The main argument in favour of the second cause is not the greater experience of the elderly, but that it is a selection mechanism that 'admits no dispute'.

In very unequal societies – which he associates with shepherding stage of civilisation – distinctions in 'birth and fortune' can also provide a secure source of subordination (which Smith treats as a kind of protection racket). In Smith's view 'birth and fortune' basically are near-universal (empirical) preconditions for authoritative leadership.

It is notable that, despite Smith's interest in parliamentary reform, and despite discussing these matters in the context of how to pay for government in commercial societies, Smith expresses so little interest in exploring the merits of 'non-natural' causes of leadership such as elections and parties – so important in various ways to Hutcheson, Burke, Hume, Madison and Montesquieu. The grounds for Smith's lack of interest in these are clear. For he thinks that, in a great society, people systematically misperceive the qualities of would-be leaders (recall how ordinary people venerate the crafty politician). This is not an expression of elite mistrust of ordinary people. Smith is famously adamant that in most contexts ordinary people's judgements should be trusted and even strengthened. And he thinks that outside a small community, where character can be revealed, it is, nearly impossible to establish good grounds for judgements of others.[124]

There is also another reason for his stance. In Smith's day, the accidents of birth (rank) played a decisive role in limiting the franchise and membership of Parliament. One cannot deny, even after centuries of widening franchises, the continued role of 'birth and fortune' in filling the ranks of parliamentary legislators.[125] And while one need not agree with Plato that wishing to be elected is itself disqualifying for good leadership, Schumpeter is unrefuted in thinking there is no reason to believe that being good at being elected is evidence at being good at governing.[126]

Even so the rhetorical utility of Smith's analysis of liberal political leadership is limited for two reasons: first, because Smith ignores rule by lot, direct democracy and elected kingship, he really fails to speak to democratic sensibilities. Second, while Smith clearly advocates for separation of powers and is very interested in liberal institutions,[127] his published works fail to explore how institutions may limit leaders.[128]

Smith also accepts the need for separation of powers:

> When the judicial is united to the executive power, it is scarce possible
> that justice should not frequently be sacrificed to what is vulgarly called
> polities. The persons entrusted with the great interests of the state may,
> even without any corrupt views, sometimes imagine it necessary to sac-
> rifice to those interests the rights of a private man. But upon the impar-
> tial administration of justice depends the liberty of every individual,
> the sense which he has of his own security. In order to make every
> individual feel himself perfectly secure in the possession of every right
> which belongs to him, it is not only necessary that the judicial should
> be separated from the executive power, but that it should be rendered
> as much as possible independent of that power.[129]

The word 'rhetorical' in the previous paragraph may raise some eyebrows.
Let me explain what I have in mind. In unpublished remarks, Sandra Peart
has suggested that for Smith 'life is a lottery and fortune determines who
is born in the various ranks of society. Then, fortune or chance selects
leaders and rulers from the higher ranks.' This is basically a correct understanding of Smith's position, as long as we recognise, as she notes, that the
game of life is not stable – there is permanent change, and in commercial
societies more so than in previously known societies. To be sure this lottery
is a *biased* lottery because for some (those lacking 'birth and fortune') there
is negligible chance of ending on top.[130]

   In fact, Smith is quite explicit that, even when there is skill in leadership, this is not what is most characteristic of successful leaders:

> the most successful warriors, the greatest statesmen and legislators, the
> eloquent founders and leaders of the most numerous and most success-
> ful sects and parties; have many of them been, not more distinguished
> for their very great merit, than for a degree of presumption and self-
> admiration altogether disproportioned even to that very great merit.[131]

It seems the most fundamental skill of a would-be great leader is a kind
of delusional or mythical belief in one's political skill. It is clear that such
a trait may well lead to great disasters. More subtly, Smith clearly implies
that successful political outcomes are non-trivially influenced by non-
meritorious factors; so, even with possession of merit, disasters need not
be forestalled.

   Because Smith also thinks that talents are very much the product of
nurture and where one ends up in the division of labour, and he thinks

landed wealth creates the possibility of some leisure to develop an understanding of a general or common interest,[132] he quite clearly thinks that 'birth and fortune' are a decent, second-best mechanism towards leadership selection. Why he thinks so is not entirely clear. Of course, in practice, many forms of wealth also create an interest/incentive to use government to advance one's own partial (commercial) interests, which is why Smith favours the participation of the class of landed wealthy. He thinks this not because he believes they are beyond corruption or that agriculture is a source of true wealth (as the physiocrats think), but rather because he argues that a broadly growing economy, which allows wages for the working poor to be high, best correlates with their material interests (because it generates a rising income from rents).[133]

Conclusion

While I would not argue that Smith is the first author to offer us a genuinely liberal theory of leadership, his thought on these matters is more ambitious than, say, Spinoza and Hume. While both of them also thought that good leaders promoted the common good (by way of rule of law, encouraging commerce and controlling religion), a good leader's primary task is for them to maintain the citizens' dispositions to minimal unity. Smith's vision is more expansive: good leaders must create conditions that break the logic of zero-sum relations and promote the flourishing of the working poor, who are the vast majority of people. It is pretty clear that for Smith this involves not only supplying public goods and solving coordination problems, but also the cultivation of social norms conducive to virtue and mutual trust.[134] This – the generation of practices conducive to virtue, trust and mutual gains – is sufficient to qualify his account of leadership as a political one (rather than the anti-political account we started out with). In addition, he has a clear account of the ameliorative nature of liberal governance. Smith reminds us that liberalism was originally conceived as a form of moral government which, while embracing various forms of impartiality, had no interest in embracing state neutrality.[135] The state has to create institutional incentives and practices conducive to become a good society.[136] Most of this is indirect, but, as we have seen, it can 'command mutual good offices to a certain degree'.[137]

I have some sympathy for this stance. Even so, Smith's thought has limited utility today because he fails to address how to create institutions which may plausibly generate public spirited political leaders who may embrace the sort of values he thinks desirable for them to hold. Presumably, he addressed this in the manuscripts he burned on his deathbed. While he clearly thought Parliament important, and thinks it can have good effects, he clearly thinks it also promotes the rise of faction and rent-seeking. And so while he offers what I take to be an attractive understanding of leadership, he seems to think even a reasonably well-organised society must be lucky to obtain it. Whether such a society can do better than luck is decidedly undecided and an urgent matter.[138]

Notes

1. See also Jerry Z. Muller, *Adam Smith in His Time and Ours: Designing the Decent Society* (Princeton: Princeton University Press, 1995). Ryan Hanley encouraged me to make this explicit. (He should not be held accountable for the Lippmann-esque manner of expression.) My claim presupposes some features of Smith's social ontology that I make explicit along the way.
2. Robert C. Tucker, 'The Theory of Charismatic Leadership', *Daedalus* 97:3 (1968), pp. 731–56.
3. John Merrington, 'Theory and Practice in Gramsci's Marxism', *Socialist Register* 5:5 (1968), pp. 145–76.
4. Carl Schmitt, 'Aufgabe und Notwendigkeit des deutschen Rechtsstandes', *Deutsches Recht* 6:9/10 (1936), pp. 181–5.
5. Tony Bush, 'From Management to Leadership: Semantic or Meaningful Change?', *Educational Management Administration & Leadership* 36:2 (2008), pp. 271–88.
6. A notable exception is Andrew Sabl, *Ruling Passions: Political Offices and Democratic Ethics* (Princeton: Princeton University Press, 2009). If one googles 'liberal leadership', one finds works in the history of nineteenth-century politics.
7. Eric Schliesser, 'Hume on Affective Leadership', in Philip A. Reed and Rico Vitz (eds), *Hume's Moral Philosophy and Contemporary Psychology* (New York: Routledge, 2018), pp. 311–33. See also, Eric Schliesser 'Walter Lippmann: The Prophet of Liberalism and the Road not Taken', *Journal of Contextual Economics – Schmollers Jahrbuch*, vol. 139 (2019), Iss. 2–4: pp. 349–63.
8. See also Joseph Cropsey, *Polity and Economy: An Interpretation of the Principles of Adam Smith* (Dordrecht: Springer, 2013 [1957]); John W. Danford, 'Adam Smith, Equality, and the Wealth of Sympathy', *American Journal of Political Science* 24 (Nov. 1980), pp. 674–95; James M. Buchanan, 'Let Us Understand Adam Smith', *Journal of the History of Economic Thought* 30:1 (2008), pp. 21–8, who emphasises Smith as the thinker of increasing returns.
9. See Christopher J. Berry, 'Adam Smith: Commerce, Liberty, and Modernity', ch. 18 in his *Essays on Hume, Smith, and the Scottish Enlightenment* (Edinburgh: Edinburgh University Press, 2018), pp. 326–46. For the political significance of Smith's economics, see Emma Rothschild and Amartya Sen, 'Adam Smith's Economics', in Knud Haakonssen (ed.), *The Cambridge Companion to Adam Smith* (Cambridge: Cambridge University Press, 2006).

10. See Donald Winch, *Adam Smith's Politics: An Essay in Historiographic Revision* (Cambridge: Cambridge University Press, 1978), where he denies that for Smith politics is about 'any specifically political qualities which [men] may be called upon to display in public settings' (p. 177). See also Emma Rothschild, 'What is Security?', *Daedalus* 124:3 (1995), pp. 53–98; see, esp., pp. 60ff.

11. Ryan Patrick Hanley, 'The "wisdom of the state": Adam Smith on China and Tartary', *American Political Science Review* 108:2 (2014), pp. 371–82.

12. I agree with Paul Sagar that (1) such 'utility' and the accompanying 'authority' grounded in the good opinion and 'assent of subjects' (p. 206) grounds Smith's account of legitimacy; and (2) that many kinds of governments can be legitimate in this sense. But this chapter shows that Smith also has a more demanding standard for good leadership. Paul Sagar, *The Opinion of Mankind: Sociability and the Theory of the State from Hobbes to Smith* (Princeton: Princeton University Press, 2019). Sagar explicitly draws on and extends the argument of Istvan Hont. See, esp., Istvan Hont, 'Adam Smith's History of Law and Government as Political Theory', in Richard Bourke and Raymond Geuss (eds), *Political Judgement* (Cambridge: Cambridge University Press, 2009), pp. 131–71.

13. For recent work along these lines, see Athol Fitzgibbons, *Adam Smith's System of Liberty, Wealth, and Virtue: The Moral and Political Foundations of the Wealth of Nations* (Oxford: Oxford University Press, 1995); Pierre Force, *Self-Interest before Adam Smith: A Genealogy of Economic Science* (Cambridge: Cambridge University Press, 2003).

14. I have argued elsewhere that Smith is a critic of stoic harmony, so I leave that aside here. See also Lauren Brubaker, 'Does the "Wisdom of Nature" Need Help?', in Leonidas Montes and Eric Schliesser (eds), *New Voices on Adam Smith* (New York: Routledge, 2006), pp. 190–214. Eric Schliesser, 'Book Reviews', *Ethics* 118:3 (2008), pp. 569–75. Michele Bee and Maria Pia Paganelli, 'Adam Smith, Anti-Stoic', CHOPE Working Paper no. 2019-02 (2019).

15. Judith Shklar, *After Utopia: The Decline of Political Faith* (Princeton: Princeton University Press, 1957), p. 10.

16. Judith Shklar, 'The Liberalism of Fear', in Shaun P. Young (ed.), *Political Liberalism: Variations on a Theme* (New York: State University of New York Press, 1989), pp. 149–66. That is to say, part of my present project is to undo a damaging self-conception within the liberal (realist) tradition.

17. Adam Smith, *An Inquiry into the Nature and Causes of the Wealth of Nations*, ed. Roy Hutcheson Campbell, Andrew S. Skinner and W. B. Todd (Oxford: Oxford University Press, 1976 [1776]), 4.2.39, p. 468.

18. So, Smith's target is *not* the Machiavellian conception of political *virtu*. Cf. Berry, *Commerce, Liberty*, p. 343.

19. Adam Smith, *The Theory of Moral Sentiments*, ed. David Daiches Raphael and Alec Lawrence Macfie (Oxford: Oxford University Press, 1976 [1759]), 6.2.2.18, p. 234. Inspired by Hayek (see, e.g., F. A. Hayek, 'Adam Smith's Message in Today's Language', *Daily Telegraph*, 9 March 1976), Hayekian

interpretations of Adam Smith tend to emphasise the dangers of the man of system. See, e.g., Jacob T. Levy, *Rationalism, Pluralism, and Freedom* (Oxford: Oxford University Press, 2015); Craig Smith, *Adam Smith's Political Philosophy: The Invisible Hand and Spontaneous Order* (London: Routledge, 2006); David Levy and Sandra Peart, 'Adam Smith and the Place of Faction', in Jeffrey T. Young (ed.), *The Elgar Companion to Adam Smith* (Cheltenham: Edward Elgar, 2007), pp. 335–45. It is not just Hayekians, of course. See, e.g., Sagar, *Opinion of Mankind*, p. 226.

20. Smith, *Wealth of Nations* 4.2.39, p. 468.
21. Smith, *Wealth of Nations* 4.2.39, p. 468.
22. Sankar Muthu, 'Adam Smith's Critique of International Trading Companies: Theorizing "Globalization" in the Age of Enlightenment.', *Political Theory* 36:2 (2008), pp. 185–212.
23. 'Those laws, at the same time, were harming the well-being of all by collecting, little by little, in the hands of a few, wealth that then became in those hands a means of oppression, and which otherwise, through the free movement of interests would have remained if not equal, at least common to all. The unequal division of taxes at last overwhelmed the inferior class who, with no property and no liberty, was reduced to rely on fraud and would cheat remorselessly, because our conscience cannot survive when it is in chains.' Letter VII in *Sophie de Grouchy's Letters on Sympathy: A Critical Engagement with Adam Smith's The Theory of Moral Sentiments*. trans. Sandrine Bergès and ed. and annot. Sandrine Bergès and Eric Schliesser (Oxford: Oxford University Press, 2020), p. 135
24. Smith, *Moral Sentiments* 6.2.2.18, p. 234; emphasis added. See also Eric Schliesser, *Adam Smith: Systematic Philosopher and Public Thinker* (Oxford: Oxford University Press, 2017).
25. 'Nothing tends so much to promote public spirit as the study of politics, of the several systems of civil government, their advantages and disadvantages, of the constitution of our own country, its situation, and interest with regard to foreign nations, its commerce, its defence, the disadvantages it labours under, the dangers to which it may be exposed, how to remove the one, and how to guard against the other. Upon this account political disquisitions, if just, and reasonable, and practicable, are of all the works of speculation the most useful. Even the weakest and the worst of them are not altogether without their utility. They serve at least to animate the public passions of men, and rouse them to seek out the means of promoting the happiness of the society' (Smith, *Moral Sentiments* 4.1.11, pp. 186–7). On the significance of the statesman's promoting the happiness of society, see below. I thank Craig Smith for reminding me of this passage.
26. See Hont p. 152.
27. Smith, *Moral Sentiments* 1.3.3.1, p. 61.
28. While Smith has egalitarian sensibilities and thought that the removal of barriers to movement and trade would have equalising tendencies, there is

no reason to assume that he thought the system of natural liberty would end up without any economic hierarchies. See Spencer J. Pack, *Capitalism as a Moral System* (Cheltenham: Edward Elgar, 1991); Deborah Boucoyannis, 'The Equalizing Hand: Why Adam Smith Thought the Market Should Produce Wealth without Steep Inequality', *Perspectives on Politics* 11:4 (2013), pp. 1051–70.

29. Maureen Harkin, 'Adam Smith's Missing History: Primitives, Progress, and Problems of Genre', *English Literary History* 72:2 (2005), pp. 429–51.

30. Smith, *Wealth of Nations*, Intro. 4, p. 10.

31. Hume tends to think they are always better; Smith thinks that mercantilist, imperial conquest generates a 'spirit of war' and undermines the ways they could be better. In Smith, there is no non-savage anarchist possibility.

32. See the Chicago School's George Stigler's somewhat grudging analysis in George J. Stigler, 'Smith's Travels on the Ship of State', *History of Political Economy* 3:2 (1971), pp. 265–77. For a thorough analysis, see Nathan Rosenberg, 'Some Institutional Aspects of the Wealth of Nations', *Journal of Political Economy* 68:6 (1960), pp. 557–70.

33. In ch. 6 of Schliesser, *Adam Smith*, I argue that 'society' is a key analytical concept for Smith. I regret not crediting Shklar with the point.

34. I suspect Shklar may have been unfamiliar with *The Theory of Moral Sentiments* when she wrote *After Utopia*.

35. Smith, *Moral Sentiments* 6.2.2.7–10, pp. 230–1.

36. In Spinozistic terms: the constitution is the nature or ratio that is preserved in a state.

37. The last few paragraphs were inspired by a very interesting talk, 'Reconstructing Adam Smith's Politics', by Glory Liu and Barry Weingast at the Adam Smith Conference at Chapman University, January 2019. For background on how Smith fits into eighteenth-century constitutional theorising, see Craig Smith, 'Forms of Government', in James Harris (ed.), *The Oxford Handbook of British Philosophy in the Eighteenth Century* (Oxford: Oxford University Press, 2013).

38. To avoid confusion: I am not claiming Smith is suggesting these privileges always need to be respected.

39. See Winch, *Adam Smith's Politics*, p. 2, who builds his interpretation on this passage. Knud Haakonssen, *The Science of a Legislator: The Natural Jurisprudence of David Hume and Adam Smith* (Cambridge: Cambridge University Press, 1989), p. 97; Samuel Fleischacker, *On Adam Smith's Wealth of Nations: A Philosophical Companion* (Princeton: Princeton University Press, 2004), p. 243.

40. Smith, *Wealth of Nations* 4.2.39, p. 468.

41. On the significance of Smith's rejection of violence, see Spenser J. Pack and Eric Schliesser, 'Adam Smith, Natural Movement and Physics', *Cambridge Journal of Economics* 42:2 (2017), pp. 505–21.

42. Gary M. Anderson and Robert D. Tollison, 'Sir James Steuart as the Apotheosis of Mercantilism and His Relation to Adam Smith.', *Southern Economic Journal*, 51 (1984), pp. 456–68.

43. Smith also thought that, with bad background theories, commerce has a tendency to create conflict; see Maria Pia Paganelli and Reinhard Schumacher, 'Do Not Take Peace for Granted: Adam Smith's Warning on the Relation between Commerce and War', *Cambridge Journal of Economics* 43:3 (2018), pp. 785–97.

44. Smith, *Wealth of Nations* 4.7.b.63, p. 590.

45. Smith, *Wealth of Nations* 5.i.f.50, p. 782.

46. This may well be indebted to Machiavelli's *The Prince*, ch. XXV, where Machiavelli argues that one must adjust one's tactics to the 'spirit of the times'. Notice, then, that the crafty politician is tactically responsive along one dimension ('directed by the momentary fluctuations of affairs') but not capable of changing tactics when more fundamental, strategic circumstances have changed.

47. Smith, *Moral Sentiments* 6.2.2.18, p. 234.

48. See Schliesser, *Adam Smith*, pp. 10, 310, 374–5.

49. Smith, *Wealth of Nations* 4.2.40, p. 469. He mixes prudential and ethical concerns in this passage.

50. Smith does not really focus much attention to demagoguery; his admirer Sophie de Grouchy applies his theory to that type of politician in Letter 4 of *Letters on Sympathy*.

51. Smith, *Moral Sentiments* 6.3.25, p. 247.

52. Smith, *Moral Sentiments* 7.2.1.49, p. 249. See Charles L. Griswold Jr, 'Imagination: Morals, Science, Arts', in Knud Haakonssen (ed.), *The Cambridge Companion to Adam Smith* (Cambridge: Cambridge University Press, 2006).

53. Even in *The Wealth of Nations*, Smith assumes that commerce occurs among fellow citizens. To quote a famous passage, 'It is not from the benevolence of the butcher, the brewer, or the baker that we expect our dinner, but from their regard to their own interest. We address ourselves, not to their humanity but to their self-love, and never talk to them of our own necessities but of their advantages. Nobody but a beggar chooses to depend chiefly upon the benevolence of his *fellow-citizens*.' Smith, *Wealth of Nations* 1.2.2, pp. 26–7.

54. Smith attacks entails, in particular, on moral grounds (*Wealth of Nations* 3.2.6, p. 284).

55. Smith, *Moral Sentiments* 4.1.11, p. 185.

56. On the significance of 'public spirit' in Hume, see Schliesser, *Hume on Affective Leadership*; and in Smith, see Jacob Viner, 'Adam Smith and Laissez-faire', *Journal of Political Economy* 35:2 (1927), p. 231.

57. Recall also Smith, *Moral Sentiments* 4.1.11, pp. 186–7.

58. While this passage with its focus on happiness suggests Smith may be a protoutilitarian (when it comes to social institutions), I have argued that Smith is best not identified with that tradition (Schliesser, *Adam Smith*, pp. 190–3).

Cf. David M. Levy, 'The Partial Spectator in the *Wealth of Nations*: A Robust Utilitarianism.', *The European Journal of the History of Economic Thought* 2:2 (1995), pp. 299–326.

59. See Winch, *Adam Smith's Politics*, p. 13.
60. Smith, *Moral Sentiments* 6.2.2.18, p. 234; emphasis added.
61. My claim is compatible with the further thought that Smith thinks it may be very dangerous to assume we can actually attain the ideal at once. I thank Ryan Hanley for conversation.
62. Smith, *Moral Sentiments* 6.2.2.15, p. 232.
63. I argue elsewhere (Schliesser, *Adam Smith*) that Smith is very concerned with the effects of intellectual speech/systems. How to promote responsible speech is one of the key challenges Smith confronts.
64. Smith, *Moral Sentiments* 3.3.36–7, pp. 152–3; 6.3.26, p. 249.
65. Smith, *Moral Sentiments* 3.3.43, p. 156.
66. Smith, *Moral Sentiments* 3.3.43, p. 156.
67. See Levy and Peart, 'Adam Smith and the Place of Faction'; Fonna Forman-Barzilai, *Adam Smith and the Circles of Sympathy: Cosmopolitanism and Moral Theory* (Cambridge: Cambridge University Press, 2010), pp. 23, 151–9, 180–1. Smith's mechanism is akin here to Hume's account of sympathy in 'Of National Character'.
68. Smith echoes here Spinoza's argument of the final pages of ch. 20 of the *Theological Political Treatise* For more on this connection, see Eric Schliesser, 'Spinoza's Economics', in Yitzhak Y. Melamed (ed.), *Blackwell Companion to Spinoza*, London: Blackwell (forthcoming).
69. I suspect Smith is thinking of Cicero's *Pro Ligario*.
70. The passage (Smith, *Moral Sentiments* 3.3.43, p. 156) I quoted is about partisanship, not partisan leaders, but Smith is also alluding to the latter: 'in times of civil discord, the leaders of the contending parties, though they may be admired by one half of their fellow-citizens, are commonly execrated by the other.' Smith, *Moral Sentiments* 6.2.2.13, p. 232.
71. Smith, *Moral Sentiments* 6.2.2.15, p. 233.
72. So, Shklar is correct in thinking that according Smith politics can undermine moral life.
73. Cf. Sagar, *Opinion of Mankind*.
74. Smith, *Moral Sentiments* 6.2.2.13–14, p. 232.
75. Aurelian Craiutu has developed the significance of this virtue in the French liberal tradition numerous books. For his most recent views, see his *Faces of Moderation: The Art of Balance in an Age of Extremes* (Philadelphia: University of Pennsylvania Press, 2018).
76. Smith's account of glory is *modern* because he rejects war and conquest. For this Hobbesian turn in the very idea of glory, see Andrew J. Corsa, 'Thomas Hobbes: Magnanimity, Felicity, and Justice', *Hobbes Studies* 26.2 (2013), pp. 130–51, and Andrew J. Corsa, 'Modern Greatness of Soul in Hume and Smith', *Ergo, an Open Access Journal of Philosophy* 2 (2015).

77. Smithian tranquillity is quite compatible with receptivity towards change and innovation.
78. Smith, *Wealth of Nations* 1.8.36, p. 96.
79. See Lisa Herzog, *Inventing the Market: Smith, Hegel, and Political Theory* (Oxford: Oxford University Press, 2013), pp. 90–5; and Maria Pia Paganelli (this volume).
80. It is possible that Smith is thinking here of Hume's description of George Monk in the *History of England*. I suspect that Nelson Mandela after the fall of apartheid would also be a good model.
81. The significance of such minimal unity in Hume's political theory is explained in Schliesser, *Hume on Affective Leadership*.
82. See Sagar, *Opinion of Mankind*, pp. 213–40, on Smith's anticipations of Max Weber's account of charismatic leadership. But Sagar errs in suggesting that such transformative leadership is the whole of Smith's account of leadership.
83. One may speculate that a true statesman is willing to lean on a crafty politician for tactical purposes.
84. Smith, *Moral Sentiments* 6.2.2.18, p. 234.
85. Smith's defence of commerce, his proposals for public education, for disestablishment and competitive religions, his advocacy of public theatre are all presented as means toward better capacities for moral judgment. See Schliesser, *Adam Smith*, and also Lisa Herzog, 'Higher and Lower Virtues in Commercial Society: Adam Smith and Motivation Crowding Out', *Politics, Philosophy and Economics* 10:4 (2011), pp. 370–95.
86. Dennis C. Rasmussen, 'Does "Bettering Our Condition" Really Make Us Better Off? Adam Smith on Progress and Happiness', *American Political Science Review* 100:3 (2006), pp. 309–18.
87. See Schliesser, *Adam Smith*, pp. 200ff.
88. It is my sense that many public choice political economists find this a congenial interpretation of Smith (via James Buchanan).
89. Smith, *Moral Sentiments* 2.1.8, p. 81. For the larger significance of this passage, see Pack, *Capitalism as a Moral System*, and Samuel Fleischacker, *On Adam Smith's Wealth of Nations*.
90. Craig Smith thinks Smith means to refer here to local government. If that is right, and it may well be, then my argument requires an extra layer of distinctions to track Smith's views on the potentially diverging proper skills of local politicians and national politicians.
91. I suspect that Smith is here distancing himself from Mandeville's 'private vices, public benefits'. Smith's position may well be thought illiberal here by those who understand liberalism as the embrace of state neutrality. But it is fully compatible with my argument that Smith is eager to promote a good society.
92. See Leonidas Montes, 'Adam Smith on the Standing Army Versus Militia Issue: Wealth over Virtue?', in Jeffrey T. Young (ed.), *The Elgar Companion to Adam Smith* (Cheltenham: Edward Elgar, 2009), pp. 315–34.

93. Note that it is not the church/parishes being commanded, but fellow citizens.
94. Smith, *Moral Sentiments* 6.2.1.20, p. 226. See also Schliesser, *Adam Smith*, pp. 213ff.
95. I borrow the term from Jacob T. Levy, *Rationalism, Pluralism, and Freedom*, p. 154. Levy is discussing Montesquieu in context. Sagar, *Opinion of Mankind*, correctly emphasises how indebted Smith is to Hume and Montesquieu.
96. Smith, *Moral Sentiments* 6.2.2.17, p. 233. Here Smith seems to embrace Stoic natural harmony. But see the rest of my analysis below.
97. Smith, *Moral Sentiments* 6.2.2.16, p. 233.
98. Smith does not say what the proper balance between rhetoric and argument is. And this requires, as Paul Sagar reminded me, judgement. For the significance of judgement in Smith, see Samuel Fleischacker, *A Third Concept of Liberty: Judgment and Freedom in Kant and Adam Smith* (Princeton: Princeton University Press, 1999).
99. See Schliesser, *Adam Smith*, p. 180.
100. The contrast with Madison is worth exploring. Madison is terrified that the masses will grab the aristocrats' property; Smith shows no such anxiety.
101. Kenneth E. Boulding, 'The Shadow of the Stationary Sstate', *Daedalus* 102:4 (1973), pp. 89–101; Paul A. Samuelson, 'A Modern Theorist's Vindication of Adam Smith', *The American Economic Review*, 67.1 (1977), pp. 42–9.
102. Smith, *Wealth of Nations* 1.9.15, p. 112.
103. Hanley, *The Wisdom of State*.
104. Smith, *Wealth of Nations* 1.9.20, p. 113. In context, Smith treats Holland as paradigmatic case.
105. Edwin George West, 'Ricardo in Historical Perspective', *Canadian Journal of Economics*, 15:2 (1982), pp. 308–26, esp. pp. 318–19.
106. 'Petty sovereigns abound, reigning in the midst of bureaucratic army institutions mobilized by aims and tactics of power they do not inaugurate or fully control. And yet such figures are delegated with the power to render unilateral decisions, accountable to no law and without any legitimate authority.' Judith Butler, *Precarious Life: The Powers of Violence and Mourning* (London and New York: Verso, 2004), p. 56.
107. David Hume, 'Of Civil Liberty', in Eugene Miller (ed.), *Essays, Moral, Political and Literary* (Indianapolis: Liberty Fund, 1987), p. 94; emphasis in original.
108. Hume, *Civil Liberty*, pp. 94–5.
109. Nobles and clergy also had separate rights to tax those under their jurisdiction. For a modern (more favorable) account, that draws on principal-agent models, see Eugene N. White, 'From Privatized to Government-administered Tax Collection: Tax Farming in Eighteenth-century France', *The Economic History Review* 57:4 (2004), pp. 636–63.
110. To return to a point from before, the relatively high interest rates reflect, in part, the risks associated with uneven enforcement of property rights.

111. I suspect that Smith's model of treating such barriers as monopolies inspired a nice argument in Grouchy's *Letters*, p. 135.
112. Hanley, *Wisdom of State*, pp. 373ff.
113. Smith, *Wealth of Nations* 5.i.d.17, p. 729.
114. Smith, *Wealth of Nations* 5.2.d.5, p. 838.
115. Smith, *Wealth of Nations* 5.1.d.17, p. 730.
116. Smith, *Wealth of Nations* 5.1.d.17, p. 730; emphasis added.
117. Smith's role as a theorist of state capacity seems to me under-theorised by the contemporary focus on Smith as a critic of state power (and made invisible by the contemporary focus on biopolitics). I thank Deborah Boucoyannis for emphasising the significance of state capacity.
118. Smith, *Wealth of Nations* 5.2.d.7, p. 839.
119. Cf. David Graeber, *Debt: The First 5000 Years* (Harmondsworth: Penguin, 2012), pp. 25ff.
120. Smith, *Moral Sentiments* 7.4.24, p. 336.
121. It is telling that Smith treats the question in terms of subordination rather than in terms of leadership.
122. Smith makes the point explicit: 'there never was . . . a great family in the world whose illustration was entirely derived from the inheritance of wisdom and virtue.' Smith, *Wealth of Nations* 5.1.b.5, p. 711.
123. Smith, *Wealth of Nations* 5.1.b.4ff., pp. 710–13.
124. See Ryan Patrick Hanley, *Adam Smith and the Character of Virtue* (Cambridge: Cambridge University Press, 2009), pp. 121ff., for the wider significance of this.
125. Martin Gilens, 'Descriptive Representation, Money, and Political Inequality in the United States', *Swiss Political Science Review* 21:2 (2015), pp. 222–8. Eric Lipton, 'Half of Congress Members are Millionaires, Report Says', *New York Times*, 10 January 2014, p. A13.
126. Joseph A. Schumpeter, *Capitalism, Socialism and Democracy* (London: Routledge, 1943).
127. See Winch, *Adam Smith's Politics*.
128. As Paul Sagar correctly insisted (in correspondence), Smith's lectures on jurisprudence and on rhetoric do offer reflections on these matters. In this chapter I adopt the method defended in Schliesser, *Adam Smith*, of focusing on Smith's writings available to a wider public in his own age.
129. Smith *Wealth of Nations* 4.7.c.54, p. 610. On Smith and liberty, cf. Christopher J. Berry, 'Adam Smith on Liberty "in our present sense of the word"', in Berry, *Essays*, pp. 385–402 with Schliesser, *Adam Smith*, pp. 216–20.
130. See Smith, *Wealth of Nations* 4.7.a.18, p. 562.
131. Smith, *Moral Sentiments* 6.3.28, p. 250.
132. Smith, *Wealth of Nations* 1.11.7–10, pp. 265–7. See Schliesser, *Adam Smith*, p. 156.
133. Smith, *Wealth of Nations*, 1.11.7–10, pp. 265–7. Pack, *Capitalism as a Moral System*.

134. Recent work by economists defines leadership in terms of norm-setting. Daron Acemoglu and Matthew O. Jackson, 'History, Expectations, and Leadership in the Evolution of Social Norms', *The Review of Economic Studies* 82:2 (2014), pp. 423–56. On the economic significance of mutual trust, see: 'When the people of any particular country has such confidence in the fortune, probity, and prudence of a particular banker, as to believe he is always ready to pay upon demand such of his promissory notes as are likely to be at any time presented to him; those notes come to have the same currency as gold and silver money, from the confidence that such money can at any time be had for them.' Smith, *Wealth of Nations* 2.3.28, p. 292.

135. See also Eric Schliesser, 'Sophie de Grouchy, the Tradition(s) of Two Liberties, and the Missing Mother(s) of Liberalism', in Jacqueline Broad and Karen Detlefsen (eds), *Women and Liberty, 1600–1800: Philosophical Essays* (Oxford: Oxford University Press, 2017), pp. 109–22.

136. Ryan Hanley (in *Wisdom of State*) has aptly called this the 'wisdom of the state'.

137. Smith, *Moral Sentiments* 2.1.8, p. 81.

138. I thank Ross Emmett for being the original cause of this chapter, and I am grateful to his students at Arizona State University for excellent comments on a presentation of some of this material. This chapter has benefitted from excellent comments by Isabel Horta Correia and Orlando Samões on an earlier draft presented in the Arrow seminar in Lisbon organised by André Azevedo Alves. I also thank the audience members in Lisbon for discussion as well as my colleagues in 'Challenges to Democratic Representation', especially Lea Klarenbeek, for critical feedback. Ryan Hanley and Paul Sagar read an ultimate draft and offered incisive comments. Special thanks to Sandra Peart, whose extraordinary generous comments at an author meets critics session January 2019 on my monograph helped prompt this chapter, and for the editors of this volume for their careful editing, generous comments and encouragement. Finally, thank you, Chris Berry, for being an encouraging mentor and model of timeless, rigorous scholarship that exhibits good judgment free from partisan rancor.

7

Adam Smith and the Virtue of Punctuality

Maria Pia Paganelli

After a lecture on luxury in Milan, Italy, a furious member of the audience approached the speaker, Christopher Berry. The content of Berry's lecture offended this person. How could someone justify rather than condemn luxury? What kind of moral values would be present in a society that values luxury? What kind of values, he asked indignantly, would Dr Berry teach his children? Berry paused a second, puzzled by the question, then, without a blink, answered: punctuality![1]

The virtue of punctuality is indeed one of the commercial virtues; like probity, it is a virtue which is the product of a commercial society. As Adam Smith claims, 'in a rude and barbarous country [the commercial virtues] are almost unknown'.[2] Rather, 'whenever commerce is introduced into any country, probity and punctuality always accompany it'.[3]

Why does punctuality gain the status of virtue in commercial societies? We can infer the explanation using Smith's logic in explaining all other moral changes: as the result of a change in opportunity cost.[4]

Smith understands virtues as endogenous. There is not necessarily a universal and eternal set of virtues installed in our heart by a divine power or nature. What we have in us is a propensity to develop morally. But what is approved as virtue adapts to our different environments, so that what is considered virtuous in one context may not be considered virtuous in a different context. The change in context changes the opportunity cost of a behaviour, and thus our moral approval of such a behaviour.[5]

And indeed, in the same section of his *Lectures on Jurisprudence* in which Smith affirmed that punctuality is a commercial virtue, as cited above, Smith also affirmed that probity is a commercial virtue. His explanation is as follows. In pre-commercial societies, commercial exchanges are rare – maybe one or two a year. In a situation like this it makes sense to cheat. It is what today we call a one-shot game. Among countries, these trade deals come every few centuries. Expecting honesty among states, and especially ambassadors, is even more absurd than expecting honesty in transactions in non-commercial societies. But when commerce is introduced and commercial exchanges are the norm, a merchant will engage in several exchanges a day. A merchant does not expect to gain that much from one transaction, but from the volume of transactions. Cheating would be shooting themselves in the foot. Others would know they are not honest dealers and would not want to deal with them. They stand to lose a lot from dishonesty, given the amount of transactions they are expecting to do – that is, in today's jargon, given the repeated nature of the game. Probity thus emerges as a virtue when there is a change in the opportunity cost of cheating. The more frequent the exchanges, the higher is the cost of cheating, as one would lose the small gain from each transaction, which amounts, cumulatively, to a lot. The fewer the transactions, the lower is the cost of cheating, because the gain from cheating more than compensates for the loss of another transaction in the very distant future.

A dealer is afraid of losing his character, and is scrupulous in observing every engagement. When a person makes perhaps 20 contracts in a day, he cannot gain so much by endeavouring to impose on his neighbours, as the very appearance of a cheat would make him lose. Where people seldom deal with one another, we find that they are somewhat disposed to cheat, because they can gain more by a smart trick than they can lose by the injury which it does their character. They whom we call politicians are not the most remarkable men in the world for probity and punctuality. Ambassadors from different nations are still less so: they are praised for any little advantage they can take, and pique themselves a good deal on this degree of refinement. The reason of this is that nations treat with one another not above twice or thrice in a century, and they may gain more by one piece of fraud than (lose) by having a bad character. France has had this character with us ever since the reign of Lewis XIVth, yet it has never in the least hurt either its interest or splendour.

But if states were obliged to treat once or twice a day, as merchants do, it would be necessary to be more precise in order to preserve their character. Wherever dealings are frequent, a man does not expect to gain so much by any one contract as by probity and punctuality in the whole, and a prudent dealer, who is sensible of his real interest, would rather chuse to lose what he has a right to than give any ground for suspicion. Every thing of this kind is [as] odious as it is rare. When the greater part of people are merchants they always bring probity and punctuality into fashion, and these therefore are the principal virtues of a commercial nation.[6]

According to Smith, the Dutch are the most honest people in his time, because they are the most commercial. There is nothing in their nature that renders them different from the people of other nations.[7] It is just that an increase in the opportunity cost of cheating has changed the habits and practices of the people.

This logic of looking at changes in opportunity cost to understand changes in morals is a constant explanation throughout Smith's work.[8] In the *Wealth of Nations* (1776), for example, Smith tells us that in societies where there is enough wealth to have wealth inequality, we observe two parallel systems of morality: an austere system of morality for the poor, and a loose system of morality for the rich.[9] The rich indulge in excesses and extravagant behaviours and are not disapproved of for that. On the contrary, extravagances and excesses are expected from people of their rank – but not from the poor. The poor have a strict moral system that values and approves firm austerity, vehemently condemning any excesses. Smith is not making any judgement on this difference in system of morals; he is simply stating it and explaining it. The consequences of excessive behaviours on the rich are imperceptible. Their wealth is such that their extravagances will dent their standard of living only after several years. On the other hand, the consequences of excessive behaviour on the poor are devastating, and are so immediately. Some debaucheries will destroy the poor and their family in a few days. It follows that the poor abhor extravagances and the rich accept them.

> The vices of levity are always ruinous to the common people, and a single week's thoughtlessness and dissipation is often sufficient to undo a poor workman for ever, and to drive him through despair upon committing the most enormous crimes. The wiser and better sort of the common people, therefore, have always the utmost abhorrence and detestation of such excesses, which their experience tells them are so immediately fatal to people of their condition. The disorder and extravagance of several years, on the contrary, will not always ruin a man of fashion, and people of that rank are very apt to consider the power of indulging in some degree of excess as one of the advantages of their fortune, and the liberty of doing so without censure or reproach, as one of the privileges which belong to their station. In people of their own station, therefore, they regard such excesses with but a small degree of disapprobation, and censure them either very slightly or not at all.[10]

Smith's logic is strictly rational: the cost of excesses is little for the rich, so they will tolerate, if not even expect, such excesses. The cost for the poor is extremely high, so they tolerate none and condemn that kind of behaviour as highly immoral.

Infanticide is another example of how a different opportunity cost changes what is morally valued. This example is present both in *The Wealth of Nations* and in *The Theory of Moral Sentiments* (1759). In Smith's own Introduction to *The Wealth of Nations*, he notes that there are some societies in which poverty is so pervasive that exposing children is the accepted practice:

> Such nations, however, are so miserably poor, that, from mere want, they are frequently reduced, or, at least, think themselves reduced, to the necessity sometimes of directly destroying, and sometimes of abandoning their infants, their old people, and those afflicted with lingering diseases, to perish with hunger, or to be devoured by wild beasts.[11]

Indeed, he reiterates in Book I, among the poorest groups in China, not only is the practice of abandoning children in ditches well accepted, but there are also acceptable professions dealing with the disposal of children by drowning them like unwanted puppies: 'In China . . . in all great towns several are every night exposed in the street, or drowned like puppies in the water. The performance of this horrid office is even said to be the avowed business by which some people earn their subsistence.'[12]

Not only do these practices generally disappear with the increased wealth in societies, but they are also condemned as morally unacceptable. If in a prosperous society the practice of discharging unwanted children persists, as a nonsensical appendix, such as in commercial ancient Greece, Smith has no hesitation in attacking it as morally repugnant:

> The extreme indigence of a savage is often such that he himself is fre-quently exposed to the greatest extremity of hunger, he often dies of pure want, and it is frequently impossible for him to support both him-self and his child. We cannot wonder, therefore, that in this case he should abandon it. One who, in flying from an enemy, whom it was impossible to resist, should throw down his infant, because it retarded his flight, would surely be excusable; since, by attempting to save it, he could only hope for the consolation of dying with it. That in this state of society, therefore, a parent should be allowed to judge whether he can bring up his child, ought not to surprise us so greatly. In the latter ages of Greece, however, the same thing was permitted from views of remote interest or conveniency, which could by no means excuse it.[13]

Smith's logic is the same: when the cost of supporting every child is high, infanticide is 'more pardonable' than when the cost of supporting every child is low.[14]

The Theory of Moral Sentiments offers other examples of changes of opportunity costs leading to changes in moral acceptance and appropriate virtues. A striking example is the substitution of the virtue of self-command with the virtue of humanity. Smith tells us that in a 'boisterous storm' the virtue of self-command is very much approved. It consists in suppressing all expressions of emotion. This facilitates addressing the life-threating dangers of the storms of life. On the other hand, the virtue of humanity flourishes in the 'mild sunshine'. The virtue of humanity, for Smith, is the free exchange of our passions, expressed at the pitch approved by an impartial spectator of course:

> The situations in which the gentle virtue of humanity can be most happily cultivated, are by no means the same with those which are best fitted for forming the austere virtue of self-command. The man who is himself at ease can best attend to the distress of others. The man who is himself exposed to hardships is most immediately called upon to attend to, and to control his own feelings. In the mild sunshine of undisturbed tranquility, in the calm retirement of undissipated and philosophical leisure, the soft virtue of humanity flourishes the most, and is capable of the highest improvement. But, in such situations, the greatest and noblest exertions of self-command have little exercise. Under the boisterous and stormy sky of war and faction, of public tumult and confusion, the sturdy severity of self-command prospers the most, and can be the most successfully cultivated. But, in such situations, the strongest suggestions of humanity must frequently be stifled or neglected; and every such neglect necessarily tends to weaken the principle of humanity. As it may frequently be the duty of a soldier not to take, so it may sometimes be his duty not to give quarter; and the humanity of the man who has been several times under the necessity of submitting to this disagreeable duty, can scarce fail to suffer a considerable diminution. For his own ease, he is too apt to learn to make light of the misfortunes which he is so often under the necessity of occasioning; and the situations which call forth the noblest exertions of self-command, by imposing the necessity of violating sometimes the property, and sometimes the life of our neighbour, always tend to diminish, and too often to extinguish altogether, that sacred regard to both, which is the foundation of justice and humanity. It is upon this account, that we so frequently find in the world men of great humanity who have little self-command, but who are indolent and irresolute, and easily

disheartened, either by difficulty or danger, from the most honourable pursuits; and, on the contrary, men of the most perfect self-command, whom no difficulty can discourage, no danger appal, and who are at all times ready for the most daring and desperate enterprises, but who, at the same time, seem to be hardened against all sense either of justice or humanity.[15]

The trade-off between humanity and self-command is loud and clear in Smith. When self-command dominates, humanity is lacking; and, vice versa, where humanity flourishes, self-command is weak.[16] Why? Think of a soldier on a battlefield whose leg is being blown off by a cannon shot.[17] What if he did not have self-command? What if he started to express his pain and fears and expected the pleasure of mutual sympathy from others? He would jeopardise the life of his fellow soldiers. The cost of the virtue of humanity is too high on a battlefield. You should not expect it. Indeed, what we commonly observe and praise in battle is the virtue of self-command. On the other hand, in the tranquillity and security of a commercial society, where the cost of properly expressing and thus sharing our emotions is low, the virtue of humanity can flourish without any catastrophic repercussions. To the contrary, the virtue of humanity, with the low cost of expressing and sharing emotions, allows for the pleasure of mutual sympathy, which would be absent with the lack of expression of emotions that self-command implies.[18]

What this means is that changes in circumstances change what is deemed morally appropriate. The system of virtues of antiquity, mostly based on (martial) courage and self-command no longer works in a commercial society.[19] But this does not imply that a commercial society is left in a virtue vacuum or becomes immoral. Its virtues adapt to the new circumstances.

And so we arrive at the virtue of punctuality: how does Smith explain the means by which punctuality evolves into a commercial virtue?

In his analysis of military might in pre-commercial societies, Smith notes that in agricultural societies raising an army is easy and cheap. Men are accustomed to the hardship of the weather by working in the fields, and, most importantly, they can leave the fields without any major economic consequences during the non-harvesting times. They have plenty of leisure time and can thus easily engage in military exercises. Shepherds have even more leisure time and can do even more military exercises. Not surprisingly they are, according to Smith, much better soldiers:

The hardiness of their ordinary life prepares them for the fatigues of war, to some of which their necessary occupations bear an analogy. The necessary occupation of a ditcher prepares him to work in the trenches, and to fortify a camp as well as to enclose a field. The ordinary pastimes of such husbandmen are the same as those of shepherds, and are in the same manner the images of war. But as husbandmen have less leisure than shepherds, they are not so frequently employed in those pastimes. They are soldiers, but soldiers not quite so much masters of their exercise.[20]

Things are different with 'artificers' – that is, the artisans – in commercial societies. Artificers have no free time. Every hour an artificer does not work is an hour in which he does not earn his source of subsistence. Doing military exercises is thus very expensive for him. This is why for Smith commercial societies have the worst militias and should rely on a professional army instead:[21]

> Though a husbandman should be employed in an expedition, provided it begins after seed-time and ends before harvest, the interruption of his business will not always occasion any considerable diminution of his revenue. Without the intervention of his labour, nature does herself the greater part of the work which remains to be done. But the moment that an artificer, a smith, a carpenter, or a weaver, for example, quits his workhouse, the sole source of his revenue is completely dried up. Nature does nothing for him, he does all for himself. When he takes the field, therefore, in defence of the publick, as he has no revenue to maintain himself.[22]

Now, use the same logic of change in opportunity costs to analyse punctuality. In pre-commercial society time is abundant. There is little one can do while nature takes its course between seeding and harvesting. Being late or on time makes no difference, because the opportunity forgone is almost non-existent. But when one does not depend on nature for one's subsistence, but on one's own labour, like an artificer in a commercial society, then one's time becomes more valuable. Having to wait for someone who is late means wasting the opportunity to produce something else which would contribute to one's life. Time becomes valuable. And when time is valuable, punctuality becomes a virtue. Being on time is an approvable conduct because it implies the recognition of the value of someone else's time, and thus a sign of respecting the other person.

Furthermore, in a commercial society, a hungry person would get their dinner by buying it from a butcher, a baker and a brewer, not through begging like a dog at the feet of their master.[23] Commercial exchanges bring all people to the same level. Everybody has equal dignity. Punctuality implies the same equalising mentality. By being on time one recognises that others are equal to you, as one's own time is not more valuable than someone else's, in the sense of the one's dignity is equal to every other person's dignity.

Dr Berry's answer was thus appropriate. Teaching his children the virtue of punctuality is to teach them to respect other people and other people's work. Punctuality, as Smith teaches us, is indeed a commercial virtue, a virtue that emerges when the opportunity cost of time rises, and when each individual acquires equal dignity through exchange.

Notes

1. On Berry's analysis of the role of luxury and commercial society on morality see, among others: Christopher J. Berry, *The Idea of Luxury: A Conceptual and Historical Investigation* (Cambridge: Cambridge University Press, 1994); *The Idea of Commercial Society in the Scottish Enlightenment* (Edinburgh: Edinburgh University Press, 2013) and 'Adam Smith and the Virtues of a Modern Economy', in *Essays on Hume, Smith and the Scottish Enlightenment* (Edinburgh: Edinburgh University Press, 2018), pp. 347–63.
2. Adam Smith, *Lectures on Jurisprudence*. ed. Ronald L. Meek, David Daiches Raphael and Peter Stein (Indianapolis: Liberty Fund, 1987 [1762]), B, p. 326).
3. See Smith, *Lectures on Jurisprudence*, B, p. 326 for a general discussion of commercial virtues; see also Deirdre N. McCloskey, *The Bourgeois Virtues: Ethics for an Age of Commerce* (Chicago: University of Chicago Press, 2006).
4. On Smith as a virtue theorist, see among others: Deirdrie N. McCloskey, 'Adam Smith, the Last of the Former Virtue Ethicists', *History of Political Economy* 40:1 (2008), pp. 43–71; Ryan Patrick Hanley, *Adam Smith and the Character of Virtue* (New York: Cambridge University Press, 2009); Samuel Fleischacker, 'True to Ourselves? – Adam Smith on self-deceit', *Adam Smith Review* 6 (2011), pp. 75–92; Maria A. Carrasco, 'Adam Smith: Self-Command, Practical Reason and Deontological Insights', *British Journal for the History of Philosophy* 20:2 (2012), pp. 391–414; Jack Russell Weinstein, *Adam Smith's Pluralism: Rationality, Education, and the Moral Sentiments* (New Haven: Yale University Press, 2013); and Berry, *Hume, Smith.*
5. Maria Pia Paganelli, 'Adam Smith on the Future of Experimental Evolution and Economics', *Journal of Bioeconomics* 20:1 (2018), pp. 23–8.
6. Smith, *Jurisprudence*, B, pp. 327–8.
7. Smith, *Jurisprudence*, B, p. 236.
8. See Paganelli, *Smith on Experimental Evolution.*
9. Adam Smith, *An Inquiry into the Nature and Causes of the Wealth of Nations*, ed. Roy Hutcheson Campbell, Andrew S. Skinner and W. B. Todd (Indianapolis: Liberty Fund 1976 [1776], V.i.g.10, p. 794.
10. Smith, *Wealth of Nations* V.i.g.10, p. 794.

11. Smith, *Wealth of Nations* Intro. 4, p. 10.

12. Smith, *Wealth of Nations* I.viii.24, p. 89.

13. Smith, *Moral Sentiments* V.2.15, p. 210.

14. Maria Pia Paganelli, '240 Years of Adam Smith's Wealth of Nations', *Nova Economia* 27:2 (2017), pp. 7–19; Berry, *Commercial Society*.

15. Smith, *Moral Sentiments* III.3.37, p. 153.

16. Maria Pia Paganelli, 'Is Adam Smith's Impartial Spectator Selfless?' *Econ Journal Watch* 13:2 (2017), pp. 319–23; Leonidas Montes, 'Adam Smith as an Eclectic Stoic', *Adam Smith Review* 4 (2008), pp. 30–56.

17. Smith, *Moral Sentiments* I.3.26, p. 147.

18. Maria Pia Paganelli, 'Boys Do Cry: Adam Smith on Wealth and Expressing Emotions', *Journal of Scottish Philosophy* 15:1 (2017), pp. 1–8; Michele Bee and Maria Pia Paganelli, 'Adam Smith Anti-Stoic', *History of European Ideas* 45:4 (2019), pp. 572–84.

19. Berry, *Hume, Smith*.

20. Smith, *Wealth of Nations* V.I.a.6, p. 693.

21. Maria Pia Paganelli and Reinhard Schumacher, 'Do Not Take Peace for Granted: Adam Smith's Warning on the Relation between Commerce and War', *Cambridge Journal of Economics* 43:3 (2018), pp. 785–97; Leonidas Montes, 'Adam Smith on the Standing Army Versus Militia Issue: Wealth over Virtue?', in Jeffrey T. Young (ed.), *The Elgar Companion to Adam Smith* (Cheltenham, UK: Edward Elgar 2009), pp. 315–34.

22. Smith, *Wealth of Nations* V.I.a.9, pp. 694–5.

23. See Smith, *Wealth of Nations* WN I.ii.2, p. 26.

8

Civility and Slavery: The Problematic Basis of Civilised Society in Hume's *History of England*[1]

Naohito Mori

Introduction

This chapter reconsiders David Hume's complex and contested idea of civilisation, with special emphasis on his enigmatic phrase binding together 'civility and slavery' in *The History of England* (1754–61). I shall explore Hume's problematic thinking that barbarous nations had to be subject to the dominion of the civilised if the former was to be civilised as well, and that this conjunction between civility and slavery was the cornerstone of European civilisation in his day. By doing so, I hope to offer a tentative reinterpretation of the often discussed relationship between Hume and Enlightenment.

As Christopher Berry comprehensively shows, Hume and his Scottish fellows advocate values of civilisation incorporated in the idea of commercial society, such as the rule of law, liberty and civility.[2] Their advocacy interestingly lacks serious political discussion, though Hume is somewhat exceptional in his theoretical and practical engagements with the politics of his time.[3] As we shall see, Hume's phrase 'civility and slavery' appears where he illustrates the Roman conquest of the ancient European nations, and suggests that those nations were first civilised by that conquest.[4] This illustration can be reasonably considered as a test case for what Berry calls the 'politics of a commercial society', regarding Hume's contemporary issue on how to 'civilise' the Highlands or how to bring about a commercial society there.[5] I will argue that the phrase 'civility and slavery' tells us much about Hume's version of the politics of a commercial society, and that he problematically thinks a commercial society and the rule of law need slavish subordination to the sovereign.

This chapter is divided into five sections. First, I shall lay out selected interpretations of Hume's idea of civilisation and its relationship with Enlightenment. Second, I will sketch Hume's harsh and controversial

argument on how to 'civilise' Ireland in his *History*. Third, I shall compare his argument on Ireland with its source, the account by the English
Jacobean politician John Davies (1569–1629), in order to examine what
Hume intends in his narratives and where he deviates from Davies. The
fourth section focuses on the strange and troubling phrase 'civility and
slavery'. I shall explore what Hume means by this phrase through comparisons with three relevant authors: James Macpherson, Davies again, and
Tacitus. Fifth, based on the foregoing arguments, I shall try to reconsider
our understanding of Hume's idea of civilisation.

1 Selected Literature on Hume's View of Civilisation

In this section, I will focus on some major studies of Hume's idea of civilisation. Since these studies centre on his arguments concerning commercial
development and the rule of law, which are essential ideas of Enlightenment, I shall further consider a few works on Hume and Enlightenment.

Studies on Hume's View of Commerce and Laws

Hume's socio-politico-economic analysis of the civilising effect of 'commerce'
has received wide-ranging commentary.[6] Commerce encourages industrious
living by circulating luxurious goods and stimulating desires for those goods.
That lifestyle in turn entails progress in mechanical and liberal arts, which further promotes multifaceted developments of human society including laws,
governments, and political liberty. Hume writes '[t]hus *industry, knowledge,*
and *humanity*, are linked together by an indissoluble chain, and are found . . .
to be peculiar to the more polished, and, what are commonly denominated,
the more luxurious ages.'[7] Thus, commerce and luxury are the most significant springs of the 'civilising' process in Hume's thinking.

It is widely admitted that the crucial precondition for this civilising process in Hume's view is the impersonal administration of laws by a regular,
centralised government.[8] With regard to the emergence of this rule of law,
we can discern two different stories in his thought. One is endogenous, the
other exogenous. According to Hume's *History*, when the habit of luxury
arose in England, the feudal barons abandoned their retainers in order to
enjoy the newly created luxurious goods by themselves, which shifted the
balance of power to the crown first, and then eventually to the Commons.[9]
In this process, the crown established a universal legal system, and the
Commons later limited the arbitrariness of its administration.[10]

Commentators have also paid attention to the other story, namely,
Hume's argument on the transplantation of laws, which first appears in his

Essays, Moral and Political (1741–2). Hume writes that it is utterly impossible for barbarous monarchies to civilise themselves, as 'no improvement can ever be expected in the sciences, in the liberal arts, in laws, and scarcely in the manual arts and manufactures', but laws can be borrowed from republics and transplanted into monarchies.[11] In Duncan Forbes's influential study, the idea of European monarchies, which are civilised by borrowing laws, constitutes the core of Hume's 'scientific Whiggism'. Based on this idea, Forbes argues, Hume attacked the 'vulgar' Whiggism prevalent then, which exclusively connected (the French) monarchy with despotism, and the (English) mixed constitution with liberty.[12]

This story of civilisation through transplantation of laws also appears in Hume's *History*. Both Hajime Inuzuka and Andrew Sabl emphasise that the Justinian Code plays a crucial role in Hume's claim, in Sabl's words, that 'many praiseworthy parts of English law had foreign origins' and the most famous origin was 'Justinian's code'.[13] Actually, Hume stresses the significance of Justinian's Code for the civilisation of Europe. In his famous illustration of 'the dawn of *civility* and sciences'[14] in Europe, he insists that what brought the 'full morning' in the fifteenth century was, among other causes, the finding of 'Justinian's Pandect'.[15] Although this reading should be annotated with Hume's nuanced differentiation of the English law from Continental law, it can be safely argued that the transplantation of laws is another significant cause that enables the civilising process in Hume's view.[16]

Studies on Hume and Enlightenment

Hume's idea of civilisation consists of the rule of law (either endogenous or exogenous) and commercial development. This leads us to consider the relationship between Hume and Enlightenment, since law and commerce constitute a significant part of what we call Enlightenment.[17] Recent studies pay considerable attention to some moderately sceptical aspects of Hume's Enlightenment thinking. Berry notes, for example, that the Scottish thinkers put some caveats on their own views on commercial society. Even the most confident advocates like Hume and Adam Smith paint a dismal picture on the darker side of that society. The dangers posed by luxury, the standing army and division of labour are the focal points of their worries, and for Hume the expansion of public credit is most striking.[18] However, as a whole, it is concluded that the Scottish thinkers (Hume included) were 'cautiously optimistic' on these issues.[19]

James Harris focuses on Hume's doubt about zeal for the reformation of religion and politics. He writes Hume's 'account of human nature, with

its subversion of the authority of reason, and its case for belief in general as
being a function of feeling not rationality, cast doubt on the very possibility
of enlightened reform and improvement'.[20] Yet, Harris thinks that Hume
should be seen as playing a part for another element of Enlightenment.
Hume intended to invite the readers to 'a certain kind of discursive space',
to 'a kind of conversation'. Thus, Hume's 'task as a man of letters was to
be part of the effort to bring that conversation, the conversation that we
call the Enlightenment, into existence'.[21]

As the title of Ryu Susato's book *Hume's Sceptical Enlightenment* shows,
Susato emphasises the sceptical aspect of Hume's Enlightenment, too.
Having examined several influential Enlightenment studies, Susato puts
forward his own working definition by shifting from 'Enlightenment' as a
project to Enlightenment as 'a shared sensitivity . . . to the on-going process of civilisation' and 'a series of questions and issues . . . based on this
historical awareness'.[22] The core of his Sceptical Enlightenment is then
illustrated as an anti-dogmatic endorsement of modern Epicureanism and
self-sceptical advocacy of modern commercial society.[23]

The latter two commentators concur on Hume's scepticism regarding
what we call the Enlightenment project and on continuing to read him as
an Enlightenment thinker in a significant sense. What is maintained as the
essence of Hume's Enlightenment is his advocacy for a society where various goods and ideas are exchanged freely and peacefully. As Berry illustrates,
this exchange is enabled by an impersonal legal system. In the later sections, I shall try to extend the sceptical aspect along with another definition
of Enlightenment. Pocock argues that this sphere of laws and commerce
must be supported by a potentially despotic power. Before moving on, let me
briefly focus on that definition in his 2005 collection of essays.

Pocock's Ironical Definition of Enlightenment

In *The Discovery of Islands*, Pocock defines Enlightenment, 'while remem-
bering that other definitions are possible and useful', as 'a programme for
bringing both war and religion into a system of civil society, based on sovereign government and international commerce'.[24] This programme is carried out through the rise of the standing army, supported by the system
of public credit, and the consequent shift of the sword from individuals
into the hand of 'Leviathan'. Pocock writes that this historical change was
made possible by a long-term social change, namely, the growth in commerce and culture.[25] In this historical explanation, once the individual
lost his own land and sword and became a mere 'generator of wealth and
credit . . . the sword might be borne by an agent other than himself, whom

he could pay Leviathan to pay for him'.[26] Thus, a commercial and luxurious society, with a standing army and public credit, was something that deprived the individuals of their independent ability to check the sovereign. Commerce and luxury are what established Leviathan.

Pocock illustrates the deprivation of individuals and the establishment of Leviathan, the changes which reoriented those individuals to 'other ends and values', as considerably relevant to his definition of Enlightenment.[27] He calls those deprived 'the individuals of Enlightenment', whose 'modern' characteristics were 'defined by theorists following Defoe as 'manners', 'politeness', 'taste' and other terms denoting an increased capacity for civilised intercourse in a society increasingly commercial, urban and reliant on the exchange of goods, ideas and cultural traits.'[28] 'Other terms' may well include 'civility', which, though somewhat older and more complicated, is at least an equally significant word that denoted civilised communication up to the middle of the eighteenth century.[29]

Thus, there is a significant sense in which Enlightenment indicates a world where something has been substantially lost. It is a world where the sword is transferred decisively from individuals to Leviathan. Leviathan, now armed with a standing army and funded through public credit, is able to command those individuals who are completely subordinate to it, and by this means the whole system of law can be enforced upon them.[30] At first blush, this sense of history does not look like Hume's, but much more like that of Adam Ferguson, whose *An Essay on the History of Civil Society* famously disappointed his friend Hume.[31] I believe, though, that the complicated composition of Hume's *History* involves full recognition of the relevance of that sense of history, although he does not choose to highlight it as Ferguson does. Hume's enigmatic phrase 'civility and slavery' encapsulates that sense. In the next section, I will sketch his aggressive narratives on Ireland, which encompass the phrase at issue.

2 Civilising through Conquest: Hume's Problematic Narratives on Ireland

Hume's problematic narratives on Ireland seem to constitute a part of his view on barbarism and civilisation. From the outset of Volume 1 of the modern edition of his *History* (although this was the volume published last together with Volume 2 in 1761),[32] Hume delivers a clear contrast between barbarism and civilisation, and goes so far as to say that 'it is rather fortunate for letters that they [barbarous ages] are buried in silence and oblivion.'[33] This disdainful attitude towards barbarity appears wherever he narrates confrontations between the 'barbaric' and the 'more civilised'. In these confrontations,

Hume exhibits his view of conquest and colonisation as the vehicle of improvement and civilisation. Among these, let me first focus on the Roman conquest over the ancient Britons, and then the English over the Irish.

The Ancient Britons and the Romans

Hume plainly illustrates the Britons before the Roman conquest as barbarians. In his view, they lacked laws and industry, and had a strong inclination towards superstition; it was the Roman conquest that brought a more civilised manner of life to them. Hume writes that Jurius Agricola:

> introduced *laws and civility* among the Britons, taught them to desire and raise all the conveniencies of life, reconciled them to the Roman language and manners, instructed them in letters and science, and *employed every expedient to render those chains, which he had forged, both easy and agreeable to them.*[34]

Although those elements of civilisation were brought to the Britons for the sake of the conquerors, Hume favours this civilising conquest. The ancient Britons were later conquered by the Saxons invading Britain. Hume describes this event as a conquest of the civilised by the barbarous. 'The Britons, under the Roman dominion, had made such advances towards arts and civil manners ... But the fierce conquerors, by whom they were now subdued, threw every thing back into ancient barbarity.'[35] These passages show Hume's favourable stance towards conquest when it brings laws, civility and a polished lifestyle.[36] He values the advancements of the Britons in these regards, in spite of the fact that they were brought about for the conquerors' sake. This evaluation applies to the case of the modern Irish.

The Irish and the English (or Scottish)

Hume's problematic narratives on the Irish have attracted several commentators' attention. As early as 1985, Hiroshi Takemoto enquired into Hume's narratives of the Irish rebellion (which will not be discussed in the present chapter), the responses they entailed among several Irish thinkers, and Hume's reply to those responses. Takemoto insightfully suggests the relevance of the Irish and Scottish contexts to reconsideration of Hume's Enlightenment thinking. Sabl also finds in Hume's narratives an aggressive aspect of Hume's 'civilisation' to justify domination over barbarous nations.[37] Eric Schliesser contrasts Hume's unreserved justification of the English rule over Ireland with Smith's more moderate thinking. Schliesser illustrates that

Smith, 'unlike Hume', does not favour 'violent extension' of civilisation, but favours only its peaceable extension, like political union between Ireland and Great Britain.[38] Schliesser also offers an evidence that Smith is critical of Hume's (problematically Anglocentric) view of the Irish massacre.[39] In addition, Luke Gibbons considers Hume as playing a part in racial discourses on the Irish.[40] Berry finds in Hume's narratives of Ireland a key to analysing his probable attitude towards the contemporary issue concerning how to 'civilise' the Highlands, which is an issue of the 'politics of a commercial society'.[41]

Hume repeatedly describes the Irish as a barbarous nation and has no hesitation in justifying the English conquest and colonisation of the Irish in order to civilise them.[42] To give an example, Hume favours James I in carrying out his task to 'civilise' the Irish successfully:[43]

> After the subjection of Ireland by Elizabeth, *the more difficult task* still remained; *to civilize the inhabitants, to reconcile them to laws and industry, and to render their subjection durable and useful to the crown of England.* James proceeded in this work by a steady, regular, and well-concerted plan . . . It was previously necessary to abolish the Irish customs, which supplied the place of laws, and which were calculated to keep that people *for ever in a state of barbarism and disorder.*[44]

Hume then explains some details of the Irish customs and narrates how James I replaced them with English laws and regular administration.[45]

Remarkably, the 'regular' administration includes putting Ireland under England's military control, withdrawing the rights of semi-independent administration formerly given to the Irish lords, confiscating all private estates, and restoring them afterwards with restrictions.[46] Although, as we shall see, Hume illustrates those policies as having been designed to restrict the tyranny of the Irish lords, the following description of Ulster is further perplexing to the retrospective eyes of modern readers. He writes that the whole province of Ulster was confiscated and distributed by the crown to the planters from England and Scotland, and '[h]usbandry and the arts were taught' to the Irish there. Consequently, 'Ulster, from being the most wild and disorderly province of all Ireland, soon became *the best cultivated and most civilized*', and to sum up, '[s]uch were the arts, by which James introduced *humanity and justice* among the people, who had ever been buried in the most profound barbarism. *Noble cares!*'[47] The last exclamation would almost look sarcastic. Hume's contemporaries, however, discussed equally violent policies in order to 'civilise' the Highlands after the '45, and the acts were passed to deprive the clan chiefs of their independent authorities.[48] This context probably invalidates that appearance.[49]

This point touches on a problematic aspect of the politics of establishing a commercial society. Berry infers that a possible lesson that Hume would suggest through his illustration of the Irish is that the civilising process based on a newly introduced legal system would take time and would not have an immediate effect. It is legitimately supposed here that, for Hume and his fellow Scots, the issue was precisely *how* to civilise the Irish/Highlanders.[50] Yet, it seems a question worth asking whether it is justifiable or not, in order to reconsider the nature of the literati's view on civilisation. An enquiry into Hume's possible answer, through a comparison of his narratives with a few historical writings before and after his, constitutes the next stage of my argument.

3 Comparison with Davies's *Discoverie*: Hume's intention and divergence

The footnotes added to Hume's harsh narratives on the Irish barbarism show that he relies, among other sources, on John Davies's *A discoverie of the true causes why Ireland was never entirely subdued, nor brought under obedience of the crowne of England, until the beginning of His Majesties happie raigne*.[51] In this section, I shall refer to this text to examine which parts among Hume's narratives are common with Davies's, and which are distinctively his own.

John Davies (baptised in 1569 and died in 1629) was a lawyer, poet, the solicitor-general of Ireland from 1603, and then its attorney-general from 1606 until 1619. He is the central figure who carried out the abolishment of the former Irish customs and the establishment of the English laws and sovereignty, which later led to 'the collapse of Gaelic society in Ireland'.[52] His narratives of the Irish 'barbarity' and its causes in *Discoverie* exerted influence on English writers thereafter and, to some extent, even on the Irish ones,[53] and his conquest doctrine laid out therein was used to justify the English rule of Ireland. Davies's narratives provide an additional reason to think that Hume's praise for James is genuine. His narratives also show that for him, and presumably for Hume too, 'conquest' is something more positive and profitable even to the conquered than our modern mindset perceives. A comparison of the two authors further indicates Hume's distinctive view of the Irish 'barbarism', which casts a light into what he means by the strange phrase 'civility and slavery'.

Davies's View of the Irish, and His Case for the 'Perfect Conquest'

Davies contends that the 'perfect conquest' of the barbarous Irish should bring civility to them. The conquered people must be entirely broken, just as the soil must be ploughed in order to be well cultivated.[54] He describes the Irish as 'rude and barbarous'[55] and provides detailed and penetrating analyses of peculiar Irish customs, which he finds to be the most barbarous in the world.[56] Specifically, he criticises the punishment by fines for serious crimes like murder, the abusive rules of property and succession with consequent instability of property, and legitimatised plunder by soldiers.[57] Thus, he writes,

> if wee confider the Nature of the Irifh Cuftomes, wee fhall finde that the people which doth vfe them, muft of neceffitie bee Rebelles to all good Gouernment, deftroy the commonwealth wherein they liue, and bring Barbarifm and defolation vpon the richeft and moft fruitfull Land of the world.[58]

In comparison with Hume, as we shall see, it is remarkable that Davies thinks most Irish customs were peculiar to them. The latter writes that their unstable rules of property 'hath bin the true caufe of fuch Defolation & Barbarifm in this land, *as the like was neuer feen in any Countrey, that profeffed the name of Chrift*'[59] and the worst custom of plunder by the soldiers 'was *originally Irifh*'.[60]

Davies, on the other hand, vigorously criticises the defects of the English rule. Besides their misconduct in the martial affairs, which hindered the full conquest, he denounces their civil policies, which he thinks perpetuated the rebellions and wars in Ireland. Even when he illustrates the destructive nature of the Irish customs, we are told that those customs became much worse when exploited by the English lords. The English, especially, did not enforce the English laws on the Irish, so that the ordinary Irish people were outside the protection of the laws, and rather treated as the enemies.[61]

> Whereby it is manifeft, that fuch as had the Gouernment of Ireland vnder the Crowne of England, did intend to make a perpetuall feparation and enmity betweene the Englifh and the Irifh; pretending (no doubt) that the Englifh fhould in the end roote out the Irifh: which the Englifh not being able to do, did caufe a perpetuall Warre betweene the nations . . .[62]

Thus, the perpetual turmoil in Ireland was caused by the English administration, not by the Irish barbarism (or not solely by it), in Davies's view.

We also have to pay attention to what he means by the word 'conquest'. He argues that, if the 'perfect conquest' had been achieved in

Ireland, it should have brought about the benefit of civilisation long before, and 'affuredly, the Irifh Countries had long fince beene reformed and reduced to Peace, Plenty, and *Ciuility, which are the effects of Lawes and good Gouernment . . .*'[63] Here, by the expression 'perfect conquest', he means not only full subjugation of the whole nation, but also equal and indiscriminating administration of laws. Immediately after the quotation above, he argues that the perfect conquest implies 'a perfect Vnion betwixt the Nations'.

> For the Conqueft is neuer perfect, till the war be at an end; and the war is not at an end till there be peace and vnity; and there can neuer be vnity & Concord in any one Kingdom, but where there is but one King, one Allegiance, and one Law.[64]

What prevented the establishment and administration of equal laws in Ireland was the malfunction of the distribution of the lands to, and self-interested behaviour of, the English lords. Since the kings of England gave such independent authority to those lords as palatines, they restrained the kings' jurisdiction and hindered the establishment of equal laws, under which their absolute authority over the native Irish should have been lost.[65]

In light of this argument of Davies, Hume can be seen as valuing James's Irish policy for the benefit of the common Irish (this probably provides his partial answer to the question on the legitimacy of the politics of a commercial society). This reading coincides with Hume's animosity against the local but arbitrary powers of the feudal barons, 'those disorderly and licentious tyrants', in his *History*.[66] Davies's view that the Irish customs were peculiar to them, on the other hand, indicates the difference between the two authors, as we shall see next.

Hume's Divergence from Davies's View of the Irish 'Barbarism'

Hume's illustration below indicates that, in contrast to Davies, he thinks that the 'barbarism' of the Irish is an instance of something general and universal, which other European nations once underwent and then overcame. The reason why the Irish still remain in that barbarity is, Hume writes, their lack of the Roman dominion:[67]

> The Irish, from the beginning of time, had been buried in the most profound barbarism and ignorance; and *as they were never conquered or even invaded by the Romans, from whom all the western world derived its civility,*

they continued still in the most rude state of society, and were distinguished by those vices alone, to which human nature, not tamed by education or restrained by laws, is for ever subject . . .[68]

Thus, in Hume's view, the watershed moment that divided the barbarous and the civilised in Western Europe was the Roman conquest, and the barbarity of the modern Irish once used to be universal among the European nations.

The citation above is not isolated. In the passage below, this time also referring to the defects of the English rule like Davies, Hume puts forward the same idea on barbarism and civilisation in Europe, through the phrase under discussion in this chapter:

> [b]y all this imprudent conduct of England, the natives of its dependent state [Ireland] remained still in the abject condition, *into which the northern and western parts of Europe were sunk, before they received civility and slavery from the refined policy and irresistible bravery of Rome.* Even at the end of the sixteenth century, when every christian nation was cultivating with ardour every civil art of life, that island . . . was . . . inhabited by a people, whose customs and manners approached nearer those of savages than of barbarians.[69]

This passage is another example of a clear conjunction between the Roman conquest and the beginning of the Western (and Northern) European civilisation, and the striking expression 'civility and slavery' encapsulates that conjunction.

This conjunction is remarkable in two ways. First, it suggests the point where Hume diverges from Davies. It is true that Davies also considers the Roman conquest as bringing about laws and prosperity.[70] He thinks, however, that the Irish barbarity is characteristic of the Irish, as we have seen. He does not consider that barbarity as common to the ancient Britons or other nations in Europe. Nor does he attribute the origin of European civilisation to the Roman dominion in the way that Hume does. For Davies, the Norman conquest of England and the English dominion over Wales are equally significant examples of beneficial conquest as the Roman conquest. He does not seem to privilege the Roman conquest in terms of dissemination of civilisation.[71]

Second, the phrase 'civility and slavery' also indicates the point where Hume deviates from one of the core values of Enlightenment. Liberty, or at least rejection of slavery, constitutes an essence of most definitions of Enlightenment. Berry writes, for example, 'any institutions such as slavery, torture, witchcraft or religious persecution . . . were to be opposed . . . as creatures of the night.'[72] Surely, the 'modern liberty' to which the Scottish thinkers subscribe is compatible with, or rather based on, allegiance to an established authority.[73] Hume indeed insists that it is this allegiance that distinguishes 'true liberty' – namely, modern liberty – from the barbarous licentiousness of the ancient Saxons.[74] Even so, slavery to conquerors is something far harder to be squared with the idea of liberty. Scottish thinkers widely (not entirely) shared the rejection of ancient liberty combined with a class of slaves, on the belief that the 'abolition of slavery was part of the civilising process brought on by the emergence of commerce'.[75] Hume's phrase, 'civility and slavery', is then considerably distinctive as well as enigmatic.

Thus, Hume deviates from Davies, and from most Enlightenment thinking on liberty, in his view that the European nations once underwent the Irish 'barbarity', and those nations overcame that barbarity through 'civility and slavery' brought about by the Romans. The next section examines what Hume precisely means by this phrase.

4 'Civility and Slavery': Its Usage and Meaning in Hume's and Other Historical Writings

The phrase 'civility and slavery' itself rarely appears in writings of Hume's time. According to the *Eighteenth Century Collections Online*, the only example other than in Hume's *History* appears in James Macpherson's *An introduction to the history of Great Britain and Ireland* (first published in 1771, although I will cite from the second edition published in 1772; hereafter abridged as *Introduction*).[76] In this section, I will try to show that both Hume and Macpherson correspondingly understand 'civility' to mean refined and attractive goods and ways of life, and 'slavery' to mean subservience to the political dominion in order to enjoy those goods and lifestyles, although they differ in their evaluations of this combination of civility and slavery. This reading will be further tried through comparison with similar wordings in Davies's *Discoverie* and Tacitus' *Agricola*.

As studies have shown, the word 'civility' has complicated, changing and interrelated meanings.[77] In addition, the relationship of civility with 'civilisation' was already controversial in Hume's time, as shown in the famous episode of Samuel Johnson's English dictionary reported by James Boswell. In his record on 23 March 1772, Boswell writes Johnson 'would not admit *civilization*, but only *civility*' to the fourth edition of *A Dictionary of the English Language*. Boswell himself thinks, though, that civilisation has an advantage in its clear sense opposite to 'barbarity', whereas civility contains two possible senses.[78] Now the *Oxford English Dictionary* provides three major meanings of civility, namely, 'citizenship and civil order', 'secularity' and 'culture and civilised behaviour', which are further subdivided into thirteen senses. Among these, 'observance of the principles of civil order; orderly behaviour', 'the state or condition of being civilised', and 'behaviour or speech appropriate to civil interaction; politeness, courtesy, and consideration' probably most fit into Hume's use.[79] Macpherson's *Introduction*, on the other hand, suggests another possible sense, though closely overlapping with the last one.

James Macpherson (1736–96) was a controversial writer well known for his Ossianic productions. He was acquainted with the Scottish thinkers in Edinburgh, such as Ferguson, John Home and Hugh Blair, the last of whom was heavily involved in the Ossian publications. After an unsuccessful time as a colonial official, in the 1770s Macpherson published three historical writings including *Introduction*, 'a work which had strong Celtic emphasis'.[80]

In this work, 'civility and slavery' appear as one of the significant causes of the decay of the Roman Empire. He describes '[t]he bad policy of Constantine and the *imbecility* which gradually arofe from advanced *civility and flavery*, though they were the great, were not the only, caufe of the ruin of Rome.'[81] Another passage (quoted below), which discusses the paradoxical continuation of the empire, shows what Macpherson means by this phrase:

> The *debility* which *tyranny and luxury* carried from Rome through all its dominions, even contributed, though the opinion is fingular, to the permanency and ftability of the empire. *The conquered nations, by being deprived of their arms, applied themfelves to thofe enervating arts which, by adminiftering to luxury, deprave when they polifh the human mind. Timid and habituated to fubmiffion, they fell in love with the tranquility of defpotifm*; and in a kind of determination to *continue flaves*, they became indifferent about title and virtues of their tyrant.[82]

Presumably, 'the debility' caused by 'tyranny and luxury' corresponds with 'the imbecility' entailed in 'civility and slavery' in the earlier citation. The words 'slavery' and 'tyranny' very likely correspond with Macpherson's depiction of the later Rome as 'absolute government', which was, in his view, despotism covered by the appearance of the old constitution of Rome.[83] In light of this, 'civility and slavery' can be seen as meaning luxury and tyranny, or despotism, in Macpherson's use.[84]

This course of argument reveals Macpherson's commitment to a then prevalent view of luxury. Luxury is the vehicle that weakened the public and martial spirit, and brought about despotism. As Berry summarises, Ferguson and Lord Kames were the most prominent advocates of this view of luxury among the Scottish thinkers, and Hume was certainly the most explicit critic.[85] It is no wonder that Macpherson, with his Highland background, his devotion to proto-Romantic writings, and his acquaintance with Ferguson, subscribes to this Fergusonian view of luxury and public spirit.

It is hard to establish whether Macpherson read Hume's *History* (though the popularity of the work suggests that he might have), and therefore whether by 'civility and slavery' they meant the same thing or not. The apparent difference between their modes of discourse also seems to make it harder to argue that they coincide in their usage of the phrase. To take just one example, Macpherson's emphasis on the corrupting effects of luxury conflicts diametrically with Hume's case for a luxurious and virtuous society.

This divide between them, though, does not necessarily exclude a possibility that they share the same understanding of the phrase, since conflicting discourses often have shared vocabularies or common goals. Studies show, for example, that the use of the language of politeness is not limited to the Whig thinkers,[86] or that conflicting authors during Queen Anne's reign sometimes use common languages to curb religious confrontations of the age.[87] We can see that Macpherson emphasises 'opinion' as the foundation of every government, in agreement with, if not directly following, Hume's hallmark argument.[88] In the remainder of this section, I would like to argue that Hume and Macpherson, when they employ the phrase 'civility and slavery', recognise the same object of luxury and servitude under the Roman dominion, whereas they make completely opposite judgements about it based on their contrasting goals. In order to support this reading, let me turn to two historical writings: Davies's *Discoverie* and Tacitus' *Agricola*. Although they do not use the phrase 'civility and slavery' itself, we can find similar (and presumably, in Tacitus' case, original) terms, with quite different judgements of civility and slavery.

Davies illustrates how the Romans were good at thoroughly and peacefully subjugating the conquered by their equal laws.[89] He continues to write:

> Therefore (*as Tacitus writeth*) Iulius Agricola the Romaine Generall in Britany, vfed this pollicy to make a *perfect Conqueft* of our Anceftours, the ancient Brittaines; They were (fayth he) rude, and difperfed; and therefore prone vpon euery occafion to make warre, but to induce

them by pleafure to quietneffe and reft, he exhorted them in priuate, and gaue them helps in common, to builde Temples, Houfes, and places of publique refort. The Noblemens fonnes, he tooke and inftructed in the Liberal Sciences, &c. . . . After that, the Roman Attire grew to be in account, and the Gowne to be in vfe among them; and fo by little and little they proceeded to curiofity & delicacies in Buildings, and furniture of Houfhold; in Bathes, and exquifite Banquets; and fo beeing come to *the heighth of Ciuility, they were thereby brought to an absolute fubjection.*[90]

Here, we can clearly discern the linkage between civility and slavery, in the sense of luxury and subjection. Davies also highly values Agricola's skilful exploitation of this linkage, as can be seen from his use of the phrase 'perfect Conqueft', which is his goal regarding policies in Ireland.

As Davies himself remarks, Tacitus' *Agricola* is his source for his description of those policies by the Roman general. The following citation from the modern translation of *Agricola* shows that Tacitus makes the linkage between luxury and subjection or civility and slavery probably clearer, though with different evaluation:

To induce a people, hitherto scattered, uncivilized and therefore prone to fight, to grow pleasurably inured to peace and ease, Agricola encouraged individuals and assisted communities to build temples, public squares and proper houses . . . Furthermore, he trained the sons of the leading men in the liberal arts . . . [O]ur national dress came into favour and the toga was everywhere to be seen. And so, they strayed into the enticements of vice – porticoes, baths, and sumptuous banquets. *In their Innocence they called this 'civilization', when in fact it was a part of their enslavement.*[91]

In contrast to Davies, Tacitus seems to illustrate the civilisation and enslavement in Britain rather bitterly, in concert with his positive evaluation of the German independence.[92]

Hume himself explicitly follows Tacitus in his description of Agricola, which we have seen above.[93] In view of these points, for the authors considered here, 'civility and slavery' commonly mean a luxurious lifestyle under the enslaving dominion of the Romans. This idea of civility and slavery presumably originated in Tacitus' *Agricola*, and was adopted by Davies, Hume and Macpherson. However, their judgements of the idea are divided. Tacitus, in spite of his admiration for his father-in-law, describes the policies of the Roman general in a comparably bitter tone.[94] Macpherson's narratives, while recognising its paradoxical effects to prolong the Roman Empire, suggest his strong antipathy against this idea. For Davies, on the other hand, this idea reveals the surest way to his ideal perfect conquest. It is clear that Hume subscribes to Davies's view.

This divide in their judgements further suggests, I believe, that it is not self-evident even in Hume's own time whether the policy of 'civility and slavery' was without any moral question, or whether the politics of a commercial society was legitimate or not. In the next section, I shall try to reconstruct Hume's possible answer to this normative issue.

5 Implications of This Reading of Hume's 'Civility and Slavery'

As we have seen, 'civility and slavery' encapsulates Hume's thinking on civilisation through conquest and colonisation. This phrase signifies a policy to enforce a legal system upon a subject people by enslaving them using both irresistible power and a fascinating luxurious lifestyle. The issue is how and to what extent can it be legitimate to abolish allegedly 'barbarous' customs and, instead, enforce laws and civility.

One would argue that this issue could be understood in the light of Hume's view of modern liberty. Modern liberty is based on allegiance to a central political power, and Hume values this 'true liberty' in contrast to the licentiousness of the ancient Germans. Though containing a serious predicament whether this 'allegiance' can be expanded to cover 'slavery' to conquerors (a point to be discussed later), this reading probably offers a key to Hume's possible thinking on this issue of legitimacy. Perhaps Hume emphasises the need for combining civility and slavery because of the licentiousness of the ancient Germans. He thinks that they were excessively independent people.[95] They were too independent to accommodate any established regular government. They did not know the benefit of obeying the political authority, that is, the benefit of living in a peaceful and orderly society. In that sense, they were licentious rather than liberal, and did not know the 'true liberty', which, in Hume's view, can be obtained only under the established political authority.[96] The civility and slavery enforced by Rome can be considered as a prerequisite to curb this excess liberty and to teach them the benefit of a society united under political authority.

This reading, however, has to be balanced by the rather favourable view of German liberty that Hume drops in his narrative on the fall of the Romans. He writes:

THE GOVERNMENT of the Germans . . . was always extremely free; and those fierce people, accustomed to independance and enured to arms, were more guided by persuasion than authority . . . The military despotism, which had taken place in the Roman empire . . . was unable to resist the vigorous efforts of a free people; and Europe, as from a new epoch, rekindled her ancient spirit, and shook off the *base servitude* to arbitrary will and authority . . .[97]

This passage seems to conflict with Hume's remark that only the civility and slavery of the Romans enabled the Europeans to leave their former barbarity. Given that this is a consciously embedded complication, I believe that Hume insinuates that the European liberty was once a synonym of barbarity, and then, only after being modified by Roman civility and slavery, had become persistent and flourishing.

If this is so, civilisation through the Roman conquest is, in his view, the prerequisite for all the other stories of civilisation. His brief comment in his last edition of *History* shows that he thinks the sovereign power must, to some extent, surpass any control upon it:

> it feems a neceffary, though perhaps a melancholy truth, that, in every government, the magiftrate muft either poffefs a large revenue and a military force, or enjoy fome difcretionary powers, in order to execute the laws, and fupport his own authority.[98]

Upon this basis, laws were enforced, then commerce, luxury and industry came to flourish, and Hume is no doubt in favour of this lawful, luxurious and polite society. This civilising process could not have occurred among the European nations without the 'civility and slavery' of the Roman dominion, as exemplified, in Hume's eyes, in the case of the Irish. Hume, here, sets forth the case for placing the cornerstone for the kind of civilisation that the other European nations now enjoy at the cost of independence and individual customs.

This understanding of the exchange of civility and slavery at the cost of independence, though, does not sufficiently answer the question of its legitimacy: who knows – and how – that the benefit of civilisation exceeds the cost of independence?[99] Is it not virtually an oxymoron to refer to modern liberty as liberty, if that liberty implies slavery under the dominion of conquerors? Perhaps there is no way to justify the concurrence of civility and slavery without falling into the dogmatism of thinking that the civilised are unconditionally superior to the barbarous. Schliesser points

out that, for Smith, this aggressive tendency for expansion is not an intrinsic feature of civilisation itself, but that of the European nations, that is,
their 'savage injustice'.[100] It seems to me that, for Hume, this is rather the
nature of European civilisation itself initiated by civility and slavery under
the Roman dominion. Probably, civility was to overwhelm slavery at last.
Both Hume's *Essays* and *History* detail the wide-ranging civilising effects
of luxury. But his 'melancholy truth' cited above may suggest that potential slavery lingers amid all the civilised societies in Europe. That being
the case, and if one's mindset has been cast and hallmarked in a political
society that was once barbarous and then civilised based on civility and
slavery, it might be an almost destined course of things, by the nature of
that mindset, for him or her to think that people that are still barbarous,
especially neighbouring ones, should be civilised through political slavery.
At least, one might need a deeply essential change in his or her civilised
nature in order to think in a different way from this course. I guess Hume's
possible answer to the question of legitimacy regarding the policy of a commercial society can be reconstructed in this way, although this reconstruc-
tion could be too tenuous.

In any case, Hume's view of civilisation encapsulated in the phrase
'civility and slavery' indicates quite an ironical aspect of his Enlightenment thinking. The modern civilised society with open, fair, refined and
comfortable communication of goods and ideas had to have at its root the
servitude closely tied to that very luxurious and refined way of life – an
irony which those thinkers like Ferguson, and Andrew Fletcher before
him, keenly expose. Hume does not highlight or criticise this irony, but
just identifies its presence at the basis of the structure and mindset of
the European civilisation. Here, Hume's version of Enlightenment coincides with what Pocock illustrates in his *Discovery of Islands* – advocacy
for the society in which to enjoy commercial development and cultural
refinement is inescapably connected to subservience to the now irresistible sword of Leviathan.

Conclusion

This chapter has examined Hume's problematic argument for civilising
the Irish through conquest, his enigmatic phrase 'civility and slavery', and
its relationship with his broader view regarding civilisation through laws
and commerce, comparing his narratives with those of Davies, Macpherson and Tacitus. A tentative conclusion is: first, that 'civility and slavery'
can be understood as a luxurious and polished way of life that makes
those who desire it submit to the ruler; second, in Hume's view, it was this

conjunction between civility and slavery that tamed the once barbarous and too independent European nations and, in so doing, placed the cornerstone of the civilising process in which the laws and commerce should play their roles.

This reading of Hume's Enlightenment thinking may have further implications. Jonathan Israel writes at the outset of his influential book that 'neither the Enlightenment itself, and still less its consequences, were limited to Europe'.[101] As a non-European (or non-'Western') student of early modern intellectual history, I fully agree with Israel's view, though with some reservations. The rational, secular and democratic aspects of Enlightenment, as Israel illustrates, have fascinated many non-Western intellectuals up to the present time, and those intellectuals have disseminated these elements of Enlightenment to a much greater world than Europe. To note only one example, Yukichi Fukuzawa in Meiji Japan vigorously argued that Western civilisation was the highest attainment of humankind and that therefore the Japanese had to follow the civilising process in Europe.[102] Without doubt, this follow-up policy, which characterises the social, economic, political and cultural transformation of modern Japan, thereafter, yielded indispensable benefits. In order to consider 'Enlightenment and its consequences' more broadly, however, a more problematic and ironical version of Enlightenment is worth examining. It is worth considering, for example, whether Fukuzawa's Enlightenment inclined more towards the democratic version or towards Hume's problematic version abridged in 'civility and slavery'. I doubt that this ominous phrase 'civility and slavery' is absent in today's 'civilisation'.

Notes

1. Chris Berry and the late Nick Phillipson gave me valuable comments, especially on the decisive relevance of Tacitus, when we talked about the very early version of the present chapter. That early version originated in my sabbatical leave in 2013–14 in Edinburgh, where Harry Dickinson so kindly supported me. I am deeply grateful for their considerate encouragement. I would also like to thank Thomas Ahnert, Charles Bradford Bow, Markku Peltonen, Sora Sato, Hiroyuki Takezawa and Paul Tonks for their beneficial questions and suggestions at seminars and conference, James Harris for his kind advice when meeting in the NLS, and Craig Smith and Robin Mills for their detailed and helpful comments on the final draft. I would also like to thank Editage (www.editage.jp) for the English-language editing. This work was supported by JSPS KAKENHI Grant Numbers JP25780145, JP15K12817, and JP16K03574.
2. Christopher J. Berry, *The Idea of Commercial Society in the Scottish Enlightenment* (Edinburgh: Edinburgh University Press, 2013), pp. 90–7.

3. Berry, *Commercial Society*, pp. 113–14.

4. David Hume, *The History of England: From the Invasion of Julius Caesar to the Revolution in 1688*, 6 vols (Indianapolis: Liberty Classics, 1983), 4, p. 312. Reference to this work hereafter is abbreviated as 'H' followed by the volume and page numbers.

5. Berry, *Commercial Society*, pp. 6–7, 115–16.

6. For example, Eugene Rotwein, 'Introduction', in *David Hume: Writings on Economics*, ed. Eugene Rotwein (Madison: University of Wisconsin Press, 1970), pp. ix–cxi; Andrew S. Skinner, 'David Hume: Principles of Political Economy', in David Fate Norton (ed.), *The Cambridge Companion to Hume* (Cambridge: Cambridge University Press, 1993), pp. 222–54; John B. Stewart, *Opinion and Reform in Hume's Political Philosophy* (Princeton: Princeton University Press, 1993); Christopher J. Berry, *The Idea of Luxury: A Conceptual and Historical Investigation* (Cambridge: Cambridge University Press, 1994); Tatsuya Sakamoto, *David Hume's Civilized Society: Industry, Knowledge, Liberty* [in Japanese] (Tokyo: Sobunsha, 1995); Carl Wennerlind and Margaret Schabas, *David Hume's Political Economy* (London: Routledge, 2008); and Berry, *Commercial Society*.

7. David Hume, *Essays: Moral, Political, and Literary*, ed. Eugene F. Miller (Indianapolis: Liberty Classics, 1987), p. 271. This work is hereafter abbreviated as 'E' and cited by page number.

8. For example, Christopher J. Berry, *Social Theory of the Scottish Enlightenment* (Edinburgh: Edinburgh University Press, 1997), pp. 7–8; Berry, *Commercial Society*, pp. 45–58, 90–7.

9. *H* 4, p. 384.

10. Berry, *Commercial Society*, p. 57.

11. *E*, pp. 124–5.

12. Duncan Forbes, *Hume's Philosophical Politics* (Cambridge: Cambridge University Press, 1975), pp. 153–87. Forbes, on the other hand, drops a critical comment on 'Hume's general theory of historical origin of law'. According to him, Hume's theory lacks historical explanation of the origin of republics, and therefore there is a gap in his theory on the genesis of law (Forbes, *Philosophical Politics*, p. 318).

13. Andrew Sabl, *Hume's Politics: Coordination and Crisis in the History of England* (Princeton: Princeton University Press, 2012), pp. 142, 284; Hajime Inuzuka, 'Explanatory Notes (appended to Kazuhisa Ikeda, Hajime Inuzuka, and Ryu Susato. Abridged Translation of Hume's *History of England* (1)) [in Japanese]', *The Economic Review of Kansai University* 54(2) (2004), pp. 304–14, esp. pp. 306–13. Possibly the first example of the transplantation of laws into a monarchy that appears in *History* seems to be that by King Egbert, who united all the Saxon kingdoms in England. Egbert, according to Hume, stayed in the court of Charlemagne, where he learned 'civility' (*H* 1, p. 48). Then, by his prudent government over all the Saxon kingdoms, 'a favourable prospect was afforded to the Anglo-Saxons, of *establishing a civilized monarchy*' (*H* 1, p. 50;

emphasis added). Definitely, we have to counterbalance this passage by noting that Hume thinks that the Saxons during the time of the Heptarchy had no great improvement in 'arts, civility, knowledge, humanity, justice, or obedience to the laws' (H 1, p. 50).

14. H 2, p. 518; emphasis added.

15. H 2, pp. 519–20.

16. Hume explains that the pandects had a direct and massive impact on Europe, whereas they only 'secretly' affected the English laws (H 2, p. 520). This effect took the form of an attempt 'to raise *their own law* from its original state of rudeness and imperfection' (H 2, pp. 520–1; emphasis added). Though Hume is not vulnerable to the belief, widespread in seventeenth-century England, that the English had the sole tradition of the Common Law, he seems to think that the English actually had a Common Law tradition that was, by comparison to other such traditions, independent to a significant degree. On the widespread belief, see J. G. A. Pocock *The Ancient Constitution and the Feudal Law: A Study of English Historical Thought in the Seventeenth Century* (Cambridge: Cambridge University Press, 1957), esp. pp. 30–2.

17. It is impossible here to delve into the details of numerous studies on the idea(s) of Enlightenment itself. I have to skip the influential series of studies on the idea by Jonathan Israel, the seminal work on narratives of Enlightenment by Karen O'Brien, the thought-provoking case for the Enlightenment by John Robertson, and so on. Those works shall be referred to just occasionally hereafter where necessary, without any systematic review.

18. Berry, *Commercial Society*, ch. 6; see also J. G. A. Pocock, *Virtue, Commerce, and History: Essays on Political Thought and History, Chiefly in the Eighteenth Century* (Cambridge: Cambridge University Press, 1985), pp. 132–41; Istvan Hont, *Jealousy of Trade: International Competition and the Nation State in Historical Perspective* (Cambridge: Belknap, 2005), ch. 4.

19. Berry, *Commercial Society*, p. 208.

20. James A. Harris, *Hume: An Intellectual Biography* (Cambridge: Cambridge University Press, 2015), p. 21.

21. Harris, *Hume*, pp. 23–4.

22. Ryu Susato, *Hume's Sceptical Enlightenment* (Edinburgh: Edinburgh University Press, 2015), pp. 6–7.

23. Susato, *Sceptical Enlightenment*, pp. 11–19.

24. J. G. A. Pocock, *The Discovery of Islands: Essays in British History* (Cambridge: Cambridge University Press, 2005), p. 110.

25. Pocock, *Discovery of Islands*, pp. 122–4.

26. Pocock, *Discovery of Islands*, p. 125.

27. Pocock, *Discovery of Islands*, p. 126.

28. Pocock, *Discovery of Islands*, p. 127.

29. Markku Peltonen, *The Duel in Early Modern England: Civility, Politeness and Honour* (Cambridge: Cambridge University Press, 2003), esp. pp. 9–11, 146–54.

30. This illustration of Enlightenment is incompatible, not only with Israel's Radical Enlightenment, but also with the Moderate Enlightenment. Jonathan I. Israel, *Radical Enlightenment: Philosophy and the Making of Modernity, 1650–1750* (Oxford: Oxford University Press, 2001), p. 11. Pocock's idea of Enlightenment here seems to stress that the modern sovereign state obtained much stronger control and therefore a new kind of domination over its subjects than before.

31. Fania Oz-Salzberger, 'Introduction', in Adam Ferguson, *An Essay on the History of Civil Society* (Cambridge: Cambridge University Press, 1995), pp. vii–xxv, at p. xvii.

32. As widely known, Hume's *History* was initially published separately and backwards. Volume 5 of the modern edition originally appeared in 1754 as the first volume of *The History of Great Britain*. Volume 6 was published as its second volume (Harris, *Hume*, pp. 349–51). Forbes remarks the latter volume was published in 1756 though dated in 1757 (*Philosophical Politics*, pp. 260–1n). Volume 3 and 4 on the Tudors appeared in 1759 as *The History of England, Under the House of Tudor*. Volume 1 and 2 came last in 1761, though dated in 1762. These publications were collected and published together in 1762 and thereafter, as *The History of England from the invasion of Julius Caesar to the Revolution in 1688* (Harris, *Hume*, pp. 374–9, 404–7).

33. *H* 1, p. 4.

34. *H* 1, p. 10; emphasis added.

35. *H* 1, pp. 23–4; emphasis added.

36. Sora Sato remarks that it was commonplace among those historians like Paul de Rapin, Thomas Carte and Tobias Smollett to acknowledge the civilising effects of the Roman conquest. Sora Sato, *Edmund Burke as Historian: War, Order and Civilisation* (London: Palgrave Macmillan, 2018), p. 47.

37. Takemoto Hiroshi, 'The Irish Rebellion in the double Circles of the Irish Sea and the Atlantic [in Japanese]', *Study Series of the Centre for Historical Social Science Literature, Hitotsubashi University*, 8 (1985), pp. 1–31, esp. pp. 10–12, 17–19, 24–25. Sabl, *Hume's Politics*, pp. 65, 266n.

38. Eric Schliesser, *Adam Smith: Systematic Philosopher and Public Thinker* (Oxford: Oxford University Press, 2017), p. 36.

39. Schliesser, *Adam Smith*, p. 165.

40. Luke Gibbons, 'Race against Time: Racial Discourse and Irish History', *Oxford Literary Review* 13 (1991), pp. 95–117, at pp. 97–101.

41. Berry, *Commercial Society*, pp. 115–16.

42. *H* 1, pp. 342–5; *H* 4, pp. 310–12.

43. 'To consider James in a more advantageous light, we must take a view of him as the legislator of Ireland; and most of the institutions, which he had framed for civilizing that kingdom . . .' (*H* 5, pp. 46–7).

44. *H* 5, p. 47. emphasis added.

45. *H* 5, pp. 47–8.

46. *H* 5, pp. 48–9.
47. *H* 5, p. 49; emphasis added.
48. Berry, *Commercial Society*, pp. 6–7.
49. Roger Emerson provides more details on the intense debates and actual poli-cies concerning 'civilising' the Highlands. Emerson instead finds Hume's dis-approval of these violent policies in the *Political Discourse*. Roger L. Emerson 'The Scottish Contexts for David Hume's Political-Economic Thinking', in Carl Wennerlind and Margaret Schabas (eds), *David Hume's Political Econ-omy* (New York: Routledge, 2008), pp. 10–30; pp. 19–25.
50. Berry, *Commercial Society*, pp. 6–7, 116.
51. *H* 5, pp. 47–9, footnotes p–y. J. Davies, *A discoverie of the true causes why Ireland was neuer entirely subdued, nor brought vnder obedience of the crowne of England, vntill the beginning of His Maiesties happie raigne. Printed exactly from the edition of 1612* (London: A. Millar, 1747). Davies's work cited hereafter as *Discoverie*.
52. Sean Kelsey, 'Davies, Sir John (bap. 1569, d. 1626), lawyer and poet', in *Oxford Dictionary of National Biography* (Oxford: Oxford University Press, 2008).
53. Sato, *Edmund Burke*, pp. 163–75.
54. Davies, *Discoverie*, pp. 8–9.
55. Davies, *Discoverie*, p. 22.
56. Davies, *Discoverie*, pp. 167–99.
57. Davies, *Discoverie*, pp. 167–75.
58. Davies, *Discoverie*, p. 167.
59. Davies, *Discoverie*, p. 170; emphasis added.
60. Davies, *Discoverie*, pp. 170, 175; emphasis added.
61. Davies, *Discoverie*, pp. 75–199.
62. Davies, *Discoverie*, p. 114.
63. Davies, *Discoverie*, p. 122; emphasis added.
64. Davies, *Discoverie*, pp. 122–3; emphasis added.
65. Davies, *Discoverie*, pp. 134–46. Remarkably, Davies thinks that the Irish themselves desired the protection under the English laws. He rebuts a view that the Irish rejected to be subject to the equal laws, by referring to charters of denisation, which the Irish successively purchased, and the petition in the reign of Edward III, which requested for general accommodation of the Irish under the English laws (Davies, *Discoverie*, p. 115). The English lords hindered the acceptance of the Irish under the English laws, and they made use of the Irish custom to exploit their people, since that custom enabled them to ignore the protections that the English laws would have provided for the people (Davies, *Discoverie*, pp. 116, 153–4). From this point of view, Davies argues for the Poynings' Act. This Act, according to him, was ben-eficial for the common Irish, since it enabled the English Parliament to curb and modify the Irish laws designed to sacrifice the commons for the interests of the great nobles (Davies, *Discoverie*, pp. 230–2). We surely have to note, though, that Davies was the person most interested in enlarging the English

rule over the Irish, and his *Discoverie* was, at least partly, written and utilised for that interest.

66. H 2, p. 525.
67. Sato refers to this point as well, though in passing: *Edmund Burke*, p. 164.
68. H 1, p. 339.
69. H 4, p. 312; emphasis added.
70. Davies, *Discoverie*, pp. 128–9.
71. Davies, *Discoverie*, pp. 127–33. Sato contrasts Edmund Burke with Hume on this point. The former finds beneficial aspects of conquest in general, whereas the latter does not acknowledge much advantage, say, in the Norman Conquest (Sato, *Edmund Burke*, pp. 47–8, 238).
72. Berry, *Social Theory*, p. 2.
73. Berry, *Commercial Society*, pp. 46–57.
74. H 1, pp. 168–9.
75. Berry, *Social Theory*, p. 129.
76. A search for the phrase 'civility and slavery' on ECCO, including EEBO, with no restriction on period and field, returns only five entries. Two are in Hume's *History of England* and *History of Great Britain*, while the remaining three are in Macpherson's *Introduction* (first edition of 1771, Dublin edition of 1771 and second edition of 1772). James Macpherson, *An introduction to the history of Great Britain and Ireland: or, An inquiry into the origin, religion, future state, character, manners, morality, amusements, persons, manner of life, houses, naviga-tion, commerce, language, government, kings, general assemblies, courts of justice, and juries, of the Britons, Scots, Irish and Anglo-Saxons* (London: T. Becket and P. A. De Hondt, 1772).
77. See, e.g., Peltonen, *The Duel*, Introduction.
78. James Boswell, *The Life of Samuel Johnson*, ed. with an introduction D. Womersley (London: Penguin Books, 2008), p. 343.
79. 'civility, n.', *OED Online* (Oxford: Oxford University Press, 2020). [https://www.oed.com./view/Entry/33581?redirectedFrom=civility (accessed 11 January 2021)]
80. Derick S. Thomson, 'Macpherson, James (1736–1796), Writer', in *Oxford Dictionary of National Biography* (Oxford: Oxford University Press, 2006).
81. Macpherson, *An Introduction*, p. 266; emphasis added. In the Dublin edition of 1771 and the first London edition of 1771 as well, we can find precisely the same use of the phrase.
82. Macpherson, *An Introduction*, p. 263; emphasis added.
83. Macpherson, *An Introduction*, pp. 260–1. However, Macpherson's narratives have a twist, as can be seen from the foregoing citation, where he argues that luxury and tyranny preserved the peace of Rome for a while. He also writes '[though] no laws could bind the emperor, the empire itfelf was governed, in fact, by a regular fyftem of laws [especially around its frontiers]; and therefore, when the tyrant fell, the ftate was not involved in his ruin' (Macpherson, *An Introduction*, p. 261). This helped that paradoxical continuation of the life of Rome, Macpherson contends.

84. Macpherson contrasts the decay among the citizens of Rome, with the martial spirits of 'uncorrupted' soldiers provided continuously from the frontiers. Although even those soldiers became depraved when they were freed from their service in the capital, '[t]hey were fucceeded . . . by new levies of hardy and uncorrupted barbarians, who preferved an appearance of vigour in the extremities of the empire, after the centre had exhibited every fymptom of political decay' (Macpherson, *An Introduction*, p. 264; emphasis added).

85. Berry, *Commercial Society*, pp. 150–72.

86. Markku Peltonen, 'Politeness and Whiggism 1688–1732', *The Historical Journal* 48 (2005), pp. 391–414, esp. pp. 395–402, 409–13.

87. Nicholas Phillipson, 'Politics and Politeness in the Reigns of Anne and the early Hanoverians', in J. G. A. Pocock, Gordon J. Schochet and Lois Shcwoerer (eds), *The Varieties of British Political Thought, 1500–1800* (Cambridge: Cambridge University Press, 1993), pp. 211–45, esp. pp. 231–9.

88. Macpherson, *An Introduction*, p. 264. This wording could have been borrowed from someone else, such as William Temple (*see* Susato, *Sceptical Enlightenment*, pp. 60–3).

89. Davies, *Discoverie*, p. 127.

90. Davies, *Discoverie*, pp. 128–9.

91. Tacitus, *Agricola and Germania*, translated from Latin by Harold Mattingly and revised with an Introduction and Notes by James B. Rives (London: Penguin, 2009), p. 15.

92. James B. Rives, 'Introduction', in Tacitus, *Agricola and Germania* (London: Penguin, 2009), pp. xiv–xliv, at pp. xl–xli.

93. *H* 1, p. 10. According to Sato, Burke similarly follows Tacitus in illustrating Agricola's policies in his *Abridgement of English History*. There, Burke concludes that the Britons 'exchange a savage liberty for a polite and easy subjection' (Sato, *Edmund Burke*, p. 32).

94. Rives, *Introduction*, pp. xxx–xxxi.

95. *H* 1, pp. 15–17. This surely corresponds with the long-lasting ethnic stereotype of the Asians, Greeks and Europeans, which goes back, at least, to Aristotle's *Politics*. Aristotle, *The Politics*, translated from Greek by E. Barker and R. F. Stalley (Oxford: Oxford University Press, 1995), 266/1327b. On the reverberations of that kind of ancient stereotype in the Scottish contexts, see an informative analysis in Ueli Zahnd, 'Civilized Scots?: Climate, Race and Barbarian North in Early Modern Scottish Philosophy', in Catherine König-Pralong, Mario Meliadò and Zornitsa Radeva (eds), *The Territories of Philosophy in Modern Historiography* (Turnhout: Brepols, 2019), pp. 127–47.

96. *H* 1, pp. 160–61, 168–9; *H* 2, p. 524.

97. *H* 1, p. 160; emphasis added.

98. David Hume, *The history of England, from the invasion of Julius Caesar to the revolution in 1688. (Esq; . . . A new edition, with the author's last corrections and improvements. To which is prefixed a short account of his life, written by himself)* (London: T. Cadell, 1778), VI, p. 163.

99. One persuasive answer to this question is that Hume's universalism enables
     him to make external evaluation of different (barbarous or civilised) soci-
     eties, as Berry compellingly shows (Christopher J. Berry, *Essays on Hume,
     Smith and the Scottish Enlightenment* (Edinburgh: Edinburgh University
     Press, 2018), pp. 146–59, 217–23, 254–8, 272–4)). Hence Hume himself
     is presumably not much worried about the question of legitimacy. And yet,
     it seems to me, his narratives regarding civility and slavery may give rise to
     another possible answer, which, though in the way of retrospective recon-
     struction, is suggested in the remainder of this paragraph.
100. Schliesser, *Adam Smith*, p. 166.
101. Israel, *Enlightenment*, p. vi.
102. Yukichi Fukuzawa, *An Outline of a Theory of Civilization* (Tokyo: Keio Uni-
     versity Press, 2008), esp. chaps 2 and 10.

9

Hume as Forerunner of the Sociology of Emotions: The Effect of Context, Comparison and Sympathy on the Genesis of Pride

Ana Marta González

Introduction

Why does Hume begin his account of the passions in *A Treatise on Human Nature* with the indirect passions, and specifically with pride and humility? Apart from the fact that pride is a common passion, 'it is not clear that there is any special significance in the fact that he chooses to give the first place in his study to pride'.[1] Since the *Treatise* is the only systematic work Hume ever wrote, a fuller answer to this question is likely to give us a clearer insight into the structure of his philosophical views.

Hume's own words in the *Treatise* provide us with a first indication of this structure. Thus, at the end of the first book, after having demolished almost all metaphysical certainties, Hume explains his philosophical endeavour as a result of his own passions and inclinations, alternating between melancholy and joy.[2] In this way, he is already offering the reader some cues about the psycho-social context of his philosophical work, and suggesting why the book *On the Passions* is placed right after the book *On Understanding*: the passions provide the ground, the starting point, for his own philosophical activity, which, as he declares at the beginning of the *Treatise*, is meant to pave the way for a new 'science of man'. As Christopher Berry has repeatedly pointed out, Hume's basic purpose in developing this 'science of man' was to explain the principles behind the constancy exhibited by human behaviour.[3] Such constancy is an implication of Hume's universalism and makes Hume's comparative approach to history and social matters possible, insofar as it makes room for trans-societal explanations.[4]

Interestingly, Hume took his 'science of man' to be articulated roughly along Newtonian lines. Indeed, 'though Newton is not here mentioned he is undeniably the inspiration';[5] 'what this Newtonian motif meant in practice was the endeavour to search for universal causes governing a range of social phenomena.'[6] For Berry, the application of causal analysis to moral subjects can be taken to be the most important consequence of Hume's commitment to the 'science of man'.[7]

Tamas Demeter has explained the specific way in which Hume's commitment to the 'experimental method' in moral subjects can be described as 'Newtonian' by reference to Newton's *Opticks* (1707), rather than to his *Principia* (1687), for while in the latter Newton follows the axiomatic, mathematical tradition, in the former he follows an analogical method, comparing different phenomena, according to analysis and synthesis. This is more in tune with Hume's own approach to human phenomena, since in in his science of human nature, human phenomena are collected from history and observation, and then compared; if analogies and similarities are found, they are ascribed to some principles of human nature that are also compared, grouped and resolved into more general ones. Once phenomena are analysed into their causal springs, the resulting principles can be construed for the purposes of explanation thereby satisfying our curiosity and facilitating the improvement of society – without the possibility of ultimate knowledge of human essence.[8]

The passions belong to those universal causes or principles; in the *Enquiry*,[9] Hume 'lists ambition, avarice, self-love, vanity, friendship, generosity and public spirit. These operate regardless of the social context.'[10] This makes them fit not only for designing comparative historical studies, but also for normative work: obviously, not in the sense that passions alone provide the basis for normative judgement:[11] normative judgements will only be possible after Hume develops his theory of artificial virtues in the third book, thereby unveiling the basic structure of social order, yet, in the meantime, Hume's focus on the passions in Book II is meant to stress their relevance in the constitution of actual human experience.[12]

Against this background, the idea I want to articulate in this chapter is that the order in which Hume chooses to develop his typology of the passions in the second book of the *Treatise* results from his desire to start with human beings as they actually live in society, that is, human beings inserted in a social dynamic marked by reference to others, and already situated in a definite social order. This starting point is consistent with his self-declared 'strong propensity' to consider objects in the light under which they appear to him.[13] It is also in line with Annette Baier's seminal interpretation of Hume's move from Book I to Book II of the *Treatise*, as showing his own conception of the self as a social self.[14] From this perspective, I argue that the indirect passions, which Hume develops in Book II, point at the social structure of that very experience – which will only be clarified in the third book. Within this framework, the fact that Hume starts his treatment of the indirect passions with the passions of pride and humility, instead of with love and hatred, could be taken as a sign of Hume's acceptance of a widespread idea among eighteenth-century philosophers, namely, that human beings have a basic tendency to assert themselves over others as a way to excel and gain the favourable opinion of their peers, and as a way to protect what for them is a constantly threatened existence.

On this reading, the book on the *Passions* becomes the keystone of Hume's plan for a science of man and ultimately for the genesis of an empirical approach to human and social affairs.[15] In my view, this interpretation represents an argument for vindicating Hume's systematic contribution to the understanding of the empirical dynamics of social life, and his anticipation of future developments in social theory.[16] While many authors have recently pointed in this direction,[17] Hume's relevance for social thought has scarcely been systematically explored, with the exception of the work of Hartmut Kliemt, Christopher J. Finlay and Claudia Schmidt.[18]

In order to explore this view, I will follow Hume's own exposition in *Treatise* II, 1, assuming that this order follows his own plan for the 'science of man'. Thus, the first part of this chapter briefly recalls Hume's division of passions, relating it to his general purpose of developing a 'science of man'. I will then analyse the psychology of indirect passions, as illustrated in the case of humility and pride. Once this general framework has been established, I will devote the final part of the chapter to analysing the alleged causes of pride and humility, making explicit the social context of these passions and the way they function psychologically. It is at this point that Hume's analysis will prove its relevance for the contemporary sociology of emotions, for Hume's indirect passions are witness to the relations and social structure that underlie them.

The Passions as a Positive Foundation of Hume's Science of Man

Recalling his division of all perceptions of the mind into impressions and ideas, Hume defines the passions as secondary or *reflective* impressions, that is, impressions which proceed from the original ones – also called 'impressions of sensation' – 'either immediately or by the interposition of its idea'.[19] While impressions of sensation pertain to anatomy and natural philosophy, reflective impressions pertain to moral philosophy.[20] Although the former can give rise to the latter, they are different since impressions of sensation do not arise with the interposition or mediation of any thought or perception: 'A fit of the gout produces a long train of passions, [such] as grief, hope, fear; but is not deriv'd immediately from any affection or idea.'[21] Thus, affections and ideas are essential to Hume's account of the passions, although passions as such cannot be further analysed in more simple elements.

As reflective or secondary impressions, passions originate in, or are caused by original impressions, impressions of sensation, either directly or with the interposition of their idea. Thus, the imaginary anticipation of pleasure or pain brings about a number of direct passions. Likewise, Hume will go on to claim that a double relationship of impressions and ideas brings about indirect passions. Among the various divisions of the passions that Hume draws in the *Treatise*, he chooses this, between indirect and direct passions, to organize Book II: 'By *direct* passions I understand such as arise immediately from good or evil, from pain or pleasure. By *indirect* such as proceed from the same principles, but by the conjunction of other qualities.'[22] 'Good' and 'evil' in this context refer to pleasure and pain. To illustrate the difference he gives some examples: 'Under the indirect passions, I comprehend pride, humility, ambition, vanity, love, hatred, envy, pity, malice, generosity, with their dependants. And under the direct passions, desire, aversion, grief, joy, hope, fear, despair and security.'[23] Later on, when he sets out to analyse the direct passions, he would repeat that they 'arise from the good and evil most naturally, with the least preparation'.[24] Accordingly, when he chooses to start his analysis with the indirect passions, we wonder if it wouldn't be more logical to start out with the direct passions since they are more basic and simpler. In my view, this choice has to do with the subtitle of the *Treatise*: the 'attempt to introduce the experimental method of reasoning into moral subjects'. Once he has concluded Book I, which represents the negative part of his endeavour, Hume is ready to lay the positive foundations of his science of man, which will be completed in Book III by introducing the theory of artificial virtues and of moral judgement. Yet, the basic elements of that science – that is, the building blocks of human experience – are provided by the passions. Not surprisingly, the way Hume analyses the passions does not follow the methodology of ancient or medieval philosophy, but rather the requirements of his own method: 'as the science of man is the only solid foundation for the other sciences, so the only solid foundation we can give to this science itself must be laid on experience and observation.'[25] Accordingly, Hume often speaks of 'experiments', making clear that, in moral philosophy, 'We must . . . glean up our experiments from a cautious *observation* of human life, and take them as they appear in the common course of the world, by men's behaviour in company, in affairs, and in their pleasure.'[26] This observation also involves 'the study of history and literature, ancient and modern'.[27] Now, human behaviour, as it appears in the common course of the world, is always embedded in a web of relationships, marked by differences in power, riches, beauty, virtue, fame and so forth. Such relationships, as Hume makes clear from sections 7 through 11 of *Treatise* 2.1, are the building blocks of pride and humility,[28] which, in turn, are the first indirect passions Hume explores in Book II, before he deals with love and hatred. A common feature of these passions is that they involve a double relation of impressions and ideas – the two types of perceptions Hume's epistemology discovers in our minds. Indeed, unlike the direct passions, 'which arise from good and evil most naturally, and with the least preparation',[29] the *peculiarity* of indirect passions is that, through a pleasant or unpleasant quality, they lead our attention to a certain *object*, which then enters into the concept of that very passion. According to Hume, in the case of both pride and humility, this object is the *self*; in the case of love and hatred, this object is the *other*.[30] Thus, while we can take pleasure in a beautiful house, so that viewing it brings us joy, we take *pride* when the beautiful house happens to be ours.

The distinction between the object and cause of indirect passions has been a matter of much debate involving the nature of intentionality in Hume's account of the passions.[31] We do not need to enter into this debate. For our purposes here it suffices to point out that, for Hume, beliefs have *causal efficacy* in the generation of these passions only through their connection with the pleasantness or unpleasantness implicit in them: pleasantness in relation to the self produces pride, unpleasantness produces humility; pleasantness in relation to the other produces love, unpleasantness produces hatred. Interestingly, pride (or humility) could grow so as to 'comprehend whatever objects are in the least ally'd or related to us. Our country, family, children, relations, riches, houses, gardens, horses, dogs, cloaths; any of these may become a cause either of pride or of humility.'[32] This suggests a dynamic idea of the self: a self that grows according to the relations it establishes. Yet, why do we take pleasure not only in the pleasantness of certain objects – virtues, properties and so on – but in the fact that those pleasant objects are related *to us*? According to Hume, this is an *original* feature of our minds, that is, it is in 'our natures'. He is careful in his choice of words, though. In his view, both pride and humility 'are determin'd to have self for their object, not only by a natural but also by an original property'.[33] His argument for sustaining the 'original' character of this property is an inductive one, namely, the 'constancy and steadiness of its operation',[34] that is, the fact that pride and humility *always* direct our attention to the self. Yet, while the *object* of both pride and humility is original – the self – the *causes* of both pride and humility are not. Those causes can be *natural* in so far as they depend on the peculiar nature of human beings, but they are not original, because they can also be produced by

artifice and civilisation.[35] Thus, people often take pride in artificial endow-
ments – technologies, manners, conventions and so forth – which clearly
do not belong to the original constitution of humanity; if they can nevertheless take pride in those things, it is only because they are connected
in some way to human nature.[36] Now, assuming that it is more in keeping
with a science of human nature to think that each of these items can produce pride 'by partaking of some general quality, that naturally operates
on the mind (T.2.1.3.5)',[37] Hume sets out to find the common element or
circumstances that are responsible for their efficacy as causes of pride and
humility.[38] It is at this point that he resorts to the principles of association
of ideas and impressions to explain the genesis of indirect passions in terms
of double relations of impressions and ideas.

For Hume, it is evident that the principles of association, explored in
the first book of the *Treatise*, hold not only for ideas but also for impressions, although with a remarkable difference, for 'ideas are associated by
resemblance, contiguity, and causation; and impressions only by resemblance'.[39] In addition, he observes that both associations of ideas and of
impressions 'very much assist and forward each other, and that the transition is more easily made where they both concur in the same object'.[40] The
example he gives is clarifying:

> Thus a man, who, by any injury from another, is very much discompos'd
> and ruffled in his temper, is apt to find a hundred subjects of discon-
> tent, impatience, fear, and other uneasy passions; especially if he can
> discover these subjects in or near the person, who was the cause of his
> first passion.[41]

Accordingly, if we take impressions and ideas as *units* of experience – something Charles Taylor once termed 'Hume's epistemological atomism' –
the psychological principles of association by resemblance, contiguity
and causation would then become the *organising principles of human experience*.[42] For sure, Hume does not intend to provide us either with any
'transcendental logic' or a 'deep psychology' theory; his only purpose is
to account for ordinary phenomena of mental life involving self and others. Yet, already at this level, he makes clear that *mental life – specifically,
emotional life – is significantly made up of social life*. This, of course, has
to do with his account of sympathy, to which I will turn later. What I
would like to stress at this point is the fact that, by advancing this view,
Hume somehow anticipates the basic thesis of the sociology of emotions,
which departs from the emotional experience to analyse social relations
and structures. Since the pioneering work of Arlie Russell Hochschild,

Theodore D. Kemper and Thomas J. Scheff, sociology has begun to recognise the potential of emotions as privileged sites of social and analysis.[43] While seeing emotions as 'carriers of meaning and value' can certainly explain their relevance for cultural analysis, the sociology of emotions has been keen also at unveiling the structural elements implicit in emotional experiences.[44] It is particularly in this regard that Hume's approach to the passions can be found inspiring and relevant. For, no matter how much he stresses the organic basis of the emotions – and specifically of pride – the way he analyses this passion shows very clearly the social background required to activate the passion.

Indeed, if on the one hand, he underlines that 'Nature has given to the organs of the human mind, a certain disposition fitted to produce a peculiar impression or emotion, which we call pride: to this emotion she has assign'd a certain idea, viz. that of self, which it never fails to produce',[45] on the other, he makes clear that such natural basis, along with the original object which it never fails to produce – the idea of self – is not enough to generate the passion, for the latter must be activated by an external cause.[46] This is proven by daily experience – since pride 'languishes when unsupported by some excellency in the character, in bodily accomplishments, in cloths, equipage or fortune'.[47] According to Hume, those external causes of pride or humility are to be found in any given cause of pleasure or uneasiness, in so far as we relate them to the self: whenever something that causes pleasure in itself is related to the self, then it results in a specific type of pleasure, that we call pride – whose object is the self. In all the examples Hume chooses to illustrate this point the social context of these passions is implicit. Yet from section 6 onwards, the social reference of these passions becomes increasingly evident. As Whelan writes:

> Hume begins with the individual conceived as the potential possessor of the various discrete states of awareness (impressions) called passions or feelings, which may be observed to occur *in certain circumstances* and to bear *certain relations* to one another.[48]

Indeed, the reference to 'certain circumstances' and 'certain relations' belongs to the specific causes that activate the passions of pride and humility, and so it is the reference to basic social conventions and structures.

Thus, in order to produce pride and not merely joy, the relation between the cause of pleasure and the self must be a narrow one.[49] In introducing the idea of *possession*, Hume is indirectly referring to the division of property, which, as it is made clear in Book III, depends on a basic social convention or artifice. A further feature required to produce pride is that the agreeable object (or disagreeable, in the case of humility) has to be peculiar to ourselves, or at least common to us with a few persons: if a beautiful object is not very different from that of my peers, then the cause of pride decreases.[50] Accordingly, comparison, which takes place in a social context, represents a crucial element to understand the origin of pride and humility. In addition, it is also convenient that 'the pleasant or painful object be very discernible and obvious, and that not only to ourselves, but to others also'.[51] If nobody else but me is able to appreciate the beauty of the object, then it may still be a cause of pleasure, but not so much of pride. If, on the other hand, I come to know the positive effect this object produces in others, then, and only then, it does become a motive of pride. Now, if others somehow enter into the constitution of the passion of pride, this amounts to saying that they enter into the constitution of its object, namely, the self. A further qualification Hume introduces to explain why we take pride or not in certain causes does not have such an obvious relation to social context, but rather with the short duration of an eventual cause of pride: in order to cause pride, the cause cannot be too inconstant or ephemeral: we do not usually take pride in ephemeral causes.[52] However, this very fact does say something about the nature of the 'self', namely, that it incorporates, in our eyes, as well as in others', the idea of duration and permanence.

Another qualification is perhaps more obviously related to the social context than the previous one. Thus, Hume argues that pride and humility are heavily influenced by general rules and custom. For instance, as a general rule, we link the ranks of men to the power or riches they enjoy, even if their personal category is not in accord with what is suggested by their power and riches, or even if they are affected by other peculiarities which deprive them of the enjoyment of their possessions. By highlighting this fact, Hume is pointing to the *social power of appearances*: even if such appearances do not correspond to a real excellence, even if the possessors are not really able to enjoy their advantages, we nevertheless tend to classify people according to those appearances. Hume thinks that this phenomenon 'may be accounted for from the same principles, that explain'd the influence of general rules on the understanding', namely:

> *Custom* readily carries us beyond the just bounds in our passions, as well as in our reasonings, it may not be amiss to observe on this occasion, that the influence of general rules and maxims on the passions very much contributes to facilitate the effects of all the principles.[53]

The power of custom, then, is relevant to account for what counts as grounds for pride or humility, and more generally of the excitement of any passion; *custom creates a sort of psychological short cut which facilitates the operation of the passions*:

> For 'tis evident, that if a person . . . were on a sudden transported into our world, he woul'd be very much embarrass'd with every object, and wou'd not readily find what . . . passion he ought to attribute to it. The passions are often vary'd by very inconsiderable principles; and these do not always play with a perfect regularity, especially on the first trial. But as custom and practice have brought to light all these principles, and have settled the just value of every thing; this must certainly contribute to the easy production of the passions, and guide us, by means of general establish'd maxims, in the proportions we ought to observe in preferring one object to another.[54]

Custom settles the value of every little thing, thereby providing the basis for any eventual stimulus of our passions, as well as of their adequate measure. This thought opens up the door for the consideration of the role of uses, fashions, practices and culture in the form and the development of any passion.

Indirect Passions in Context: The Specific Causes of Pride and Humility

Every positive quality we regard as part of ourselves *may* be cause for pride, and every negative quality *may* be cause for humility. However, that this positive quality so narrowly linked to us *in fact* becomes a cause for pride or humility depends largely on the social context. It is the social context which clarifies to what extent that positive quality is peculiar to us, providing us with a sufficient ground for pride. It is only within a certain context, where this positive quality becomes obvious not only to us but to others, that it can really be cause for pride and not merely for joy, and, most importantly, it is only the social context which ensures that the operation of each passion upon human nature is sufficiently backed up by shared practices and customs.

Once these considerations have been introduced, Hume pays attention to common causes of pleasure that, to the extent that they belong to us and are displayed in the appropriate contexts, constitute common causes of pride: virtue and vice; beauty and deformity; external advantages or disadvantages; property and riches; and fame. I will go quickly over the aspects involved in these causes, which enrich in some point the basic thesis I am developing here.

When speaking of virtue and vice in the book on the passions, Hume is not interested so much in discussing different moral theories, as in noting the relationship between vice and pain, virtue and pleasure, since, in his view, this is all that counts to become a cause for pride or humility.[55] Likewise, beauty and deformity, and more generally, every bodily accomplishment or deficiency, constitute some other quality which may produce pride or humility when they are closely related to the self.[56]

In passing, Hume mentions that people are often proud of the surprising events they have experienced,[57] the adventures they have met with, the dangers they have been exposed to, and regards this as a further proof of the specific quality of the pleasure we find in pride: the fact that it directs attention to ourselves. Indeed, the pleasurable quality we find in referring or exhibiting unusual experiences derives from the fact that they make us appear as unique.[58] This fact, however, is directly related to the social context in which we conduct our lives, and can help explain the role novelty and fashion can play in the definition of a specifically modern social pattern of taste.[59]

The only objection Hume seems to find for his general account of pride and humility as based in pleasurable/displeasurable qualities of the body is the fact that we are not usually proud of being healthy, something he attributes to the fact that health is not peculiar to any man, and very often is inconstant.[60] Yet, that even health can become a source of pride in certain social contexts is proved by the proud way people nowadays exhibit their healthy constitution. In addition, Hume's point could be also recognised if we realise that lack of health, when it is chronic and there is no hope of recovery, often becomes a source of humility.[61] Be that as it may, the consideration of health and sickness provides Hume with an occasion to stress one of the points highlighted above, *comparison and the judgement of others – that is, the social context – make up most of the value we place in certain qualities:*

> Bodily pain and sickness are in themselves proper causes of humility; *tho' the custom of estimating everything by comparison more than by its intrinsic worth and value*, makes us overlook these calamities, which we find to be incident to everyone, and causes us to form an idea of our merit and character independent of them . . . *Men always consider the sentiments of others in their judgement of themselves.*[62]

Apart from the qualities of mind and body, human beings find occasion for pride in many other foreign objects, as long as they acquire a particular relation to themselves.[63] Hume wonders why this is so, and goes on to analyse the kind of relation of ideas and impressions involved in this phenomenon. This type of pride, he thinks, cannot be grounded merely in resemblance – as it is the case when someone takes pride in his or her resemblance to a great man – but rather in contiguity or causation.[64] He further notes that, in these cases, 'an association of ideas, however necessary, is not alone sufficient to give rise to any passion'.[65] In addition, a previous relation of affections (or emotions) is required. According to Hume, it is only because there is a positive emotion about that foreign object that the relation of ideas, which links that object to our selves, may result in a positive passion such as pride. Thus, *ideas work merely as connectors*; they are instrumental vehicles to force emotions; the closer the relation they exhibit between the original emotion and the object of the passion, the greater the passion they help produce. Accordingly, 'every change in the relation produces a proportionable change in the passion'.[66] Based on these principles, Hume explains very familiar facts, such as the pride men find in the 'beauty of their country, of their county, of their parish'. While the idea of beauty produces a pleasure, since the object or cause of this pleasure is, by the supposition, related to self, the double relation of impressions and ideas facilitates the transition from one impression, of beauty, to the other, of pride.[67]

More interestingly, he resorts to the same principles to explain the *opposite* phenomena, namely, that of some people who 'discover a vanity of an opposite kind, and affect to depreciate their own country, in comparison of those, to which they have travelled'.[68] In cases like these, the ground of vanity changes because of the social context:

> these persons find, when they are at home, and surrounded with their countrymen, that the strong relation betwixt them and their own nation is shar'd with so many, that 'tis in a manner lost to them; whereas their distant relation to a foreign country, which is form'd by their having seen it and liv'd in it, is augmented by their considering how few there are who have done the same. For this reason they always admire the beauty, utility and rarity of what is abroad, above what is at home.[69]

The same principles explain why we can be vain 'of the qualities of those who are connected with us by blood or friendship'[70] and ashamed of their disgrace; why people 'who boast of the antiquity of their families, are glad when they can join this circumstance, that their ancestors for any generations have been uninterrupted proprietors of the same portion of land.'[71]

However, *property and riches* are by far the most common causes of pride and humility. Not so much because of their intrinsic importance – one could argue that virtues of the mind or moral virtues are more important; and so is any bodily accomplishment – but because property serves to the purpose of enhancing our individuality, our difference from others in a very special way:

> The relation, which is esteem'd the closest, and which of all others produces most commonly the passion of pride is that of property. This relation 'twill be impossible for me fully to explain before I come to treat of justice and the other moral virtues. 'Tis sufficient to observe on this occasion, that property may be defin'd, such a relation betwixt a person and an object as permits him, but forbids any other, the free use and possession of it, without violating the laws of justice and moral equity.[72]

Again, while the understanding of this phenomenon – and, specifically, its social roots – will increase when we come to the discussion on the nature of property, it does not depend on any specific theory of justice. The crucial point for Hume is that

> the mention of the property naturally carries our thought to the proprietor and of the proprietor to the property; which being a proof of a perfect relation of ideas is all that is requisite to our present purpose. A relation of ideas, join'd to that of impressions, always produces a transition of affections; and therefore, whenever any pleasure or pain arises from an object, connected with us by property, we may be certain, that either pride or humility must arise from this conjunction of relations.[73]

Nevertheless, in order to clarify further the connection between property and pride, Hume develops an argument in three steps: (1) riches are 'the power of acquiring the property of what pleases'[74] and taking pleasure in something is requisite for pride; (2) power consists in the probability of its exercise; and (3) the probability of exercise already brings about a certain pleasure, which increases with the actual exercise of the power.

While he had previously rejected in the *Treatise* the distinction between power and its exercise, in trying to explain the peculiar connection of property and pride, he has to resort to it, because he observes that many things operate upon our passions 'by means of the idea and supposition of power, independent of its actual exercise. We are pleas'd when we acquire an ability of procuring pleasure, and are displeas'd when another acquires a power of giving pain.'[75] In this context, he offers a suggestive definition of power, which provides the background for the generation of certain passions, such as fear or anxiety. Power, says Hume, is 'the possibility or probability of any action, as discover'd by experience and the practice of the world'.[76] Thus, if riches and property are causes of pride it is because they usually bring with them the power of acquiring pleasures. While the actual presence of pleasure is a bigger source of satisfaction than the mere probability of it,[77] the satisfaction which riches brings is not merely grounded on actual power, but in probability – as in the case of the miser.[78] At any rate, perception of the power of others can generate fear and anxiety on my side:

> Wherever a person is in such a situation with regard to me, that there is no very powerful motive to deter him from injuring me, and consequently 'tis uncertain whether he will injure me or not, I must be uneasy in such a situation, and cannot consider the possibility or probability of that injury without a sensible concern.[79]

This experience is proof of the effects of uncertainty on our passions, but also provides the background to understand the desire of expelling fear through the acquisition of property, for property is experienced as a means of increasing our power.[80]

Comparison and Sympathy: The Mechanics of Social Psychology

The account given so far of the specific relation between property and pride would not be complete unless we realise the effect of *comparison* on human happiness. Likewise, the account of pride and humility would not be complete unless we explain the specific force these passions take as a result of the operation of *sympathy*. This is something Hume explicitly considers in *Treatise* 2.1.11, when he reflects on the influence of the opinion of others on these (and other) affections.[81] Comparison and sympathy represent the key mental operations in charge of linking psychology and social contexts. 'Only in comparison with others does one judge oneself happy or unhappy.'[82] This Kantian line was already fully at work in the social theory of the Scottish Enlightenment, and specifically in Hume who argues that: 'Comparison is in every case a sure method of augmenting our esteem of anything. A rich man feels the felicity of his condition better by opposing it to that of a beggar.'[83] Hume takes comparison to be a powerful force in human behaviour; so much so, that it very often prevails over reason; it is only by taking this fact into account that we understand the mechanism of indirect passions such as malice and envy:

> As we seldom judge of objects from their intrinsic value, but form our notions of them from a comparison with other objects, it follows, that according as we observe a greater or less share of happiness or misery in others, we must make an estimate of our own, and feel a consequent pain or pleasure. The misery of another gives us a more lively idea of our happiness, and his happiness of our misery. The former, therefore, produces delight; and the latter uneasiness.[84]

Comparison would produce this effect not only in regard to others, but also when we consider our own life in perspective, and compare our pleasurable present condition with a former miserable one.[85] What Hume presents as an almost mechanical reaction can fall on both sides of the moral spectrum since comparison of our pleasure with the disgrace of others could in principle provoke either a positive reaction such as compassion, or a negative one such as envy. Yet, what counts is the relative weight of a passion previously at work:

> 'Tis from the principle of comparison that both these irregular appetites for evil arise. A person, who indulges himself in any pleasure, while his friend lies under affliction, feels the reflected uneasiness from his friend more sensibly by a comparison with the original pleasure, which he himself enjoys. This contrast, indeed, ought also to enliven the present pleasure. *But as grief here suppos'd to be the predominant passion, every addition falls to that side,* and is swallow'd up in it, without operating in the least upon the contrary affection.[86]

He develops a similar explanation for the relief a criminal may find in penance.[87] In both cases, Hume is merely interested in explaining the psychological relations of ideas and impressions involved in the mechanical production of certain psychological effects or passions, regardless of their moral content. Thus, he finds also that comparison plays a crucial role in both the genesis of envy and malice, although with a significant difference: 'That envy is excited by some present enjoyment of another, which by comparison diminishes our idea of our own: whereas malice is the unprovok'd desire of producing evil to another, in order to reap a pleasure from the comparison.'[88] At any rate, a crucial factor in the operation of comparison is the resemblance and proximity between the ideas compared, which provides the basis for the imagination to play its part. Indeed, 'a poet is not apt to envy a philosopher, or a poet of a different kind, of a different nation, or of a different age. All these differences prevent or weaken the comparison, and consequently the passion.'[89] In all these cases it is apparent that *the operation of these passions depends on previously established social differences, and competitiveness among those who belong to the same social sphere.* Hume tests these principles to explain political behaviours,[90] and even rules of art,[91] only to conclude that:

> no ideas can affect each other, either by comparison, or by the passions they separately produce, unless they be united together by some relation, which may cause an easy transition of the ideas, and consequently of the emotions or impressions, attending the ideas; and may preserve the one impression in the passage of the imagination to the object of the other.[92]

Indirect passions, whose operation depends on comparison, unveil the differences and similarities embedded in the social structure. Yet, for Hume,

> No quality of human nature is more remarkable of this sociality, both in itself and its consequences, than that *propensity we have to sympathize with others*, and to receive by communication their inclinations and sentiments, however different from, or even contrary to our own.[93]

In accounting for the receptivity to 'hatred, resentment, esteem, love, courage, mirth, melancholy', communication through sympathy would play a more prominent role than 'natural temper and disposition'.[94] It is this sort of communication that Hume wants to elucidate. While the explanation he provides is somewhat mechanical, it refers to ideas and impressions. Thus, in order to sympathise with another person, we would first get to know the other's affections through their effects and external signs: from these we would form an idea; this idea would be then converted into an impression, which would in turn replicate the passion itself, producing an emotion similar to the original one. For Hume, this process is explained through resemblance and contiguity with the original sources of the passion; the fact that we share in the same nature, country, character and so forth with other human beings, makes us all the more receptive to the passions they feel.[95]

Of course, this resemblance would hardly generate a passion in us were it not because of our strong receptivity to any impression related to ourselves.[96] In other words: we can reproduce the emotion we see in others only because resemblance with them brings to mind the idea of ourselves being affected in a similar manner.

Feeling an emotion similar to the emotion another person is feeling would then be the natural effect of understanding/imagining how we would be affected by their situation. This explains why our ability to understand/ imagine their situation, and hence conceive their passion 'in the strongest and most lively manner'[97] increases with resemblance and other relations, such as contiguity, acquaintance, relations of blood and so on. Hume can resort to his own psychological principles: all ideas are borrowed from impressions, 'two kinds of perceptions differ only in the degrees of force and vivacity with which they strike upon the soul', so that 'the lively idea of any object always approaches its impression', something which

> is most remarkable in the opinions and affections: and 'tis there princi-pally that a lively idea is converted into an impression. Our affections depend more upon ourselves, and the internal operations of the mind, than any other impressions; for which reason they arise more naturally from the imagination, and from every lively idea we form of them. This is the nature and cause of sympathy; and 'tis after this manner we enter so deep into the opinions and affections of others, whenever we dis-cover them.[98]

From these principles follow that: 'when we sympathize with the passions and sentiments of others, these movements appear at first in our mind as mere ideas, and are conceiv'd to belong to another person, as we conceive any other matter of fact', but then, 'the ideas of the affections of others are converted into the very impressions they represent, and that the pas-sions arise in conformity to the images we form of them.'[99] This 'conver-sion of an idea into an impression', which takes place in the operation of sympathy, is founded on 'the relation of objects to ourself. Ourself is always intimately present to us.'[100] This principle, which resembles the Stoic idea of *oikeiosis*, is at the heart of the ability we display to understand the point of view of others.[101]

The relevance of the sympathy principle in Hume's science of man is well known. Yet, it is worth noting that, to the extent our passions are boosted by social life, sympathy is at the basis of the enhancement of all indirect passions. As Paul Russell puts it, 'due to the influence of sympathy, approval and disapproval may serve as a "secondary" source of our sense of pride and humility';[102] this secondary source becomes a primary one, however, when we analyse the influence of *reputation* or fame in the genesis of pride or humility, for reputation or fame depend *solely* on the opinion of others, and hence on how we are affected by the emotionally charged opinion of others about our own achievements or failures.

In considering the influence of sympathy on pride and humility, Hume focuses directly on the genesis of these passions in praise and blame. His consideration of this phenomenon introduces us to the paradoxes of this sort of pride and humility. On the one hand, he notes that 'no person is ever prais'd by another for any quality, which wou'd not, if real, produce, of itself, a pride in the person possest of it'.[103] Yet, on the other, he realises that every time a person considers himself 'in the same light, in which he appears to his admirer', this provokes a separate pleasure. It is this pleasure that he specifically has in mind, as a *separate* source of pride. Given his precedent analysis of sympathy, he finds it entirely natural 'for us to embrace the opinions of others in this particular; both from sympathy, which renders all their sentiments intimately present to us; and from reasoning, which makes us regard their judgement, as a kind of argument for what they affirm.' Yet, in addition to the principle of sympathy, in the readiness we show to be influenced by the opinion of others he also finds the influence of the principle of *authority*: two principles which are especially active when the opinions expressed refer to our own worth or character, because 'such judgements are always attended with passion'. Indeed, 'we are peculiarly pleas'd with any thing that confirms the good opinion we have of ourselves, and are easily shock'd with whatever opposes it.'[104]

Of course, as Aristotle had already pointed out, we do not take the same pleasure in the approval of people we do not hold in great regard as we do with approval by people we esteem and appreciate. Likewise, Hume observes that

> Tho' fame in general be agreeable, yet we receive a much greater satisfaction from the approbation of those, whom we ourselves esteem and approve of, than of those, whom we hate and despise. In like manner we are principally mortify'd with the contempt of persons, upon whose judgement we set some value, and are, in a great measure, indifferent about the opinions of the rest of mankind.[105]

Hume takes this as a proof that our desire for fame is not based on an original instinct; rather, he implicitly contends that it is made up of a 'composite reality', based on the operation of sympathy, to the extent that this operation conveys a real knowledge of us. This, however, does not exclude the fact that many people find pleasure even in popular opinion entertained by people whom they otherwise despise, even if that opinion is known to be false.[106] Recognising that affective consonance or dissonance with our fellows may override our own personal opinion represents a further sign of the deeply social character of our nature.

Hume considers and explains usual social phenomena, in which pride and humility result from reputation and fame. He mentions, for instance, how often 'men of good families, but narrow circumstances, leave their friends and country, and rather seek their livelihood by mean and mechanical employments among strangers, than among those, who are acquainted with their birth and education',[107] just to avoid that particular humility – or shame – derived from living among their fellow citizens. Indeed, to the extent that sympathy entails a 'communication of sentiments', grounded 'on the relation of objects to ourselves', both our pain and our pleasure increase with sympathy.[108] Thus, when this sympathy serves only to increase our pain, 'we seek to diminish this sympathy and uneasiness by separating these relations, and placing ourselves in contiguity to strangers'.[109]

Concluding Reflections

Hume's decision to start Book II of the *Treatise*, 'On the Passions', with the analysis of indirect passions is not an arbitrary one. It is in tune with his purpose to study phenomena as they appear to him. Human passions are to be observed in a social context, marked by social differences, the perception of which have an impact in the conception one entertains about oneself, and in the emotions each individual experiences. The fact that emotions reflect our social experience is at the basis of the sociology of emotions. To the extent that Hume has unveiled the relations and structures underlying our emotional experience, he can be taken to be one of the forerunners of this sociological approach.

The connection between self and society is particularly clear in the case of indirect passions such as pride and humility. According to Hume, the connection between pride/humility and the self is an original one. It belongs to the very structure of these passions. Each instance of pride and humility involves the recognition of the relation between a certain pleasant/unpleasant qualities with the self; pride originates not merely when we are pleased by beauty, but also when we associate this beauty with ourselves, through a relation of property: that beautiful object is *mine*. This suggests the idea that property represents an extension of the self, and precisely one which comes to light against the background of society, since, according to Hume, property is established only in so far as the frontiers between yours and mine become clear, with the introduction of a basic social convention.

While the basic social conventions establishing property are at the basis of many instances of pride and humility, we take pride also in many other qualities, such as virtue, beauty and many other bodily accomplishment. Yet neither of these pleasant qualities become actual causes of pride if we abstract of a social context marked by comparison; in addition, the connection between those qualities and pride is boosted by the operation of sympathy, whose logic is especially at work in cases where pride is originated in reputation and fame, even when this fame is lacking in substance.

Based on this analysis, I think it is legitimate to conclude that an analysis of instances of pride, such as the one attempted by Hume in the *Treatise*, represents a gateway into the social structure and the cultural ideas entertained in social interactions, as claimed by the sociology of emotions. In so far as this conclusion is grounded on Hume's 'science of man', we are invited to recognise the potential of that science for analysing the different social contexts in which human beings conduct their lives.

Notes

1. Frederick G. Whelan, *Order and Artifice in Hume's Political Philosophy* (Princeton: Princeton University Press, 1985), p. 149.
2. Donald W. Livingston, *Hume's Philosophy of Common Life* (Chicago and London: University of Chicago Press, 1984), p. 38.
3. Christopher J. Berry, *Essays on Hume, Smith and the Scottish Enlightenment* (Edinburgh: Edinburgh University Press, 2018), p. 147.
4. Berry, *Essays*, pp. 208, 209.
5. Christopher J. Berry, *Social Theory of the Scottish Enlightenment* (Edinburgh: Edinburgh University Press, 1997), p. 59.
6. Christopher J. Berry, *David Hume* (New York: Continuum, 2009), pp. 13, 25.
7. Berry, *Social Theory*, p. 59.
8. Tamás Demeter, 'Hume's Experimental Method', *British Journal for the History of Philosophy* 20:3 (2012), pp. 577–99, at p. 587.
9. David Hume, *An Enquiry Concerning Human Understanding*, ed. Lewis Amherst Selby-Bigge, rev. P. H. Nidditch (Oxford: Clarendon Press, 1975), p. 83.
10. Berry, *Essays*, p. 21.
11. Berry, *Essays*, p. 212.
12. Whelan, *Order and Artifice*, pp. 137–8.
13. David Hume, *A Treatise of Human Nature*. The text will be referred to by 'T' and by the book, section, part and paragraph; pages will be given according to the Selby-Bigge edition (SBN), ed. Lewis Amherst Selby-Bigge, rev. P. H. Nidditch (Oxford: Clarendon Press, 1978); and the Fate Norton edition (FN) ed. David Fate Norton and Mary J. Norton (Oxford: Clarendon Press, 2011). (T 1.4.7.3; SBN, p. 265; FN, p. 172).
14. Annette Baier, *A Progress of Sentiments: Reflections on Hume's Treatise* (Cambridge: Cambridge University Press, 1991).

15. Claudia M. Schmidt, *David Hume: Reason in History* (University Park: Pennsylvania State University Press, 2003), p. 161.
16. Ana Marta González, *Sociedad civil y normatividad. La teoría social de David Hume* (Madrid: Dyckinson, 2013).
17. Russell Hardin, *David Hume: Moral and Political Theorist* (Oxford: Oxford University Press, 2007), p. 28.
18. Hartmut Kliemt, *Moralische Institutionen. Empiristische Theorien ihrer Evolution* (Freiburg, 1985); Christopher J. Finlay, *Hume's Social Philosophy. Human Nature and Commercial Sociability in A Treatise of Human Nature* (London and New York: Continuum, 2007); and Schmidt, *David Hume.*
19. *T* 2.1.1.1; SBN, p. 275; FN, p. 181.
20. *T* 2.1.1.2, p. 276; FN, p. 181.
21. *T* 2.1.1.2, p. 276; FN, p. 181.
22. *T* 2.1.1.4, p. 276; FN, p. 182.
23. *T* 2.1.1.4, pp. 276–7; FN, p. 182.
24. *T* 2.3.9.2; SBN, p. 438; FN, p. 280.
25. *T*; SBN, p. xvi; FN, p. 4.
26. *T*; SBN, p. xix; FN, p. 6.
27. David Owen, 'Hume and the Mechanics of the Mind', in F. David Fate Norton & Jacqueline Anne Taylor (eds), *The Cambridge Companion to Hume* (Cambridge: Cambridge University Press, 2009), pp. 70–104, p. 101.
28. In speaking of 'humility' as a passion, Hume departs verbally from the moral tradition which distinguished between the virtue of humility and the sentiment of humiliation, but most likely he is also making a point, namely, rejecting the virtuous quality of certain attitudes which in his view are not compatible with a worldly existence. See James Moore, 'Hume and Hutcheson', in Michael Alexander Stewart and John P. Wright (eds), *Hume and Hume's Connexions* (University Park: Pennsylvania State University Press, 1995), pp. 23–57, p. 30.
29. *T* 2.3.9.2; SBN, p. 438; FN, p. 280.
30. *T* 2.2.1.2; SBN, p. 329; FN, p. 214.
31. Rachel Cohon, 'Hume's Indirect Passions', in Elisabeth S. Radcliffe (ed.), *A Companion to Hume* (London: Wiley-Blackwell, 2008), pp. 159–84, at p. 164. Donald Davidson observed that the cause of pride is not to be differentiated from the object of pride at least in one respect: pride is constituted by certain (propositional) beliefs – for example, the house is beautiful, the house is mine – and it is these (intentional) beliefs that work as causes of the feeling of pride. Donald Davidson, *Essays on Actions and Events* (Oxford: Oxford University Press, 1980).
32. *T* 2.1.2.30; SBN, p. 279; FN, p. 183.
33. *T* 2.1.3.2; SBN, p. 280; FN, p. 184.
34. *T* 2.1.3.2; SBN, p. 280; FN, p. 184.
35. 'Mankind is an inventive species, and where an invention is obvious and absolutely necessary, it may as properly be said to be natural as any thing that

proceeds immediately from original principles, without the intervention of thought or reflexion' (*T* 3.2.1.19; SBN, p. 484; FN, p. 311).

36. *T* 2.1.3.5; SBN, p. 281; FN, p. 184.
37. See Owen, *Mechanics of the Mind*.
38. *T* 2.1.3; SBN, pp. 281–2; FN, p. 185.
39. *T* 2.1.4.3; SBN, p. 283; FN, p. 186.
40. *T* 2.1.4.4, p. 284; FN, p. 186.
41. *T* 2.1.4.4; SBN, p. 284, FN, p. 186.
42. Charles Taylor, *The Explanation of Behaviour* (London: Routledge, 1964).
43. Arlie R. Hochschild, *The Managed Heart: Commercialization of Human Feeling* (Berkeley: University of California Press, 2003 [1983]); Arlie R. Hochschild, *The Commercialization of Intimate Life: Notes from Home and Work* (Berkeley, Los Angeles and London: University of California Press, 2007); Theodore Kemper 'Themes and Variations in the Sociology of Emotions', in Kemper (ed.), *Research Agendas in the Sociology of Emotions* (New York: State University of New York Press, 1990); Thomas Scheff, *Microsociology. Discourse, Emotion and Social Structure* (Chicago: The University of Chicago Press, 1990); Thomas Scheff, *Emotions, the Social Bond and Human Reality: Part/Whole Analysis* (Cambridge: Cambridge University Press, 1997).
44. Ana Marta González, 'In Search of a Sociological Explanation for the Emotional Turn', *Sociologia, problemas e práticas* 85 (2017), pp. 27–45, at p. 39; Ana Marta González, 'Emotional Culture and the Role of Emotions in Cultural Analysis', in González (ed.), *The Emotions and Cultural Analysis* (London: Routledge, 2012), pp. 1–15.
45. *T* 2.1.5.6; SBN, p. 287; FN, p. 188.
46. *T* 2.1.5.7; SBN, p. 287; FN, p. 188.
47. *T* 2.1.5.7; SBN, p. 288; FN, p. 188. There is also a further reason for this requirement of an external cause of pride, for, were pride to depend on nature alone, then we would be perpetually proud; and since humility is in the same situation as pride, none of them would ever make its appearance (*T* 2.1.5.7; SBN, p. 288; FN, p. 188). In other words: the need for an external cause to activate these passions prevents their reciprocal neutralisation. And, on this basis, we could add: the fact that unequal external causes of both humility and pride are present in everybody would account for the diversity of temperaments.
48. Whelan, *Order and Artifice*, p. 161; emphasis added.
49. *T* 2.1.8; SBN, p. 301; FN, p. 196.
50. *T* 2.1.6.10; SBN, p. 291; FN, p. 191.
51. *T* 2.1.6.6; SBN, p. 292; FN, p. 191.
52. *T* 2.1.6.7; SBN, p. 293; FN, pp. 191–2.
53. *T* 2.1.7.8; SBN, p. 293; FN, p. 192.
54. *T* 2.1.7.9; SBN, pp. 293–4; FN, p. 192.
55. *T* 2.1.7; SBN, p. 295; FN, p. 193.
56. *T* 2.1.8; SBN, p. 298; FN, p. 195.

57. *T* 2.1.8; SBN, p. 301; FN, p. 196.
58. *T* 2.1.8; SBN, p. 301; FN, p. 197.
59. Colin Campbell, *The Romantic Ethic and the Spirit of Modern Consumerism* (Oxford: Oxford University Press, 2005), p. 158.
60. *T* 2.1.8; SBN, p. 302; FN, p. 197.
61. *T* 2.1.8.8; SBN, p. 302; FN, p. 197.
62. *T* 2.1.8.8, pp. 302–3; FN, pp. 197–8.
63. *T* 2.1.9.1; SBN, p. 303; FN, p. 198.
64. *T* 2.1.9.2; SBN, p. 304; FN, p. 198.
65. *T* 2.1.9.4, p. 305; FN, p. 199.
66. *T* 2.1.9.5; SBN, p. 306; FN, p. 200.
67. *T* 2.1.9.6; SBN, p. 306; FN, p. 200.
68. *T* 2.1.9.8; SBN, p. 307; FN, p. 200.
69. *T* 2.1.9.8; SBN, p. 307; FN, p. 200.
70. *T* 2.1.9.9; SBN, p. 307; FN, p. 200.
71. *T* 2.1.9.11; SBN, p. 307; FN, pp. 200–1.
72. *T* 2.1.10.1; SBN, pp. 309–10; p. FN, 210.
73. *T* 2.1.10.1; SBN, p. 310; FN, p. 202.
74. *T* 2.1.10.3; SBN, p. 311; FN, p. 203.
75. *T* 2.1.10.4; SBN, p. 312; FN, p. 203.
76. *T* 2.1.10.6; SBN, p. 313; FN, p. 204.
77. *T* 2.1.10.7; SBN, p. 314; FN, p. 204.
78. *T* 2.1.10.9; SBN, p. 314; FN, p. 204.
79. *T* 2.1.10.7; SBN, p. 313; FN, p. 204.
80. *T* 2.1.10.7; SBN, p. 313; FN, p. 204.
81. *T* 2.1.11.12; SBN, p. 316; FN, p. 205.
82. Immanuel Kant, *Religion within the Boundaries of Mere Reason*, trans. Allen Wood (Cambridge: Cambridge University Press, 1998), p. 51.
83. *T* 2.1.10.12; SBN, pp. 315–16; FN, p. 205.
84. *T* 2.2.8.8; SBN, p. 375; FN, p. 242.
85. *T* 2.2.8.10; SBN, p. 376; FN, p. 242.
86. *T* 2.2.8, SBN, pp. 376–7; FN, pp. 242–3.
87. *T* 2.2.8.11; SBN, pp. 376–7; FN, p. 242.
88. *T* 2.2.8.12; SBN, p. 377; FN, p. 243.
89. *T* 2.2.8; SBN, p. 378; FN, p. 244.
90. For instance, the fact that any party in a civil war always choose to call in a foreign enemy at any hazard rather than submit to their fellow citizens (*T* 2.2.8.17; SBN, p. 379; FN, p. 244).
91. *T* 2.2.8.18; SBN, p. 379; FN, p. 244.
92. *T* 2.2.8.20; SBN, p. 380; FN, p. 245.
93. *T* 2.1.11.2; SBN, p. 316; FN, p. 206.
94. *T* 2.1.11.2; SBN, p. 317; FN, p. 206.
95. *T* 2.1.11; SBN, p. 318; FN, p. 207.
96. *T* 2.1.11.3; SBN, p. 317; FN, p. 206.

97. T 2.1.11.5; SBN, p. 318; FN, p. 207.
98. T 2.1.11.7; SBN, p. 319; FN, pp. 207–8.
99. T 2.1.11.8; SBN, p. 319; FN, p. 208.
100. T 2.1.11.8; SBN, p. 320; FN, p. 208.
101. Ana Marta González, 'Humean Keys for Social Theory: From Natural Circles of Sympathy to the Formation of an Impartial Moral Judgment', in Alejandro G. Vigo (ed.), *Oikeiosis and the Natural Bases of Morality: From Classical Stoicism to Modern Philosophy* (Hildesheim, Zürich and New York: Georg Olms, 2012), pp. 231–62.
102. Paul Russell, *The Riddle of Hume's Treatise. Skepticism, Naturalism and Irreligion* (Oxford: Oxford University Press, 2008), p. 252.
103. T 2.1.11.9; SBN, p. 320; FN, p. 208.
104. T 2.1.11.9; SBN, p. 321; FN, p. 209.
105. T 2.1.11.11; SBN, p. 321; FN, p. 209.
106. T 2.1.11.19; SBN, p. 324; FN, p. 211.
107. T 2.1.11.14; SBN, p. 322; FN, p. 209.
108. T 2.1.11.19; SBN, p. 324; FN, p. 210.
109. T 2.1.11.15, p. 322; FN, p. 210.

10

The Reception and Study of David Hume's Economic Thought in China

Zhang Zheng-ping

David Hume's economic ideas are an indispensable part both of his own science of human nature and the wider history of economic thought. As studies on David Hume's economics have developed, we have acquired a better appreciation of the internal logic of his economic thought. This chapter outlines the reception of Hume in China since 1930. It aims to introduce Western scholars to the main trends in the Chinese understanding of Hume and his works. During the past 100 years David Hume has appeared in various guises to the eyes of Chinese scholars. We can identify three broad stages in the Chinese study of Hume: before 1980 he was first seen as a philosopher who had great influence on Immanuel Kant and whose scepticism and agnosticism needed to be criticised; between 1980 and 2000 he was then seen as a British philosopher and essayist who argued for a science of human nature; and since 2000, Hume the historian and political economist has come to be known to Chinese readers. To understand the various stages in the Chinese study of Hume, we need to understand both broader trends in Hume studies and the economic development of China in the context of international competition.

When he was lingering on his deathbed in 1776, David Hume wrote 'My Own Life', which was short and 'without vanity' and contained 'little more than the History of my Writings'. Most of the important writings in Hume's life did not meet with much luck on their first publication: *The Treatise of Human Nature* (THN), in Hume's words, 'fell dead-born from the press, without reaching such distinction, as even to excite a murmur among the zealots'; *An Enquiry concerning the Principles of Morals* (EPM), which was very highly thought of by Hume, 'came unnoticed and unobserved into the world'; and *The History of England* (HE), did not attract enough attention when first published, though it 'was better received' when the second book was published. It seemed that, during Hume's whole life, only the *Political Discourses* (PD) 'was successful on the first publication'.[1]

Paradoxically, however, the reception of these writings by later generations was almost the opposite to their fortunes during Hume's life. *THN* has always been regarded as one of the great philosophical works, *HE* was a must-read for English students in the nineteenth century, and *An Enquiry concerning Human Understanding* (*EHU*) and *EPM* have been considered seriously by scholars since the nineteenth century. On the other hand, *PD* has not attracted much scholarly attention. This does not mean that scholars have not attached importance to *PD*. Of course, some scholars have still paid attention to Hume's political thought and economic ideas and interpreted the texts from different points of view.[2] But among the thousands of articles and hundreds of monographs on Hume, articles, collections and monographs on Hume's economic thought are much fewer in number than those on Hume's philosophy and other writings. Among these few studies are *Writings on Economics* (Nelson, 1955) edited by Eugene Rotwein, which included the editor's long introduction to Hume's economic psychology and economic philosophy, and *David Hume's Political Economy* (Routledge, 2009), which included thirteen articles, edited by Carl Wennerlind and Margaret Schabas. Since monetarism arose in the 1980s, there have been dozens of articles about Hume's monetary ideas, such as the connection between Hume's monetary theory and the monetarism of American economists.[3] The publication of these papers and chapters is significant and contributes to our understanding of Hume's economic studies.

Hume's introduction into China came a little later than that. Smith's *Wealth of Nations*, which had long been regarded as a guide to how to make a nation and its people rich and strong, was translated by Yan Fu in 1902.[4] In the late nineteenth century and the early twentieth century Chinese intellectuals were eager to learn from Smith, Thomas Henry Huxley and others. They wanted to learn how to improve China and make the country more economically and politically powerful. Some three decades later, David Hume came to be known to Chinese intellectuals as one of the great philosophers of the Great Britain. Hume's main works had been introduced to Chinese readers one after another from the 1930s: first, the philosophical works, then the economic and political writings, and finally the historical works. It took nearly 100 years and several generations of the translators for this process to take place.

Accordingly, Chinese scholars have always explored the different facets of Hume's thought, including the philosophical, political, ethical, aesthetic, historical and even the economic aspects of his writings, but the focus of these studies has shifted with the gradual availability of Chinese translations of his various works. The reception of a particular thinker has its own historical and academic background, and this context is distinct from the context in which the author in question wrote his work. When David Hume's writings were introduced to Chinese scholars, which essays the translators chose to translate and the arguments that scholars had about them were shaped by the intellectual interests of that period. To trace the evolution of the Chinese understanding of Hume, we need to understand how the translation and the intellectual context in Chinese scholarship shapes the issues that are discussed. It is difficult to answer this definitively as Hume's writings ranged so widely, but by tracking the details of the scholarly debates we can trace the evolution of Chinese thinking about Hume. The rest of this chapter will give a sketch of the reception of Hume in China since the 1930s and then focus on Chinese study and analysis of Hume's economic ideas. This chapter is divided into three parts: first, there is a brief outline of the translation of Hume's writings in China and some typical examples of research on Hume's philosophical works; second, there is a survey of Chinese scholars' studies on Hume's economic thought; and third there is a discussion of the reasons behind Hume's changing image in China.

The Reception of Hume in China and Chinese Translations

I will divide the short history of Chinese translation and reception of Hume's ideas into three periods according to the different images of Hume in Chinese eyes: the first period lasts roughly from 1930 to 1980 when he was viewed as a great British philosopher who had an important influence on Immanuel Kant; the second lasts from 1980 to 2000 when he was primarily viewed as a philosopher of human nature and as an empirical philosopher; and the third has lasted since 2001 when Hume as polymath, historian, political philosopher and also enlightened thinker has been to the fore.

Among Hume's writings, *EHU*, parts of *THN* and 'My Own Life' were the first works introduced into China. The first Chinese version of Hume's works was divided into three volumes, translated by Wu Guang-jian into vernacular Chinese, and published using vertical typesetting into three volumes in 1930, and reprinted in one book in 1933 by the Commercial Press. In the preface to the three-volume version, the publisher introduced Hume as a philosopher who influenced Kant and as a historian superior to Robertson and Gibbon, but whose achievements in philosophy were greater than those in historiography.[5] From this introduction, we can see that Chinese intellectuals' first acquaintance with Hume was primarily as a philosopher. Hume was juxtaposed with Kant, doubtless because of Kant's famous words that 'Hume's works awakened him from a dream'.

This reminded later readers that Kant's philosophy had close connections with Hume, and so it was Chinese interest in Kant that led them to Hume. So in China the relationship between Kant and Hume influenced the way Hume was introduced to Chinese scholars at the beginning of the period in which European scholars began to be received in China.

It is not surprising that the translators always linked Hume with Kant. In fact, British empiricism and German rationalism are not quite the opposite poles that they are depicted as being in introductions to the history of philosophy. Indeed, contemporary Kant scholars still find the shadow of Hume's philosophy in Kant. When Chinese intellectuals introduced Western philosophy to the reader, they tended to prefer rationalism to empiricism, and preferred Kant to Hume, partly because there had been a long empirical tradition in the intellectual history of China, and they hoped for a new kind of rationalist philosophy to enlighten the Chinese. Empiricism was too familiar to Chinese people, and so interest in Kant surpassed interest in Hume. At that period, Chinese scholars were willing to accept all sorts of Western philosophical ideas, so it was not only the writings of Kant that became popular but also those of Hegel, Karl Marx, Locke and Berkeley. In the 1950s Marxism and historical materialism formed the mainstream of Chinese academic life, and so the agnosticism of Hume and Kant became subject to criticism.[6] There were three papers critiquing Hume's and Kant's philosophy – *Critique on Hume's Agnosticism*, *Critique on Kant's Agnosticism* and *Agnosticism is the Secret Idealism*, which were published in the *Guangming Daily* between 1955 and 1956. The target of these three papers was idealism, the opposite of materialism, and it seems that their authors thought that agnosticism was equal to idealism; according to their arguments, the agnosticism seemed to lie in Hume's scepticism and Kant's ideas on belief and the limit of human knowledge. To some extent, such critiques of Hume and Kant showed the Chinese philosophical response to the political circumstances of the period.

In 1937 another translation of *EHU* in modern Chinese – by Guan Wen-yun – was also published with horizontal type by the Commercial Press, a very authoritative publishing institution in the translation of Western classical texts which was responsible for publishing most of Hume's philosophical writings in Chinese. In 1962 the same press published the first Chinese translation of *Dialogues concerning Natural Religion* (DNR). The two translators were Chen Xiu-zhai and Cao Mian-zhi, the former dedicated to European philosophy and the famous translator of the works of Gottfried Wilhelm Leibniz.

With regard to the early period of translating famous Western works into Chinese, covering the fifty years between 1930 and 1980, there are two points worth noting: (1) only two *complete* works by Hume (*EHU* and *DNR*) were translated into Chinese, and Hume's philosophical and religious ideas were compared with those of Kant and criticised by Chinese scholars from the viewpoint of Marxist historical materialism; (2) the translators were not Hume scholars and in general otherwise did little research on Hume – Wu Guan-jian translated a number of English and French novels and translated not only Hume's work but also other British thinkers such as John Locke and George Berkeley; Chen and Cao taught Western philosophy in the universities and wrote about the history of European philosophy but were not what you would call Hume scholars.

The 1980s were an open, vibrant period for intellectual circles in China. A large number of Western philosophical works, ancient, modern and contemporary, were introduced to Chinese readers at this time. The first complete translation of *THN* by Guan Wen-yun was published in 1980 and reprinted several times. This is still the authoritative version that students refer to today. After that, there was an upsurge in the translation of Hume's writings, with a focus on Hume's *Essays, Moral, Political and Literary* (*EMPL*), *PD* and *EPM*.

Between 1981 and 2000 the first new Chinese translation of Hume was the economic essays, though this is less surprising than it might first appear given the burgeoning Chinese interest in economic development at this time. Since the 1979 reforms in China, economic development has become the main business of the government, and Chinese scholars needed new theories of economic policymaking and economic behaviour. The edited collection *Hume's Economic Writings* (translated by Chen-Wei), which included nine essays, appeared in 1984. Hu Qi-lin, a Chinese economist, wrote a long preface to introduce Hume's economic theories, especially his theory of money and the idea of free trade. Subsequently nineteen of his political essays were chosen and translated into Chinese, and published with the title *Hume's Political Writings* in 1993. A preface by the translator, Zhang Ruo-heng, provided a short sketch of Hume's political thought. The two prefaces showed that the authors recognised the connections between the science of human nature and Hume's political and economic thought. They believed that Hume's philosophy of human nature was the basis of his theory of economics and politics, although they did not analyse the details of the relationship.[7]

Most of Hume's essays (*EMPL* and *PD*) have been picked out and translated. To date, there have been at least five translations of Hume's essays,[8] which shows that the translators and the publishers regarded Hume as a successful essayist who was good at discussing taste, tragedy, the writing of essays, study of history and other topics. It seemed that, in the eyes of

Chinese publishers, Hume was an acute critic of the literary and philosophical currents of the eighteenth century. The essay is also an important genre in Chinese writing. Different translators have had different understandings and representations of Hume's rhetoric and style.

In 1999 there was a new translation of *EHU* by Commercial Press, and the translator was moreover a Hume scholar.[9] In the same year, *EPM* also had its first modern Chinese translation, by Wang Shu-qin. Another Chinese version of *EPM* by Zeng Xiao-ping, a scholar whose studies had focused on empiricism, was published by the Commercial Press in 2001. Since 2001 Hume's writings have been published in new Chinese versions and won more readers. For example, there have been four versions of *THN* and two versions of Hume's *Natural History of Religion* (NHR) by different publishers, though only one translation of *DNR* has been reprinted several times by Commercial Press. In 2010s a translation of Hume's six-volume *History of England* was published by the Ji-lin Publishing Group, although some readers and scholars pointed out there were many errors included a misunderstanding of the key term 'British History'[10] in this version.[11] Hume's *PD* and *EMPL* were freshly translated and published under different titles – *Hume's Essays: Politics and Economics* and *Hume's Essays: Literary and Morals* – by Zhejiang University Press in 2011, their translators making reference to various editors' important notes such as those found in Eugene F. Miller's edition of *EMPL* (Liberty Classics, 1985) and Knud Haakonssen's edition of *PD* (Cambridge University Press, 1994). Two volumes of Letters of David Hume have been translated by Zhou Bao-wei, who had also translated Ernest Campbell Mossner's *The Life of David Hume* (Cambridge University Press, 1980), but the volumes have been not published yet.

To date, nearly all of Hume's writings have been introduced to Chinese readers, the exception being minor works or edited collections such as the *New Letters of David Hume* (Oxford University Press, 1954). In addition to these, nine English studies on Hume's philosophical ideas have been translated into Chinese since 1980. Three of them were by A. J. Ayer, with his *Hume* (Oxford University Press, 1980) available in two translations – one published on the mainland, another in Taiwan. Barry Stroud's *David Hume* (Routledge & Kegan Paul, 1977), Elizabeth S. Radcliffe's *On Hume* (Wadsworth, 2000), Donald W. Livingston's *David Hume's Philosophy of Common Life* (University of Chicago Press, 1986), Christopher J. Berry's *David Hume* (Bloomsbury Academic, 2013); Ernest Campbell Mossner's *The Life of David Hume* (Oxford University, 1980); and David Edmonds and John Eidinow's *Rousseau's Dog: A Tale of Two Philosophers* (Faber & Faber, 2006) have also been made available Chinese readers.

Translations, of course, contribute to academic studies, and further to the publication of these books, some Chinese scholars also published their research on Hume's philosophy. Between 1980 and 2000 there were only six monographs on Hume published by four authors, and three of them were by Zhou Xiao-liang, a scholar dedicated to Hume's philosophical studies. Most of these studies discussed Hume's philosophy of human nature, while only one book focused on Hume's epistemology.[12] There were more than 100 papers and articles on Hume's philosophy, with epistemological questions, such as the 'cause–effect' and 'is–ought' problem', and methodological questions, such as induction, or Hume's attitude towards religion and agnosticism being the main topics. If one inputs 'David Hume' into the Chinese National Knowledge Infrastructure (CNKI) with the time limit from 1980 to 2000, one gets 162 items, some eight items per year. These articles cover a wide range of Hume's thought – philosophical, aesthetic, ethical, economic and political – but only a few were about Hume's economic thought. By that period, most of Hume writings had been translated into Chinese except for the letters and *The History of England*. It was worth noting that by this period Hume was not perceived merely as a key influence on Kant but as a great thinker in his own right who has an important place in European philosophical history.

Since 2001 an increasing number of scholars have become interested in Hume's ideas, and there have been twenty-three monographs on Hume published since that year. Hume's political philosophy is one of the most popular topics. Gao Quan-xi, notably, published his *Hume's Political Philosophy* focusing on Hume's theory of justice in 2004, while in 2013 Li Wei-bin engaged with Gao's views in his *New Inquiry into Hume's Political Philosophy* emphasising the role of naturalism.[13] The 'cause–effect' and 'is–ought' problems and epistemology have remained important subjects in studies of Hume's philosophy, but there has been increasing interest in his moral and political writings as well.[14] Hume's aesthetics became a new theme especially for Ph.D. dissertations, with scholars discussing questions such as what taste meant and the role of reason and sentiment in Hume's texts.[15] Obviously, the research during this period has become deeper, and there have been attempts to understand Hume from fresh perspectives. Hume's economic thought, the theory of trade, and his religious thought also became new topics for Chinese scholars' work. [16]

During the last nineteen years the number of papers on Hume have been increasing rapidly. There are 926 items relating to David Hume between 1 January 2001 and 31 October 2019 in CNKI, including

165 Master's and doctoral dissertations. It is surprising that the number is five times that of the second period. This academic phenomenon may be due to the increasing number of students, researchers and journals and the enlargement of Chinese universities. Scholars began to do more detailed studies on more varied subjects (political theory, aesthetic judgement, etc.) and discussed key notions, such as sympathy, artificial versus natural virtue, justice/property, utility, taste and so on. It is worth noting that more students and scholars have also begun to pay attention to Hume's economic ethics and his economic philosophy more generally.

With this expansion of research on Hume, Hume's image in China began to change. Chinese scholars have come to know more theoretical aspects of Hume's thought, in particular the great system that he himself called the 'science of man': 'all the sciences have a relation, greater or less, to human nature', 'even Mathematics, Natural Philosophy and Natural Religion, are in some measure dependent on the science of Man'.[17] Chinese studies on Hume and the Scottish Enlightenment have increasingly come back to this idea of a systematic 'science of man'.

Hume as a Political Economist in China

As mentioned above, Hume's monetary theory was first introduced to Chinese readers in the 1980s. In the Preface to *Hume's Economic Writings*, entitled 'A Short Review of Hume's Economic Thought', Hu Qi-lin analysed Hume's quantity theory of money as well as the foundation of his economic theory and the claims about free trade and commerce. Hu asserts that the philosophical basis of Hume's economic theory is his *A Treatise of Human Nature*. The account of human nature in *THN* provide a strong argument that selfishness and avarice are innate to human beings, and that selfishness should not be restrained if an individual does not threaten the public interest when he or she pursues his or her self-interest. However, it may be worth discussing whether Hume's theory of monetary quantity is scientific or not. Hu contended that the theory was not scientific but admitted that the theory was significant as an argument against mercantilism. That Hu thought Hume's theory not scientific might be a reflection of ideology. When he analysed Hume's monetary theory from the viewpoint of Marxist political economy, he believed that Hume fell foul of Marxism in two regards: (1) Hume's theory of monetary quantity was based on the faulty hypothesis that money and commodities have no value before they enter circulation and only formed their value in circulation; (2) Hume turned the order of the circulation between money and commodities upside down.[18] Both of these reflect a Marxist analysis of Hume. Moreover, Hu's overview was the first introduction of Hume's economic thought to Chinese readers, and his conclusion that Hume was one of the opponents of mercantilism was different from the standard Western opinion that Hume was one of the last of the mercantilists.

Chinese economists became interested in Hume's theory of monetary quantity partly because of the influence of the monetarism of American economists. Monetarism became popular with the emergence of the monetary theories of John Maynard Keynes and Milton Friedman. The theory was introduced to China very quickly, and became popular with Chinese economists in the 1980s. So, when Hu introduced Hume's economic thought, he put the emphasis on his monetary theory because monetarism was the fashionable topic of discussion of that time. However, the fashion for monetarism was transitory. There was only one paper on Hume's monetary theory before the year 2000, which only introduced the main points of Hume's theory and reviewed Hume's attainments in the historical context, before offering a short criticism of Hume's theory from the viewpoint of Marxist political economy.[19]

Hu Qi-lin also introduced Japanese economists' studies on Hume. He translated Ohno Seizaburo's 'Hume's Theory of Civil Society' (おおの せ いざぶろう), adding it as an appendix to *Hume's Economic Writings*. Ohno Seizaburo examined Hume's evolving understanding of civil society from 1739 to 1752.[20] He argued that, if we want to understand Hume better, we should link his moral philosophy with political economy in our mind and not separate these two issues. Indeed, Hume scholars have acknowledged that it is necessary to examine his political philosophy, economic ethics and aesthetics in the frame of Hume's system of human nature.

From 1980 to 2000 Chinese economists paid little attention to Hume, except for one piece on 'Hume's Economic Ethical Thought',[21] which claimed to explore the methodology of *THN* and its influence of his economic ethics. The author asserted that Hume got rid of abstract moral principles and instead explored human nature and ethical matters from an economic and social standpoint, which paved the way for the union of economics and ethics. The paper made a good attempt to study Hume's economic ethics, and some scholars became interested in Hume's economics as a result of it. As mentioned in the first section, there have been more than ten papers and dissertations on Hume's economic thought since 2001, involving his analysis of consumption, economic growth, the balance of international trade and other arguments. The authors like to talk about two strands in Hume's economic thought. One of these is the problem of the homo economicus hypothesis in economic theory. The hypothesis of the selfish homo economicus runs counter to the Confucian tradition, so Chinese scholars have needed to think more about it.

Since the birth of political economy, the supposed selfish economic man has been considered to stem from Adam Smith's claims in *The Wealth of Nations* (Book I, Chapter 2) about the case of the butcher, the brewer and the baker. However, this passage in itself cannot explain all the problems associated with the economic man hypothesis, so some economic scholars have begun to look for other bases for the idea as it appears in modern economic thinking. The origin of this supposition was regarded to be Hume's THN by Yao Hui and Yang Zhong-jun. In their *The Hypothesis of Human Nature in Western Economics: From Hume's Philosophy of Human Nature to Bowles's Hypothesis of Social Preferences*, the two authors argue that Hume stated clearly that man is selfish and that selfishness and avarice were the sole motive of his labour. However, they also note that he also mentioned that man feels sympathy for others, so there is also an altruistic disposition in human nature; and this led to a tension in the relation between selfishness and altruism. In response to this, Yao and Yang turned to the work of Samuel Bowles to rectify the hypothesis of selfish man.[22] The study represents an attempt, to some degree, to explore the theme of economic thought and Hume's system. In addition to the hypothesis of economic man, the 'invisible hand' is another important notion of economics. The nature of the connection between the economic systems of David Hume and Adam Smith became a feature of the scholarship.[23] This analysis is a little cursory because the authors emphasised Smith was influenced by Hume on the subject of the selfishness of human nature, without noting that 'selfish man' was the major characteristic of Mandeville's and others' texts.

The second strand in Chinese discussions of Hume's economic thought concerns itself with particular Humean concepts, such as consumption, economic growth and the balance of international trade. Almost all the papers are based on an analysis of Hume's economic essays and merely give interpretations of concrete economic matters. For example, in his 2009 paper Yan An talks about 'Hume's Theory of Economic Growth and Its Influence', but only analyses the notion of wealth and Hume's ideas of growth in brief.[24] Another paper, on 'Hume's Moral Concept of Consumption',[25] noted that the desire to consume is located in human nature, the aim of consumption being to increase human happiness, and should thus not be seen as blameworthy, and that utility and sympathy are two principles for the judgement of consumptive actions.

Since 2010 there have been some new studies on Hume's accounts
of commerce and economic ideas. Moving on from the analysis of mere
economic theory and the economic ethics of Hume, the new studies have
paid more attention to context and interdisciplinary methods in Hume
studies. For example, 'utility' is one of the key concepts in both Hume's
moral philosophy and his economic philosophy. Cheng Qi-qi has examined the significance of Hume's notion of utility from the perspective of
the history of economic thought and research into behavioural economics. In his *Hume's Utility Theory and Its Implications*, Cheng pointed out
that, if, like Hume, we consider the source of all utility to be the feelings
of pain and pleasure, and discuss the impact of the feelings and imagination on the calculation of utility, it is conducive to understand individual
utility and to construct a utility function which is close to reality. Cheng
observes that the diversity of feelings determines the diversity of utility and that the characteristics of feelings and imagination determine
their presentation and strength, and so finally determine the forms of
utility.[26] He also attempts to find the relations between the motives of
human feelings and economic behaviour. He thinks that this generalised
model of human behaviour may provide valuable insights into contemporary behavioural economics, which is 'a large and rapidly growing field,
and is just beginning to move towards a unified theory that provides a
cohesive alternative or supplement to the standard economic model'.
There are at least two reasons for this proposition. First, this generalised
theory of human behaviour is itself a unifying theory, which is an objective of contemporary behavioural economics because the main significant findings and topics given by different models in the field of modern
behavioural economics can be properly incorporated into this unifying
theory; second, this generalised theory not only implies heuristic mechanisms which have been widely used in interpreting bounded rational
human behaviour, but also, more importantly, contains the transmission
mechanism of the motivational force of a passion, making this theory
more consistent and integrated.[27] Cheng's research on Hume here is not
undertaken from the perspective of the main currents of contemporary
economics, but from that of behavioural economics and experimental
psychology. Through a highly detailed and close perusal of Hume's texts,
he tries to find a causal relationship between passion and behaviour in
Hume's *THN*.

In recent years there have been a further two Chinese-language monographs on Hume's political economy: one focuses on Hume's accounts of
the passions and wealth and makes an attempt to find a coherence in
his science of human nature and political economy; the other scrutinises

Hume's discussions of commerce and politics since the Tudors in his *History of England*. The first is *Passions and Wealth: The Science of Human Nature and Political Economy of David Hume* by Zhang Zheng-ping (Zhejiang University Press, 2018). Zhang describes the ways in which we can understand Hume's economic thought: first, from the perspective of economic history; second, within the framework of theoretical economics; and third, as part of the system of the science of human nature.[28] Zhang tries the third way. She scrutinises *THN*, *EMPL* and *PD*, especially the second book of *THN*, combined with *A Dissertation on the Passions* and other writings such as the letters on economic problems and some chapters of *History of England*. She analyses the mechanism of sympathy and some elements that lead interested affections to prevail over all other passions in human nature. She discusses the relation between interest and utility and researches the market, morality and Hume's theory of human nature with one eye on the tension between wealth and virtue. How do the motivations of economic behaviour arise from the various passions like pride and humility, love and hate? How do one's passions come into concord with the opposing passions of others? The first part of *Passions and Wealth* argues that the passions are the sole origin of human actions, and sympathy is a very important instrument for the communication of the passions. The second part discusses Hume's attitudes to commercial society and his defence of luxury in the eighteenth-century context. *Passions and Wealth* is helpful for Chinese scholars since it helps them 'to understand the philosophic basis of British classical political economy systematically'; 'it is a classical resource for the transformation of modern economics'.[29] It also serves to remind Chinese readers and scholars that there is a political economist Hume.

The second monograph is *Commerce and Politics in David Hume's History of England* (The Boydell Press, 2017; Fu-dan University Press, 2018) by Wei Jia. Wei's intention here is to undertake a systematic study to determine 'the relationship between the three Humes: Hume the political thinker, Hume the historian, and Hume the political economist'.[30] Obviously, political economy is an important theme in Hume, and *The History of England* unfolds broad social, economic and institutional changes. In the first part of *Commerce and Politics*, Wei examines 'Hume's argument that commerce had fundamentally transformed English society and consequently the nature of its government', while in the second part she explores 'Hume's analysis of foreign, financial, and domestic policies by connecting his views on contemporary politics to his account of the seventeenth-century constitutional crisis in Stuart history',[31] One of the explicit purposes of *Commerce and Politics* is to explain Hume's idea of modern commercial society, in other words, the origin and development of commercial society. The distinctiveness of Wei's research lies in her analysis of and focus on Hume's *History of England*. As mentioned above, Hume's *History of England* had long been ignored in China, its scholars seemingly having no interest in Hume as a historian. The belated translation of *The History of England* was a symptom of this. What interested the Chinese for the most part was the philosopher Hume. Wei's *Commerce and Politics* served to remind Chinese readers of Hume's important historical works and was thus very significant for Chinese Hume studies.

Hume in the Context of the Scottish Enlightenment

Roger Emerson said that, 'Hume scholarship is a curious business. It tends to concentrate on the philosophic, religious and political writings, glances occasionally at the historical work and largely ignores Hume's political-economy.'[32] However, Hume did contribute to the discussions of the economic problems in the eighteenth century. Mark Blaug points out that 'Hume made three specific contributions to economic thought: "the so-called specie-flow mechanism;" the notion that there is an inherent connection between the growth of political liberty in the modern commercial societies and that individualism and political freedom flow from economic freedom; and the theme you cannot deduce "ought" from "is."'[33] In the 1980s some Chinese scholars discussed Hume's theory of money while Western economists talked up the quantity theory of money, but Hume had never been regarded as a political economist or economic thinker even when Chinese scholars had discussed his economic notions before 2000.

Influenced by the work of translators, Hume's image in China has changed gradually since 2000. These translations have included not only Hume's writings and studies on Hume's thought but also works on the historical background and other thinkers of the age. Around the year 2000, under the influence of F. A. Hayek's liberal politics and economics, Chinese scholars began to pay attention to research into the Scottish Enlightenment and its ideas. Yu-sheng Lin, a student of Hayek, published an essay 'Of the Scottish Enlightenment' in *Du-shu* – a very popular academic journal at that time – in which he introduced the Scottish Enlightenment as one of Hayek's intellectual sources.[34] Subsequently, in 1997, the first Chinese translation of Adam Smith's *The Theory of Moral Sentiments* was published – nearly 100 years after that of *The Wealth of Nations*. A translation of Adam Ferguson's *An Essay of the History of Civil*

Society followed in 1999. Adam Smith has since come to be regarded as a moral philosopher of the market economy, not only as a classic political economist of Britain. The number of papers and monographs on Smith's moral philosophy have increased rapidly. Various translations of Smith's two main works – *The Wealth of Nations* and *The Theory of Moral Sentiments* – have been sold on the Chinese book market, especially after former prime minister Wen Jia-bao endorsed *The Theory of Moral Sentiments* on several occasions. It seems that, in twenty-first-century China, Smith the moral philosopher has become more significant than Smith the economist. This reversal in Chinese understanding of Smith might in part be due to the Chinese politician's advocacy but it is also a result of the rise in serious research into Smith's moral philosophy. This research on Smith, as a Scottish Enlightenment thinker – not as a classical political economist or a moral philosopher – has begun to be acknowledged by Chinese readers. Unlike the reversal in Smith's image, the reversal in Hume's image is not dependent on the political promotion of Hume's economic thought. It should instead be understood as the consequence of the growth of Hume and Scottish Enlightenment studies in China.

A small group of Chinese scholars have recognised the importance of the Scottish Enlightenment since the late 1990s. Since 2000 Luo Wei-dong and other scholars have organised a series of translations of the works of eighteenth-century Scots like Francis Hutcheson, Adam Ferguson and Thomas Reid, none of whom were previously familiar to Chinese students. They have also translated research on the Scottish Enlightenment such as Christopher J. Berry's *Social Theory of the Scottish Enlightenment* (Edinburgh University Press, 1997) and *The Idea of Commercial Society in the Scottish Enlightenment* (Edinburgh University Press, 2013);[35] the collection *Wealth and Virtue* (Cambridge University Press, 1989), edited by Istvan Hont and Michael Ignatieff; Knud Haakonssen's *Science of Legislator: The Natural Jurisprudence of David Hume and Adam Smith* (Cambridge University Press, 1985) and *Natural Law and Moral Philosophy: From Grotius to the Scottish Enlightenment* (Cambridge University Press, 1996), and others. Ian Ross's *The Life of Adam Smith* (Oxford University Press, 2010) and Ernest Campbell Mossner's *The Life of David Hume* – two important biographies – have also been published by Zhejiang University Press in 2013 and 2017, respectively. The first conference on the Scottish Enlightenment in China was held in 2009, and work in this area continues to today. Younger scholars and students have increasingly become interested in the Scottish Enlightenment, and they are discovering a different intellectual understanding of the eighteenth century with the addition of Hutcheson, Hume, Smith, Reid and other Scots to their reading.

Of course, Chinese economic development forms the great background for the rise of research into British political economy of the eighteenth century. Chinese policymakers and academics are increasingly interested in economic growth and the nature of international competition and tensions between the different nations. Hume and Smith discussed these questions in the eighteenth century and were a source of guidance for Great Britain in that transformative period. China has been undergoing a massive transformation from a traditional society to a modern one, from an agricultural society to a commercial one, and needs a new kind of political economy and moral philosophy to underpin this. The Scottish thinkers Hume, Smith, Ferguson and their contemporaries debated political and economic problems and also reflected on the most appropriate ethic for the emergence of a commercial society. One of the most striking features of their advice was that it did not lead to the sort of violent revolution often associated with the French Enlightenment philosophers. On the contrary, they managed to contribute to the development and progress of Great Britain without aligning themselves with revolutionary movements. It is this aspect of their thinking that makes them attractive to many in contemporary China.

Conclusion

This chapter's examination of the reception and study of Hume in China has shown us the different images of Hume across three distinct periods, and has illustrated the thinking of different generations in the changing China. At each stage Chinese thinkers have approached Hume as a resource for solving the problems that faced China in the throes of transformation. The political economist Hume has been discovered as the Chinese study of the Scottish Enlightenment has expanded and the political and economic development of China has gathered pace. The historian Hume will also come to Chinese readers in the future. But Hume, as he said in 'My Own Life', took himself to be 'a man of letters', not simply a philosopher, a historian, or an essayist like Joseph Addison. The political economist Hume may be important for a present-day China that is involved in trying to understand international trade conflict and which is looking forward to taking on a growing role in the world. But Hume, the Enlightenment thinker and man of the eighteenth century, will continue to appeal to scholars and future generations of Chinese scholars as they uncover new aspects to Hume that speak to their own interests and concerns.

Appendix: Hume's main writings and the details of Chinese translations

Title in Chinese translation	The Original English copyright	Time of first Chinese translation	The translator(s)	Chinese Publisher
EHU	Open Court Publishing Company, 1907	1930	Wu Guang-jian	Commercial Press
	Unknown	1937	Guan Wen-yun	Commercial Press
	Oxford, 1894	1999	Lv Da-ji	Commercial Press
EHU & EMP	Oxford, 1902	2001	Zhou Xiao-liang	Shen-yang Press
DNR	Oxford, 1935	1962	Chen Xiu-zhai & Cao Mian-zhi	Commercial Press
THN	Oxford, 1946	1980	Guan Wen-yun	Commercial Press
	Oxford, 1946	2009	Shi Bi-qiu	Jiu-zhou Press
	Unknown	2009	Jia Guang-lai	Shan-xi Normal University Press
	Unknown	2016	He Jiang	Tai-hai Press
EMP	Oxford, 1902	1999	Wang Shu-qin	China Social Sciences Press
	Oxford, 1902	2001	Zeng Xiao-ping	Commercial Press
Hume's Economic Writings	Longmans, Green & Co. New York, 1912	1984	Chen Wei	Commercial Press
Hume's Political Writings	David Hume's Essays, Warwick House, London (unknown date)	1993	Zhang Ruo-heng	Commercial Press
Hume's Classical Essays	Unknown	2002	Yu Qing	Shanghai University Press
The Natural History of Religion	Adam & Charles Black, edited by H. E. Root, 1956	2003	Xu Xiao-hong	Shanghai People Press
	Unknown	2014	Zeng Xiao-ping	Commercial Press
Hume's Essays	Unknown	2006	Xiao Yu	China Social Sciences Press
Hume's essays on Politics and Economics & Literature and Morality	The Philosophical Works of David Hume (Vol. III), Edinburgh, 1854 reprinted by Thoemmes Continuum, 1996	2011	Zhang Zheng-ping & Ma Wan-li	Zhe-jiang University Press
History of England (Vols 1–6)	Unknown	2012–13	Liu Zhong-jing	Ji-lin Publishing Group

Notes

1. See David Hume, 'My Own Life', in Ernest Campbell Mossner, *The Life of David Hume* (Cambridge: Cambridge University Press, 1980), p. 613.

2. See Walt Whitman Rostow, *Theorists of Economic Growth from David Hume to the Present: With a Perspective on the Next Century* (Oxford: Oxford University Press, 1990).

3. See Arie Arnon, *Monetary Theory and Policy from Hume and Smith to Wicksell: Money, Credit, and the Economy* (Cambridge: Cambridge University Press, 2011).

4. Cheng-chung Lai, *Adam Smith and Yan Fu: The Wealth of Nations and China* (Hangzhou: Zhejiang University Press, 2009).[赖建诚：《亚当·斯密与严复：<国富论>与中国》, 杭州: 浙江大学出版社, 2009]

5. See David Hume, *Enquiry concerning the Human Understanding*, trans. Wu Guang-jian (Open Court Publishing Company, 1907; Commercial Press, 'the publisher's words', 1930), p. [伍光建：《人之悟性论》, 商务印书馆1930年, "出版人序", 第2页]

6. See Fang Shu-chun, Ge Li and Huang Dan-sen, *Criticism of the Agnosticism of Hume and Kant* (Shanghai: Shanghai People Press, 1956); 方书春、葛力、黄枬森著：《批判休谟和康德的不可知论》, 上海人民出版社, 1956.

7. See *Hume's Economic Writings*, preface by Hu Qi-lin, trans. Chen Wei (Commercial Press, 1984); and *Hume's Political Discourses*, preface and trans. Zhang Ruo-heng (Commercial Press, 1993). [《休谟经济论文选》, 陈玮译，商务印书馆,1984;《休谟政治论文选》, 张若衡译, 商务印书馆, 1993]

8. There are several versions of these essays: in 1988, Hume's essays were collected under the title *Of the Dignity and Meanness of Human Nature: Hume's Essays* (trans. Yang Shi and others, and published by Shanghai SDX joint Company); in 1996, *Essays on Broken Human Nature* included a number of Hume's essays (trans. Feng Yuan and published by Guangming Daily Press); in 2002 came *Hume's Classical Essays* (trans. Yu-qing and published by Shanghai University Press), followed by, in 2006, *David Hume's Essays* (trans. Xiao Yu, published by China Social Sciences Press), which collected twenty essays, including 'My Own Life'. [《论人性的高贵与卑劣》, 杨适译, 上海: 三联书店, 1988；《人性的断裂》, 冯援译, 北京: 光明日报出版社, 1996；《休谟经典文存》: 瑜青译, 上海: 上海大学出版社；《休谟散文集》, 肖聿译, 北京: 中国社科文献出版社, 2006]

9. David Hume, *An Enquiry concerning the Human Understanding*, ed. Selby Bigge (Oxford: Clarendon Press, 1894), trans. Lv Da-ji (Commercial Press, 1999) [休谟:《人类理智研究》, 吕大吉译, 商务印书馆, 1999]

10. The term 'British history' is the same as 'history of England' in the Chinese context, and thus the translation of Hume's *History of England* has always been as the 'British History'.

11. Sun Jian, 'On the Differences between Britain and England, Parliament and Congress: Review of the Chinese Version of David Hume's *History of Britain*', *Journal of World History* 6 (2013), pp. 118–25. [孙坚：《试论"不列颠"和"英格兰"、"议会"和"国会"之间的差别－－大卫·休谟＜英国史＞中译本读后有感》,《世界历史》, 2013年第6期, 第118–125页]

12. Zhou Xiao-liang, *Hume and His Philosophy of Human Nature* (Social Sciences Academic Press, 1996); *Hume* (Hu-nan Education Press, 1999); *On Hume's Philosophy* (People Press, 1999); Luo Zhong-shu, *Inquiry on Human Nature: Reviews of Hume's Philosophy* (Si-chuan University Press, 1995); Huang Zhen-ding, *On the Way of Human Nature: Inquiry concerning Hume's Treatise of Human Nature* (Hu-nan Education Press, 1997); Yin Xing-fan, *The Myth of Knowledge: Analysis on the Western Epistemology from David Hume* (Jiang-xi People Press, 1998) [周晓亮：《休谟及其人性哲学》（社会科学文献出版社,1996)、《休谟》(湖南教育出版社, 1999)、《休谟哲学研究》（人民出版社, 1999）；罗中枢：《人性的探究：休谟哲学述评》（四川大学出版社,1995）；黄振定：《通往人学途中：休谟人性论研究》（湖南教育出版社, 1997）；尹星凡：《知识之谜：休谟以来的西方知识论及其评析》（江西人民出版社, 1998）]。

13. Gao Quan-xi, *Hume's Political Philosophy* (Beijing University Press, 2004); Li Wei-bin, *New Inquiry on Hume's Political philosophy* (Social Sciences Press of China, 2013). [高全喜：《休谟的政治哲学》, 北京大学出版社, 2004; 李伟斌：《休谟政治哲学新论》, 中国社会科学出版社, 2013]

14. Zhao Ming-da, *The Competition of Theories: The Hume Problem in the Perspective of the Information Sciences* (Ji-lin Publishing Company, 2019); Luo Chang-jie, *On Hume's Cause-Effect-Doctrine: Critics and Reflections on the New Hume Debate* (Commercial Press, 2016); Sun Wei-ping, *Facts and Values, the Hume Problem and Its Solution* (Social Sciences Academic Press, 2016); Chen Xiao-ping, *Bayes's Method and Scientific Rationality: Reflections on the Hume Problem* (People's Press, 2010); Zhang Zhi-lin, *The Idea of Cause-Effect and the Hume Problem* (People's University Press of China, 2010). [赵明达：《理论的竞争：信息科学视角下的休谟问题》, 吉林出版集团, 2019; 骆长捷：《休谟的因果性理论研究：基于对"新休谟争论"的批判与反思》, 商务印书馆, 2016; 孙伟平：《事实与价值：休谟问题及其解决尝试》, 社会科学文献出版社, 2016; 陈晓平：《贝叶斯方法与科学合理性：对休谟问题的思考》人民出版社, 2010; 张志林：《因果观念与休谟问题》, 中国人民大学出版社, 2010]

15. Zhang Zhao-xia, *The Dimensions of Experience: On Hume's Aesthetic Thought* (An-hui University Press, 2010); Chen Hao, *Sentiments and Tastes: On Hume's Empirical Aesthetic Thought* (Beijing University Press, 2017). [张朝霞：《经验的维度：休谟美学思想研究》, 安徽大学出版社, 2010; 陈昊：《情感与趣味：休谟经验主义美学思想研究》, 北京大学出版社, 2017]

16. Wei Jia, *Commerce and Politics in David Hume's History of England* (Fudan University Press, 2018); Zhang Zheng-ping, *Passions and Wealth: The Science of Human Nature and the Political Economy of Hume* (Zhejiang University

Press, 2018); Liu Jin-shan, *Philosophical Inquiry Concerning the Idea of Miracle: The Case of Hume's 'Of Miracles'* (People Press, 2015). [魏佳：《贸易与政治：解读大卫·休谟的＜英国史＞》，复旦大学出版社，2018；张正萍：《激情与财富：休谟的人性科学与其政治经济学》， 浙江大学出版社，2018；刘金山：《"神迹"概念的哲学探究：以休谟的"论神迹"为中心》，人民出版社，2015]

17. David Hume, *A Treatise of Human Nature*, vol. 1, ed. David Fate Norton and Mary J. Norton (Oxford: Clarendon Press, 2011), p. 4.

18. See Hu Qi-lin, 'A Brief Review of Hume's Economic Thought', see *Hume's Economic Writings* (Commercial Press, 1984), pp. 4–5. [胡企林：《休谟经济思想简析》，见《休谟经济论文选》，陈玮译，商务印书馆，1984，第4–5页]

19. See Lu Xiao-ming, 'On the Theory of Monetary Quantity of David Hume', *Jiangxi Social Sciences* (J), 1986 (3), pp. 35–9. [陆晓明：《休谟货币数量论研究》，见《江西社会科学》，1986年第3期，第35–9页]

20. Ohno Seizaburo, *Hume's Theory of Civil Society*, trans. Hu Qi-lin; see also *Hume's Economic Writings*, trans. Chen Wei (Commercial Press, 1984), pp. 170–81.

21. Zhao Xiu-yi, 'On Hume's Economic Ethical Thought', *Journal of Eastern China Normal University* (Philosophy and Social Sciences) (J), 1998 (6), pp. 3–10. [赵修义：《试论休谟的经济伦理思想》，见《华东师范大学学报（哲学社会科学版）》，1998年第6期，第3–10页]

22. Yao Hui and Yang Zhong-jun, 'The Supposition of Human Nature of Western Economics: From Hume's Philosophy of Human Nature to Bowles's Supposition of Social Preferences', *Journal of Central China Normal University* (Social Sciences and Humanities), 2011 (3), pp. 20–4 [姚慧、杨忠君：《西方经济学的人性假设：从休谟人性哲学到鲍尔斯社会偏好假设》，见《华中师范大学学报（哲学社会科学版）》，2011年第3期，第20–24页]

23. Qian Meng-dan, 'On the Foundation of Human Nature of an Invisible Hand: On the Influences of Hume's Theory of Human Nature on the Theory of Adam Smith's "an Invisible Hand"', *Hei-he Journal*, 2010 (8), pp. 30–1. [钱梦旦：《"看不见的手"的人性论基础研究：论休谟的人性论对亚当·斯密"看不见的手"理论的影响》，见《黑河学刊》，2010年第8期，第30–1页]

24. Yan An, 'Hume's Theory of Economic Growth and Its Influence', *Study on Productive Power* (J), 2009 (17), pp. 16–17. [燕安：《休谟经济增长思想及其影响》，《生产力研究》，2009年第17期，第16–17页]

25. Zhao Ling, 'On Hume's Morals of Consumption', *Jiang-hai Academic Journal* (J), 2004 (5), pp. 213–17. [赵玲：《休谟的消费道德思想论析》，《江海学刊》，2004年，第10期，第213–17页]

26. Cheng Qi-qi, 'Hume's Utility Theory and Its Implication', *Zhejiang Social Sciences*, 2013 (03), pp. 29–36. （程奇奇：《休谟的"效用"理论及其启示》，《浙江社会科学》，2013年第3期，第29–36页）

27. See Cheng Qi-qi, *Passion, Imagination and Behaviour: On Hume's Theory of Economic Behaviour*, PhD thesis, 2012. 12, Zhejiang University. [程奇奇：《激情、想象和行为：休谟经济行为理论研究》，博士论文，浙江大学2012年]

28. Zhang Zhengping: 'Conclusion: The Political Economy in the Frame of the Science of Human Nature', in *Passions and Wealth: The Science of Human Nature and Political Economy of David Hume*, pp. 225–31. [张正萍："余论：人性科学体系中的政治经济学"，《激情与财富：休谟的人性科学与其政治经济学》，浙江大学出版社，2018年，第225–31页]

29. Luo Wei-dong, 'Passions, Reason and the Origin of "Economic Man"', *China Reading Weekly*, 29 August 2018, Tenth Layout. [罗卫东：激情、理性与"经济人"的思想起源，《中华读书报》，2018年8月29日，第10版]

30. Wei Jia, *Commerce and Politics in David Hume's History of England* (The Boydell Press, 2017, p. 3; Fu-dan University Press, 2018), pp. 4–5. [魏佳：《贸易与政治：解读大卫·休谟的＜英国史＞》，复旦大学出版社，2018，第4–5页]

31. Wei Jia, *Commerce and Politics* (The Boydell Press, 2017, p. 3; Fu-dan University Press, 2018), pp. 8, 9. [魏佳：《贸易与政治：解读大卫·休谟的＜英国史＞》，复旦大学出版社，2018，第8页、第9页]

32. Roger L. Emerson, *Essays on David Hume, Medical Men and the Scottish Enlightenment: 'Industry, Knowledge, and Humanity'* (London: Ashgate, 2009), p. 155.

33. Mark Blaug, 'Introduction', in *David Hume (1711–1776) and James Steuart (1712–1780)*, ed. Blaug (Cheltenham: Edward Elgar Publishing Limited, 1991), pp. 1–2.

34. Yu-sheng Lin, 'Of the Scottish Enlightenment', *Du-shu*, 1993 (1), pp. 89–96.[林毓生：《从苏格兰启蒙运动谈起》，《读书》，1993年，第1期，第89–96页]

35. Li Hong-tu's article 'The Theory of the "Commercial Society" in the Scottish Enlightenment of the Eighteenth Century: A Study Focused on Adam Smith' (*Journal of World History* 4 (2017) [李宏图：《18世纪苏格兰启蒙运动的"商业社会"理论——以亚当. 斯密为中心的考察》，《世界历史》，2017年第4期] is to some extent a review of Christopher J. Berry's *The Idea of Commercial Society in the Scottish Enlightenment*. Chinese translations of Christopher Berry's research on the Scottish Enlightenment have proved useful for Chinese scholars in their understanding of the key concepts of eighteenth-century social theory.

Index

Note: 'n' indicates chapter notes.